W9-AEW-193

Ethical Considerations
in Educating Children Who Are
Deaf or Hard of Hearing

Ethical Considerations in Educating Children Who Are Deaf or Hard of Hearing

Kathee Mangan Christensen, Editor

Gallaudet University Press / Washington, DC

Gallaudet University Press Washington, DC 20002
http://gupress.gallaudet.edu

© 2010 by Gallaudet University

All rights reserved. Published 2010

Printed in the United States of America

Library of Congress Cataloging-in-Publication Data

Ethical considerations in educating children who are deaf or hard of hearing
/ Kathee Mangan Christensen, editor.
    p. cm.
  Includes index.
  ISBN-13: 978-1-56368-479-1 (hbk. : alk. paper)
  ISBN-10: 1-56368-479-9 (hbk. : alk. paper)
  1. Deaf children–Education–Moral and ethical aspects. I. Christensen, Kathee Mangan.
HV2430.E83 2010
174'.9371912–dc22
                                  2010037167

For

KING, ALFIE, HUGO, AND BEATRIX

Contents

Part Three. Interpreting Decisions

Acknowledgments

Writing about ethics can be risky business. It involves developing an objective, logical stand on controversial topics. Using a "both/and" point of view, the chapter authors of this text have done a masterful job of examining some of the common challenges in the education of students who are deaf or hard of hearing, unpacking the controversy which surrounds these challenges, and offering insights based on real life experience. I am grateful to all of the chapter authors for their dedication to the task of provoking thought around the issue of enhanced educational opportunities for *all* deaf and hard of hearing students.

This book has benefitted from the support of many people. Foremost are the insights of Mary Kane, John Blackwell and Phil Kerstetter, the technical skills of Ron Richardson and Vincent Hernandez, the web site wizardry of Tony Haffner and the moral support of Clay Blair. Ivey Wallace and Deirdre Mullervy of Gallaudet University Press organized, edited, and made amazing suggestions that strengthened the manuscript. Thanks to all!

I am fortunate to live among a family of writers and editors. An enormous amount of credit, along with an equal portion of gratitude, is owed to Chip for meticulous editing, to Kyra and JD for creative feedback, and to my husband, Ben, for hours of reading, re-reading, and thoughtful discussion!

This book is primarily a collection of stories bolstered by research and reflection. Thank you to all of the Deaf adults, Deaf children and their families that I have had the pleasure of knowing and working with over the years. I hope that the stories we share will bring smiles of recognition and hope for progress toward a time when the rocky shores of controversy in our field give way to strong and secure common ground!

Kathee Mangan Christensen, Editor

Introduction: Rethinking Ethical Decision Making: Why Now?

KATHEE MANGAN CHRISTENSEN

There is no period so remote as the recent past.

—Alan Bennett, *History Boys*

My father was a teacher of the deaf. So was my mother. My first five years of life were spent in a house owned by the Michigan School for the Deaf and provided to our family as part of my father's job as dean of boys. I can still remember the address of that house: 1661 Miller Road, Flint, Michigan, just down the hill from the primary unit where I played with the deaf students on the weekends. My first languages were acquired simultaneously. I used both spoken English and American Sign Language (ASL), although, at that time, the term *ASL* had not been coined. Simply put, I used the sign language. I learned to sign from signers and to speak from speakers. At an early age, I figured out which language to use through trial and error, along with careful observation. In my world, everyone signed and some spoke. I was never formally taught about Deaf culture; however, I did intuit several rules as a very young child. For example, around the age of 3 or 4, I figured out that when I answered the door, I signed first. If the person started speaking, then I spoke. At a residential school, I made the assumption that most people who came to our door would know sign language, whether they were deaf or not.

When I started kindergarten, I realized that my communication skills were unique and not particularly respected. One of my earliest memories is the face of my kindergarten teacher, who sternly told me that "we don't use deaf-and-dumb hand signals here!" I'm sure I wondered, "Why not?" This was, indeed, my first experience with marginalization, albeit a unique variety. Much later, as a teenager, I dreamed of becoming a writer, an artist, a philosopher . . . it did not occur to me that I could parlay my natural lifestyle into a career. In retrospect, I believe that my kindergarten teacher must have provided an early challenge to what would be an enduring quest.

Serendipity played a role. During the week of my graduation from MacMurray College with a bachelor's degree in English, my parents introduced me to Alice Streng, then head of the teacher-preparation program in education of the deaf at the University of Wisconsin. Alice had taught both of my parents in their undergraduate days at Milwaukee State Teachers College. In fact, in the days of posteconomic depression, she recruited my mother from theater and my father from prelaw into the deaf education program with the assurance that they would find meaningful and satisfying careers. Law and theater, in Alice's opinion, were financially risky. Years later, she again used her considerable charm and intuition on me, also, offering me a full scholarship if I agreed to begin the deaf education program that fall. I canceled my plans to attend Bread Loaf School of English at Middlebury College that summer and instead packed up and moved to Milwaukee. Alice had trumped Robert Frost and my plans to become a writer. At the University of Wisconsin–Milwaukee, I joined eight white, hearing women in a master-of-science-degree program designed to teach deaf children to speak English. Literacy, it seemed, would follow speech. Sign language was not an approved part of the teacher-preparation program; however, most of my classmates were eager to learn it. The much-anticipated student-teaching experience at the Wisconsin School for the Deaf in Delavan was an incentive, and I was glad to help them out.

My near-native sign language ability was an asset to me in student teaching. My degree in English helped me to find parallels in signed and spoken languages and improvise ways to explain the nuances of English to my students through signs and visual support. I did not realize at the time that I was applying the techniques of bilingual education. It seemed instinctive . . . intuitive. Of course, only a person with fluency in both languages would be able to intuit this approach, and, in the 1960s, teacher preparation in education of the deaf was "English only," even at Gallaudet. I was fortunate to be able to communicate with my students, with deaf faculty and community members, and with hearing professionals throughout my years as a teacher and professor. This, I believe, gave me the freedom to think about issues that were not part of my own teacher-preparation experience but were fundamental to success in the classroom and beyond. This is where I became concerned—in fact, fascinated—with the ways in which educational decisions were made, particularly at public residential schools for deaf students, the ethical considerations around these decisions, and the eventual ramifications for deaf individuals. This book is based on true-to-life ethical dilemmas that the other authors and I have encountered in several decades of work with children, youth, and adults who are deaf or hard of hearing.

In an issue of the *Ethics in Science and Technology Center Update* (Spring, 2007, p. 4), Dr. Michael Kalichman wrote, "It is our personal responsibility to engage in an ongoing effort to identify ethical challenges and approach them through transparent and inclusive discussions. The answers we find will not always be complete or satisfactory, but the alternative (to not try at all) would be itself unethical."

These words guide the content of this book. The overall goal is to promote constructive conversations around current issues and explore ways in which the diverse needs of individual deaf students may become the primary focus of educational decision making.

Reaching consensus on a definition of the term *ethics* as it applies to the education of individuals who are deaf involves consideration of diverse perspectives within a variety of situations. Deaf people, their families and social circles, along with professionals from the fields of education, medicine, communication, and culture, constitute the primary circles that overlap in a discussion of what is "best" for a given person in a specific situation at a particular time in that person's life. Ethical decision making is not a static concept. Rather, it is an evolving phenomenon that is dependent upon situations that occur in contemporary society. Past practice can inform or guide current decision making; however, an ethical decision takes into account the facts of the moment and issues of fairness and justice in a certain situation. Although efforts are made to achieve consensus, those who are involved in decision making may not agree on what is "best." Without guidance, decision-making efforts may result in what may be labeled a "standoff," effectively postponing important decisions until one constituent group "wins" the debate. This, of course, results in the feeling among other constituent groups that they have "lost" in the effort to secure what they have advocated.

In order to create a more positive decision-making environment, we must have a flexible working framework to use as a guide during discussions. The goal of such a framework is to respect multiple points of view and to negotiate without condemnation. The basis of the framework proposed in this text is an adaptation of *situation ethics*, which can be defined as a system in which acts are judged within their contexts instead of by categorical principles (Merriam-Webster Online Dictionary, 2010.) This approach incorporates the view that ethical decision making applies to whole situations with varying features. That is, rather than weeding out what some consider to be "wrong," the dominant approach becomes one of considering how various features interact in a situation and then determining what is most helpful in that situation. Given a variety of options, what is the best option *now*? How can we engage a "both/ and" rather than an "either/or" mind-set when making complex decisions that have profound implications for the lives of individuals? The objectives of this book are to raise questions about current educational practice, present a way to apply an ethical framework to educational decision making, and provide a catalyst for further professional dialogue with regard to a perceived disconnect between an existing human condition and pedagogy.

Why ethics? Simply because little attention has been given to accountability in educational decision making up to this point. This text requires the readers to step back from their "professional personae," take a hard look at what is happening in the education of deaf children, and address the following questions: What social footprint is being left for those that follow us? What is being done effectively in our field? Where are the gaps? Are we, as professionals, maintaining high ethical standards? At the end of the day, what is being accomplished that makes us proud?

A close look at the contemporary education of deaf students reveals a field that is fraught with irony. A few "What the - ?" examples come to mind:

1. Hearing infants, young children, and their families are encouraged to learn American Sign Language so that they can communicate with each other early on and avoid the frustration that lack of oral communication can incur. Signing babies are "trendy." Speech-language pathologists who know basic ASL are among those who teach "baby signs" to hearing families for use with infants, toddlers, and "late talkers." Deaf infants and toddlers, however, are frequently denied early access to ASL and are placed in oral/aural programs that focus on oral communication only.
2. The federal Individuals with Disabilities Education Act (IDEA) was designed, in part, to ensure that the rights of children with disabilities are protected, to provide for the education of *all children* with disabilities, and to assess the effects of educating these children. Despite legislation intended to address the needs of the overall special education population, more and more profoundly and congenitally deaf children are, in fact, being left out and left behind with regard

to natural, spontaneous peer socialization and accessible communication with hearing peers and teachers. According to Mitchell and Karchmer (2006), 19% of deaf children in mainstream settings are "solitaires"; that is, they are the only deaf student in the school, and deaf children continue to be among the groups considered at risk for failure on state-mandated assessments.

3. Medical insurance may pay for cochlear implant (CI) surgery; however, there is little or no financial support for the years of follow-up therapy required for young CI users in order for them to benefit maximally from the technology.

4. Hearing children of Deaf adults (coda) who know much about life and communication in both Deaf and hearing cultures are often marginalized in both. Some codas report feeling discriminated against (as young children) by hearing people because of their animated use of sign language while at the same time being made to feel "different" in their family situation. One young hearing woman described the heartbreak she felt when her deaf sister told her that she could never, never understand "what it means to be deaf." Even though the hearing woman was a fluent signer, a staunch participant in culturally Deaf events, and a certified ASL interpreter, she at times felt that she did not fit in. I had similar experiences as an early signer, although I was not a coda. In my opinion, some of the best graduate students I have taught are codas. The intuitions they share about culture and communication in their bilingual worlds have been valuable additions to graduate seminar discussions.

5. Schools for children who have difficulty acquiring their native language (spoken English) emphasize speech-language pathology. No parallel program exists to provide ASL services to those deaf children who have difficulty acquiring their native or most accessible language, ASL. This is true despite the fact that some deaf children have additional special needs that make oral communication impossible and signed communication a challenge.

6. Real-time captioning is available at most large meetings and other functions for deaf and hearing audiences. The captions, however, are keyed by a person listening to English and result in some errors due to homonyms and other listening obfuscations. One recent example involved a speaker who said "hide out," while the stenographer typed "high doubt." Persons who use English as a second language often need to go through an additional translation process in order to access the meaning of presentations in real-time captions.

7. A deaf couple wanted to make sure that they had a deaf child. They sought out a sperm donor with five generations of deafness in his family in much the same way hearing couples seek donors with high IQs, artistic or athletic talent, and so forth. The deaf couple was condemned for deliberately inflicting a "disability" on a child. The deaf couple, of course, viewed their deafness from a linguistic and cultural perspective and did not see themselves as "disabled" (Sandel, 2007).

8. It has been known for decades that hearing children require from 18 months to 2 years of consistent, comprehensible language input before they begin to talk in a meaningful way. Their initial expressive communication constitutes a natural "child grammar," which differs significantly from adult grammar (Brown, 1973). Over time and with consistent input, most hearing children naturally acquire the spoken language of their families. Deaf children, on the other hand, the majority of whom have not experienced consistent, comprehensible language input at home, are

expected to express themselves in English phrases and short sentences soon after they begin school, usually between the ages of 2 and 4 years. We know with deaf children that early acquisition of a signed first language (L1) supports later learning of the written form of a spoken language and that "delayed exposure to an accessible L1 in early life leads to incomplete acquisition of all subsequently learned languages" (Mayberry, 2007, p. 548). Yet deaf children are denied early access to visually accessible, comprehensible linguistic input again and again in programs throughout the country.

Furthermore, of course, there are the issues of technology and the application of innovative strategies to a field that is struggling to prepare deaf citizens to succeed in a rapidly advancing society. The fields of education, science, and technology appear to be moving forward without the requisite ethical discussions that build a moral foundation on which to base critical decisions. Consider the following excerpt from the *New Yorker* magazine. It has implications for education:

> The 21st century has seen the advent of "feature creep," a problem which results when engineers design products with bells and whistles that enhance products for the general public but, for the most part, are too complicated for the general public to use effectively. A recent study showed that "at least half of all returned products have nothing wrong with them. Consumers just couldn't figure out how to use them." (Elke den Ouden, Phillips Electronics, *New Yorker,* May 28, 2007)

The engineers and marketers of these products had the well-being of the public in mind, but they were not in touch with the public's needs and capabilities. Ironic as it may seem, more options may create confusion and make a product less useful. Education is needed in order to help consumers make smart, ethically appropriate choices for individual use. The field of education of deaf students, in turn, has the same need. Although the National Technological Institute for the Deaf (NTID) at the Rochester Institute for Technology and PEN-International are taking the lead in providing symposia on technology and deaf education, the widespread use of current technology in teacher preparation and classrooms for deaf and hard of hearing students has yet to be realized beyond an experimental or cursory basis. Much of the educational technology available to support deaf students is missing, misunderstood, or misused in contemporary classrooms. From cochlear implants to "talking gloves," there is much to learn about the application of technology with deaf and hard of hearing students (Hyde & Power, 2006; Parton, 2006).

The issues and ironies mentioned earlier challenge us to recognize our assumptions, perceptions, or biases and determine to what extent they may interfere with ethical decision making. Indeed, it is the observation of these and other situations that, in large part, has motivated the contributions to this book.

Overview of the Book

The intent of this book is to set the stage for a situation ethics approach to the concept of decision making. This approach is based on the following fundamental points. There is no "right way" that can be applied to every situation:

- Situations are examined not with regard to what is "right or wrong" but rather to what is useful. "Either/or" thinking is replaced by "both/and" thinking.

- It is understood that no one can be absolutely objective because an individual's own power interests and social influences prevent it.
- "Common knowledge" is ruled out in favor of "common awareness." One cannot speak for everyone, and claiming to know the ultimate "truth" is at best naïve and at worst arrogant. (Adapted from Critchley, 2001)

The text is divided into three parts, and each part considers the decisions that must be made in three crucial areas in a child's education—parental choices, educational services, and interpreting.

Part One: Parental Decisions

Chapter 1 provides an inside look at a state residential school for students who are deaf or hard of hearing. Marybeth Lauderdale utilizes her considerable expertise as a teacher and administrator to detail the benefits of residential school placement from educational, social, and cultural perspectives. She introduces the Illinois School for the Deaf as a rich, barrier-free environment where students develop a sense of Deafhood "at first hand," so to speak.

In chapter 2 Mathew Call explores the threefold condition of triplicity. In this case, triplicity means life in three cultures (American Deaf culture, mainstream culture of the United States, and Latino/Chicano culture) and use of three languages (American Sign Language, English, and Spanish). In a situation where a deaf child from a monolingual Spanish-speaking family enters school in the United States, what responsibility do educators have to provide trilingual education? Call presents the apparent barriers to successful trilingual, tricultural education and poses the following question: Is it ethical to deny a language, especially a heritage language, to a child who is deaf? He considers the potential advantages of access to trilingual education. Given the fact that the birth rate of Hispanics in the United States is increasing, this chapter helps us to anticipate future needs in education.

No current book on the topic of ethics in the education of children who are deaf or hard of hearing would be complete without a chapter by a member of the medical community. Much controversy revolves around issues that spring from a medical perspective and stream beyond the boundaries of the medical community and into the cultural and educational world of deaf children and their families. In chapter 3 Katrin Neumann presents state-of-the-art findings on the issue of cochlear implantation in young children who are deaf. Neumann has extensive experience working with families with young deaf children in her practice at the University of Frankfurt am Main, Germany. The insights she has gained from this work, along with an overview of current international research on cochlear implantation, make chapter 3 essential reading for persons engaged in, perhaps even struggling with, decision making with regard to the pros and cons of cochlear implantation.

Part Two: Educational Decisions

The fourth chapter lays the foundation for an honest discussion on the most apparent ethical challenges present in decision making in the field of education of the deaf. I argue that the logical starting place for these discussions is at mandated Individual Educational Program (IEP) team meetings. As educational decision makers approach the task of choosing among the options for education of deaf and hard of hearing students, they must consider the complexity of the issues faced by these students and their families. The vast array of situations includes understanding the needs of individuals who are culturally Deaf; American Sign Language users; cochlear implant users; those who use hearing aids/FM systems; those who use signed English, sign-supported speech, contact signing, and nonverbal communication in various educational and social settings; those who are hard of hearing; and those who experience deafness after they have acquired spoken language. The dynamics of families from diverse cultural and linguistic backgrounds, along with the world of innovation and technology, are issues that overlap the broad topic of educational decision making. A framework based on situation ethics is suggested to treat all educational issues with justice, respect, dignity, and care, above all treating each person as an individual with unique strengths.

In chapter 5 Wendy Harbour expands the concept of partnership to include categories other than deaf or hard of hearing. She breaks the dichotomy and includes persons who do not identify with either group even though they are members of the larger Deaf community (e.g., those with changes in hearing levels over time). An "either/or" mode of thinking can be harmful on many levels to deaf and hard of hearing students. "Both/and" thinking is more advantageous as substantiated by a carefully described rationale. Using a bricolage approach, Harbour examines her own biases and challenges readers to do the same. She provides clear definitions of terms, discusses hearing loss as a social construction, and explores ways in which disability studies may expand thinking beyond the deaf/hearing duality.

Chapter 6 evokes thoughts of civil rights law and other laws that prohibit discrimination against historically underrepresented groups. Melissa Herzig and Kary Krumdick, both teachers in a self-contained program for deaf and hard of hearing students, challenge the assessment practices proscribed by the No Child Left Behind legislation and describe the need for assessments designed for and validated with the deaf school-age population. They offer the ASL Scale of Development as an alternative process for ethical assessment of visually oriented deaf and hard of hearing learners, many of whom use ASL as their primary means of access to the educational curriculum.

In chapter 7 James J. DeCaro and Patricia A. Mudgett-DeCaro share stories that frame a general discussion of ethical leadership. They challenge educational leaders to provide an environment in which deaf students can learn to take full responsibility for making the best decisions for themselves in life and find the energy to overcome the momentum of the status quo . . . to surmount barriers.

Part Three: Interpreting Decisions

Chapter 8 paints a broad-brush view of the overall situation of educational interpreters in various settings. We see interpreting through the eyes of the interpreters who bring to light issues of how they are assessed, how they participate, and how they are valued in the total educational process. The findings from Rico Peterson and Christine Monikowski's research can inform not only the fields of effective interpreter training and teacher preparation but also the larger field of education of deaf persons in general, particularly with regard to collaboration among interpreters, teachers, and administrators.

Have you ever wondered what actually happens in a classroom where one deaf student is mainstreamed with an interpreter? In chapter 9 Melissa Smith places the reader directly into a mainstream science lesson in a public school classroom. She compares the work of the educational interpreter to a choreography of visual movement. Smith describes the competing visual demands on a deaf student in a mainstream class and emphasizes the need for a well-defined working relationship that involves the student, the educational interpreter, and the general education teacher. The reader is left to draw conclusions about the benefits of a mainstream situation with a highly qualified educational interpreter. This chapter could serve as a primer for general education teachers and administrators with regard to the challenges faced by educational interpreters on the job.

Chapter 10 concludes the book with a justification of the benefits of a "both/and" approach to the education of students who are deaf. I present a model for "eventual bilingualism," along with an identification of the over-arching themes explored in this book. It is my hope that these themes will challenge readers to seek common ground and to get to know someone whose views differ dramatically from their own. While opinions may not change, educators and other professionals will see other perspectives and, in so doing, learn important information that can help them make decisions that will enhance the lives of deaf and hard of hearing students. As a result, we can reduce the biases that so often undermine even the best intentions of our professional discussions and "ensure that all of today's children are adequately educated and nourished, that they reach adulthood untraumatized and able to face the future with resilience and a willingness to learn" (Bateson, 2000, p. 157).

References

Bateson, M. C. (2000). *Full circles, overlapping lives: Culture and generation in transition.* New York: Random House.

Brown, R. (1973). *A first language: The early stages.* Cambridge, MA: Harvard University Press.

Critchley, S. (2001). *Continental philosophy: A very short introduction.* New York: Oxford University Press.

Hyde, M., & Power, D. (2006). Some ethical dimensions of cochlear implantation for deaf children and their families. *Journal of Deaf Studies and Deaf Education, 11,* 102–111.

Kalichman, M. (Spring, 2007). What do we mean by "ethics"? *Ethics Center Update.* San Diego: University of California–San Diego Center for Ethics in Science & Technology.

Mayberry, R. (2007). When timing is everything: Age of first-language acquisition effects on second-language learning. *Applied Psycholinguistics, 28,* 537–549.

Merriam-Webster Online Dictionary. (2010). Retrieved June 14, 2010, from http://www.merriam-webster.com, s.v. situation ethics.

Mitchell, R. & Karchmer, M. (2006). Demographics of deaf education: More students in more places. *American Annals of the Deaf, 151,* 95–104.

Parton, B. (2006). Sign language recognition and translation: A multidisciplined approach from the field of artificial intelligence. *Journal of Deaf Studies and Deaf Education, 11,* 94–101.

Sandel, M. (2007). *The case against perfection: Ethics in the age of genetic engineering.* Cambridge, MA: Belknap Press of Harvard University Press.

Part One

Parental Decisions

1

Looking at Residential Schools for Deaf Students

Seeing a Viable Option

MARYBETH LAUDERDALE

> The way that children are trained and schooled is a crucial demonstration of the way that they are perceived and treated in a given society. . . . Discovering who was taught, and when and how, is related far more to the social, political, legislative, economic, and religious forces at work in a society than it is to the unique social and educational needs of . . . persons. At the same time, this history mirrors our progress toward appreciating the basic humanity of all people.
>
> —Winzer, *The History of Special Education: From Isolation to Integration*

A deaf student and his parents arrive at noon on our campus. We walk up the stairs to the cafeteria. The student takes a quick glance around and asks curiously, "Where do the deaf kids sit?" As I respond with a smile, "Anywhere they want; they're *all* deaf kids!" the student reacts with incredulity as he studies the area and notices that everyone in the entire room—students and staff—is seated at round tables signing.

As superintendent of the Illinois School for the Deaf (ISD), I never tire of this scenario; each time is as powerful as the first and even more so when the student is a *singleton*—the only deaf student in his district, school, or class, an individual who has possibly never met another deaf person face to face.

Introduction

"Residential school" sounds sterile and uncaring—the dictionary definition states that it is merely a synonym for "boarding school." Residential schools for deaf and hard of hearing students have gotten a bad rap in the past thirty years or so since the passage of PL 94-142 and the interpretation of "least restrictive environment" as being educated in a neighborhood school with peers without disabilities.

The deaf people I have known in my decades in the field of Deaf education, whether educated in residential schools or not, do *not* consider themselves as having a disability.

Overall, those who were educated in a residential school consider themselves fortunate to have gotten an education among their deaf peers in a caring, twenty-four-hour environment where they could communicate without barriers, join extracurricular activities with equal access, and feel free to be themselves. Those who were mainstreamed often tell of childhoods of isolation: trying to fit in with their hearing counterparts, trying to master the guessing games of speechreading and accommodating the majority, hoping not to be singled out as deaf or spoken to as a person who is inferior. This observation has been supported in the literature (Kent, 2003).

Educational Options from the Start

On March 1–3, 1993, the National Institute on Deafness and Other Communication Disorders, together with the Office of Medical Applications of Research of the National Institutes of Health convened a Consensus Development Conference on the Early Identification of Hearing Impairment in Infants and Young Children. Cosponsors of the conference were the National Institute of Child Health and Human Development and the National Institute of Neurological Disorders and Stroke. The conference brought together specialists in audiology, otolaryngology, pediatrics, neonatology, neurology, speech and hearing sciences, speech-language pathology, health care administration, epidemiology, education, counseling, nursing, and other health care areas, as well as representation from the public. Following 1–1/2 days of presentations by experts in relevant fields and discussion by the audience, an independent consensus panel weighed the scientific evidence and prepared a draft statement in response to the following key questions:

- What are the advantages of early identification of hearing impairment and the consequences of late identification of hearing impairment?
- Which children (birth through 5 years) should be screened for hearing impairment and when?
- What are the advantages and disadvantages of current screening methods?
- What is the preferred model for hearing screening and follow-up?
- What are the important directions for future research? (http://consensus.nih .gov/1993/1993HearingInfantsChildren092html.htm)

The panel called for all infants to be screened for hearing impairment, preferably prior to hospital discharge. At that time, there were only 11 hospitals in the United States screening more than 90% of babies.

Nationally, the rates have increased significantly over time. The National Conference for Hearing Assessment and Management reported the following:

> [D]ata show that of more than four million infants born in the United States in 2005, 93 percent were screened for hearing loss. States have taken a variety of approaches to this issue: some mandate that all hospitals or birthing centers screen infants for hearing loss before they are discharged; some mandate that insurance policies cover the cost of the screening, while others use state dollars to fund screening programs. Still other states require that information on hearing screening be available to parents before they leave the hospital. Fourteen states allow newborns to be exempt from universal hearing screening programs if a parent objects to the testing.

Thanks to newborn hearing screenings, parents are finding out that their child is deaf or hard of hearing much earlier than in the past. From a linguistic perspective, this is positive; theoretically, comprehensible language input can start much earlier than it has historically. However, in the United States, the controversy still continues over which methods will be chosen for the child: Will the child be fitted with a cochlear implant or hearing aids, or will the child be taught sign language or spoken language or both? Many birth-to-three education programs strive to respect the parents' wishes while providing balanced, unbiased parent education that addresses the needs of the child and the family as a whole (Yoshinaga-Itano, 2003).

By the time the child starts school, the parents are addressing new decisions and perhaps still struggling with how best to communicate with the child and the family. The educational decisions the parents of a deaf child face with regard to school placement are similar to those that all parents face. However, the parents of a deaf child must also consider the education that occurs outside of the classroom—extracurricular activities, socialization, and career counseling, to name a few. Students are in the classroom for 6 or so hours a day and in the dormitory and recreation programs the remaining 18 hours in a 24-hour period. A crucial factor in determining the placement most comfortable for the student and the parents will be the strength of their relationship and partnership with the school staff. They will come to rely on mutual trust and honest, effective communication in order to foster the child's healthy development.

The continuum of educational options should be considered as a realm of possibilities. The family may move closer to the residential school so that the child can attend as a day student. Alternatively, the family may choose to send the child to the residential school and make arrangements for the youngster to come home every weekend. In some cases, the family may send the child to a residential school and see their son or daughter only on scheduled breaks. Fortunately, the development of videophones and Skype can ease the adjustment for families in the latter two situations, as it offers them an opportunity to communicate face to face at any time. Alternatively, the parents may decide that the child should stay in the local school district, with or without an interpreter, or go to a cluster site, where the child can be with hearing peers part of the day and also with deaf peers part of the day. *The important issue is to address the needs of both the child and the family.*

As the child grows, parallel play and physical socialization give way to social interaction through language. It becomes more difficult for older students who are deaf or hard of hearing to follow the conversations and rapid repartee that characterizes most junior high school social structures, as well as to participate in organized sports or other team activities. In addition, at this age the presence of an interpreter may no longer be openly welcomed. Junior high social activities, for instance, often do not accept the presence of an extraneous adult, no matter what that person's function is. Direct communication is preferable, and, when that cannot be achieved, the relationship is often dropped. At this time many families reassess their educational options and decide to give the residential school a try. Again, technology can help with the transition as videophones, text pagers, and computer technology allow instant visual communication.

Historically, the "tween" years have marked a turning point for the reassessment of educational options, especially if a child has been deemed a "failure" in whatever method the school endorses. Years ago, the Illinois School for the Deaf was divided into three units based on methodology: the Oral Unit, in which spoken language was used; the Acoustic Unit for hard of hearing students who could benefit from auditory training; and the Manual Unit, in which signing was used as the language of instruction and most of the teachers were themselves deaf. While one could argue that this previous structure may have fostered discrimination, each unit provided a critical mass of students who "belonged," and ISD has many educational success stories from these years.

The high school years present another set of challenges. In addition to the need to be socially active and involved, high school students may want to participate in clubs, teams, and activities. As students grow older, activities and academics become more competitive. There is also a need for guidance counseling, as the students begin contemplating their future plans as they relate to transitioning to work or postsecondary education. In addition, during this phase many parents and students decide to transfer to a residential school in order to take full advantage of these opportunities in a communication-rich, barrier-free environment.

The Illinois School for the Deaf participates in the Central States Schools for the Deaf (CSSD) tournaments in volleyball, basketball, and track. Throughout the country, other regional tournaments for Deaf students mirror those sponsored by the CSSD, such as the regional and national Academic Bowl competitions that Gallaudet University has organized since 1996. ISD has been participating in the Illinois High School Association Scholastic Bowl since 1998. It also participates in the Western Illinois Valley Conference, wherein our school competes with public schools in Illinois in all sports programs. Several residential schools also participate in the national Laurent Clerc Basketball Tournament. Interstate Deaf sports are inspiring because, at those tournaments, the playing field is truly level, both competitively and socially. Those events can be likened to state tournaments in public schools because of the critical mass of Deaf students involved.

Factors to Consider

Parents have many factors to consider when choosing a public or residential school for their child:

1. **Language- and communication-driven program.** The program must be centered around the acquisition, learning, and use of language(s). Educators, parents of deaf children, and Deaf adults have long debated the best way to teach language to deaf children. Some say that exposure to and development of ASL is a prerequisite for the development of English skills and literacy, whereas others counter that literacy is best developed if deaf and hard of hearing children learn English orally or through an English-based signing system. Research increasingly shows that deaf children who develop a natural, signed language learn to read and write much like hearing children for whom English is a second language and that the development of a strong first language base is necessary for literacy growth in English as a second language (Johnson, Liddell, & Erting, 1989). Fish, Hoffmeister, and Thrasher (2005) tested all students above the age of 7 who had no identified disabilities at two bilingual/bicultural schools for the Deaf in the northeastern United States ($n = 190$, ages 7–20 years old). Forty of the students had Deaf parents and 150 had hearing parents. The authors reported highly significant correlations between students' ASL proficiency and an English

vocabulary measure from the Stanford Achievement Test. These correlations held for both the entire sample and within each of the Deaf groups. In addition, Deaf students with Deaf parents performed better on both the ASL and English vocabulary measures than Deaf students with hearing parents.

This communication debate has been raging for hundreds of years, with no end in sight. Ultimately, it is essential that parents understand the difference between natural languages and signing systems, as well as between all signed and oral-aural language options. Parents should be fully informed and knowledgeable so that they can make the best decisions for the deaf or hard of hearing child. Regardless of the parents' communication choice, all deaf and hard of hearing children should have access to what all other children in our nation take for granted: communication, the chance to develop language skills, and a rich educational environment in which they can communicate directly with their peers and teachers.

The need for communication illustrates the complex ways in which hearing loss is fundamentally different from any other condition. It underscores both the difficulties perpetuated by current law and policy and the reasons that language access and development must become a right rather than an afterthought in our educational system. Lawrence Siegel (2008) succinctly said, "John Dewey said that 'society exists in and through communication.' So it is for deaf and hard of hearing people."

At ISD, we are committed to the additive bilingual approach, which uses visual-spatial American Sign Language while also presenting English print. We rely heavily on technology to make learning as visual as possible. ISD works in conjunction with the Center for ASL/English Bilingual Education Research (CAEBER), headed by Dr. Steven Nover at Gallaudet University. Collaboration with this program has enhanced the education at the school by providing our teachers and staff with solid, research-based instructional theory and practice, resulting in conscious language planning for optimum educational benefit. The program is known as the ASL/English Bilingual Professional Development program and was formerly known as Star Schools. According to Beverly Trezek (2008), the primary goal of the CAEBER program is:

> to provide professional development that promotes bilingualism, multilingualism and respect for all languages through the use of school-based language planning. Educators at the Illinois School for the Deaf have been engaged in school-based language planning since the Fall of 2004, although actively involved in bilingual language development since 1999. During the 2007–08 academic year, school-based language planning extended to reading instruction when ISD adopted the Direct Instruction reading curricula supplemented by Visual Phonics as its core reading curriculum for students in kindergarten through high school.

In keeping with the bilingual approach, ISD has collaborated with Dr. Trezek in an effort to enhance literacy through phonemic- and phonics-based reading instruction. In order to teach the phonemic awareness and phonics tasks included in the curricula, Visual Phonics is used. Visual Phonics, or See the Sound/Visual Phonics (STS/VP), is a multisensory system of 46 hand cues and written symbols used in conjunction with speech and speechreading to represent phonemes. The use of Visual Phonics to support the implementation of the Direct Instruction curricula has been the subject of recent research investigations conducted with students who are deaf or hard of hearing (Trezek & Malmgren, 2005; Trezek & Wang, 2006). Educators at ISD received training in Visual Phonics in 1999; however, prior to 2007–2008, implementation of this instructional tool was limited to an application for speech development. It makes sense to provide a consistent visual supplement for an invisible task.

2. **Well-trained, certified, highly qualified teachers and other staff**. The program must require certified educators and have a stringent hiring process for other staff. The program must follow all state rules and regulations for certification and accreditation. There should also be a strong professional development component present and in use at the school for all personnel, not only the educational staff.

3. **A rigorous curriculum that affords access to the state's general curriculum.** The program must present standards and benchmarks to students at the same pace and at the same age/grade levels as those for hearing students. Assessments should measure what is being taught in a way that is accessible to students who are deaf and hard of hearing. Placement should not be determined by a single assessment measure but rather should be triangulated.

4. **A research-based modified curriculum for students with special needs**. The program should have specialists to support students who have additional needs and challenge these students to achieve personal bests, as measured on their individualized education plans (IEPs).

5. **Related services personnel and programs**. The program should have appropriate personnel such as health practitioners, school psychologists, social workers, speech and language therapists, audiologists, cochlear implant specialists, and ASL specialists to provide all of the services required by the student's IEP.

6. **A safe and secure environment.** The program should follow legal requirements regarding student-to-staff ratios and be able to prove it is a *safe and secure* location, complete with safety equipment designed for deaf and hard of hearing students. A tested safety plan and procedures must be in place, be current, and be practiced during regular drills.

7. **Appropriate use of state-of-the-art technology.** The program should integrate appropriate technology into both the curriculum and everyday life as soon as it is feasible to do so. In these days of limited funds, grant funds may allow the purchase of state-of-the art equipment and technology, which further levels the educational playing field, most notably making all educational materials as visual as possible for students who are deaf and hard of hearing and presenting materials simultaneously in American Sign Language and in English. When investing in any new technology, the program must also invest in training, maintenance, sustainability, and expandability to ensure that the technology will be used. It is also imperative to not invest in technology for technology's sake (i.e., just because it "looks cool"). This results in the counterproductive phenomenon of the "technology tail wagging the education dog." At the Illinois School for the Deaf, we constantly guard against doing this.

8. **Communication**. The program should exhibit fluid and consistent communication between departments and with parents. Parents should feel comfortable working with the school in providing the best education possible for their children. This is especially true for a residential school: Parents should not feel that they just *drop off* their children for the school to care for. Optimal education is a partnership between the parent, the child, and the school.

9. **A comfortable, homelike atmosphere.** Students and parents must feel like empowered team members with the school and view the school as a supportive, safe, and caring *home away from home* for the child. There should be nothing sterile or uncaring about the program. If the parents and the child feel this fit, then the results will be positive.

10. **Finally, a critical mass.** A popular cultural literacy dictionary defines critical mass as the minimum needed to produce a given effect. In physics, for instance, it is the amount of material that must be present before a chain reaction can sustain itself. Here is a specific example: "A town needs a critical mass of industry to attract more business." With regard to the education of a deaf child, a critical mass of students who are deaf is needed in order to achieve a feeling of belonging in the students and to foster the development of self-esteem. Steven Pinker (1997) reported extensive relevant research:

    > [C]hildren everywhere are socialized by their peer group, not their parents. . . . At all ages children are driven to figure out what it takes to succeed among their peers and to give those strategies precedence over anything their parents foist on them. Weary parents know they are no match for a child's peers, and rightly obsess over the best neighborhood in which to bring their children up. (p. 447)

Stories from Our Students

Administering a 24-hour program for students who are deaf and hard of hearing presents many challenges, beginning with the fact that a program is only as strong as its weakest link. Along with academics, health and safety, and room and board, we must ensure that the entire program and educational system are communication and language driven. This provides empowerment and confidence by teaching students to become the best "you" possible, not a faulty facsimile of a hearing person. The following stories illustrate three separate experiences of personal growth and confidence.

Daniella, fourth grader (original written work, followed by corrected version as a class project):

> I went to hearing school. I was 2 grade. I in the hearing school there have interpreter. Then teather speak then I watch interpreter sign later she stop sign so I told her "please sign" She say "no I need rest I will sign soon" I say "how I understand and how I learn?" so I ask my friend only can sign then she explian me what teacher say. I told my dad and mom what happend in school and interpreter. My mom and dad say "really?" I say "yes" so my mom talk with my dad. Both decide I move another they find ISD I visit then I like I want join so they say ok. Then live dorm and go school then I like because there have sport and have activities. I was in 4 grade. I learn many and understand what teacher say. I love ISD!

> (Corrected English): I went to hearing school when I was in second grade. I was the only deaf student in a hearing class. They had an interpreter. Her signing was not good. Sometimes I did not understand her signing. It was so hard for me to learn. Once, the interpreter stopped signing. I asked her to please sign. She told me she was tired and needed to rest. One of my friends could sign, so I asked her to tell me what the teacher said. After school I told my parents what

happened in school. My parents decided to send me to ISD. Now I live in the dorm and go to school at ISD. I love it! I love it because there the teachers sign clearly, and it is easy for me to learn. I have lots of deaf friends. There are many activities and sports.

Rachel, sophomore, written in English:

There was a time in my life where I felt I did not fit in anywhere. I felt out of place and all alone. Being the only deaf at my old school was hard. Nobody understood me and never really cared to. I tried to be involved in sports and clubs but it was hard because of my hearing loss. I never knew what was going on and nobody bothered to take the time to explain it to me. The kids mostly just pushed me away and ignored me. I had only one friend, whom was also hard of hearing but nobody knew it. She wasn't open about herself and having hearing aids. She felt embarrassed and ashamed to tell. Plus she could hear a lot better than I could. As my hearing started getting worse in high school around freshman and sophomore years I became more and more of a loner. It hurt. I could go home and cry for hours to my mom about how sad I was and how I longed to just have more friends or be a part of the "popular crowd." That's when my parents got fed up and looked up a deaf school for me. They thought maybe it was time I could go somewhere where I fit in more and belonged. That's when Illinois School for the Deaf came into the picture.

Immediately after they told me what they had researched I started to cry and I accepted the offer. Within a month we were discussing the changes and making plans to visit. After my visit I fell in love with the school. I was transferred a month later.

Now, after being at ISD for a little over a year I would say I have changed a lot. I have learned to be able to communicate with others like me through sign language/ASL. I have learned how to live in a facility with other girls and get along and be respectful. Yes, I do miss my family so much more than words could say but sometimes it is nice to be out. I feel so much older and mature. Compared to my old school, I feel I can get a better education. I can retain so much more information here being able to understand it more and I feel that the teachers really listen to kids and help them out more. They have more of a relationship with kids, including me.

At my old school I had no idea what my future goals were. I didn't really think I could do much. ISD has opened many new doors for me. And has showed me all the different kinds of people there are and given me opportunities to help them. ISD shows me college options, helps me to apply, and helps me get the credits and things I need to qualify for the colleges. As a junior I already know what my goals are and what I right now plan to spend my life doing. I thought I would never find something to fit me or that I could do without having trouble because of my hearing loss. ISD has opened my eyes and changed my life.

Nathan, alumnus, age 28:

"Dad" is often the first word that a toddler would utter, after having heard the word dozens of times from mom when dad comes home from work. Thereafter, the vocabulary base grows, form sentences, and dialogues are fostered between parents and the child. Then, education continues to grow as the child is able to read, write and ask questions to gain more knowledge.

Except that wasn't the case for me. I came to Chicago, USA, as a three years old adoptee fresh out of Korea. Furthermore, I was deaf, and that means I was language-less too. No utterances of "dads" for me. But who were there at the O'Hare airport to receive me as their first and only child on the day of December 22nd, 1984? My parents who, like me, were deaf and they were more than just deaf. They were Deaf, meaning they conversed in American Sign Language as their means of communication and did not rely on oralism to function in the society. For all I could remember, when I saw my dad for the first time, he made a big welcoming smile and our eyes locked to each other. Unlike all other people before him, he did not try to come down and use his mouth to try to talk to me. He used his hands to talk to me. He probably signed to mom and said "that's our boy!" and held me up in his arms. From that moment, I knew something was different about them. Probably because we're all Deaf.

Out of all places, my education happened in a car on way home. I was growing hungry, and out of a car window, I saw something familiar. The sight was that of golden arches shaping like a big M. I had noticed that my parents were using hands, signing. I decided to mimic them. I raised my hand and pointed my finger at that big M and followed the letter's shape. Imagine my amazement when my dad quickly communicated to the driver, my uncle, and the car quickly moved and steered onto the next exit to the big M. The first time that anyone actually understood what I said. That's American Sign Language. My meal order was also accurate—I got a Happy Meal! Happily full, my mom brought children's books and taught me signs associated to the book. My mom likes to say that by the time we arrived home, I had finished the whole book and knew all the signs for it. Then, one week later, I'd learned enough signs to be able to communicate with my parents like any other three years old would.

Like I mentioned, my parents were Deaf, they graduated from a residential school for the deaf in Jacksonville, Illinois. I was up next. My mom spent the first two years working with me full-time and took me to school. My education continued through the communication means of ASL and was further stimulated by my peers. Some of them had Deaf parents like I did. There were also Deaf teachers and counselors working at the school that served as role models and spoke in ASL to keep up the language simulation in all of us.

My class was one of the best classes in the school history, faring well in sports (a rare qualification earned to the football playoffs), academics (performed well in quiz bowls and ACT scores), and most importantly, we had a sense of well-being individuals who were prepared to go into the society and the world at large. I graduated at top of my class, received a scholar-athlete award from Jacksonville Rotary Club, and were admitted into the Rochester Institute of Technology where I received my B.S. degree in Information Science. Now I work for Google as a webmaster. Not too bad for a kid who had wanted a Happy Meal when he first arrived from Korea! None of this would have happened without my parents' involvement and the support/environment that my residential school fostered.

Conclusion

A residential school for deaf/hard of hearing students is a viable academic option that offers obvious and lasting cultural and communication benefits. As perhaps all ISD alumni would attest, the bonds forged at the school last a lifetime. A testimony to this is any annual homecoming weekend—thousands of alumni attend and interact. They have a unique, lifelong bond with each other and with the school as a second home. Corrie Tijsseling (2004, p. 111) referenced Paddy Ladd's insight: "The difference of deaf children (compared to hearing children) should not be seen as a disability but as a cognitive process of its own—the process of creating knowledge—in which the child explains its own existence to itself and to others." Ladd names this epistemic process "Deafhood": a knowing and explaining of oneself that is defined by being deaf. Being deaf is an undeniable aspect of identity, one that can lead to identity confusion in deaf children from hearing families unless positive opportunities for self-identification are provided. Foster and Kinuthia (2003) suggest a model for the development of self-identity that includes four basic components: individual characteristics, situational characteristics, social conditions, and societal conditions. A residential school setting has the critical mass of students to address all of these factors both in and outside of the classroom setting. Residential schools for deaf students have been and will continue to be a unique and valued agency for assisting students who are deaf and hard of hearing develop into productive and successful members of "Deafhood."

Editor's Note

In the spring of 2009, when Superintendent Lauderdale was writing this chapter, the State of Illinois, in an effort to meet its budget, considered closing the Illinois School for the Deaf. This called into question the ethics of such a potential decision . . . one that would affect the lives of hundreds of deaf and hard of hearing students, their families, and their teachers. The immediate response of the Deaf community attests to its loyalty and commitment to ISD and its programs. Numerous ISD alumni, parents, and others organized e-mail blasts, a letter-writing campaign, and a rally at the state capitol in Springfield. In addition, ISD students made dramatic and articulate appeals on YouTube to save their school. As a result of this widespread collaboration, the governor withdrew the proposal, and ISD opened with Tiger pride in the fall of 2009.

References

American Heritage New Dictionary of Cultural Literacy, third ed. (2005). Houghton Mifflin. Dictionary.com. http://dictionary.reference.com/browse/criticalmass, s.v. critical mass.

Fish, S., Hoffmeister, R. H., & Thrasher, M. (2005). Knowledge of rare vocabulary in ASL and its relationship to vocabulary knowledge in English in Deaf children. Paper presented to the IASCL conference, Berlin.

Foster, S., & Kinuthia, W. (2003). Deaf persons of Asian American, Hispanic American, and African American backgrounds: A study of INTRAINDIVIDUAL diversity and identity. *Journal of Deaf Studies and Deaf Education, 8*, 271–290.

Johnson, R., Liddell, S., & Erting, C. (1989). *Unlocking the curriculum: Principles for achieving assess in deaf education.* Washington DC: Gallaudet University.

Kent, B. (2003). Identity issues for hard of hearing adolescents aged 11, 13, and 15 in mainstream settings. *Journal of Deaf Studies and Deaf Education, 8*, 315–324.

Ladd, P. (2003). *Understanding deaf culture: In search of deafhood.* Buffalo, NY: Multilingual Matters.

National Center for Hearing Assessment and Management. (2008). Newborn hearing screenings. Retrieved March 8, 2009, from http://www.infanthearing.org/screening/index.html.

National Conference of State Legislatures. "Newborn hearing screening laws." Retrieved March 8, 2009, from http://www.ncsl.org/programs/health/hear50.htm.

Pinker, S. (1997). *How the mind works.* New York: Norton.

Siegel, L. (2008). *The human right to language: Communication access for deaf children.* Washington, DC: Gallaudet University Press.

Tijsseling, C. (2004). *From deafheid to Deafhood: A different perspective on deaf children.* Nijmegen: Radboud University.

Trezek, B. (2008). *Moving in the right DIRECTion: Integrating direct phonics instruction into the bilingual model at the Illinois School for the Deaf.* Jacksonville: Illinois School for the Deaf.

Trezek, B., & Malmgren, K. (2005) The efficacy of utilizing a phonics treatment package with middle school deaf and hard of hearing students. *Journal of Deaf Studies and Deaf Education, 10*, 256–271.

Trezek, B., & Wang, Y. (2006) Implications of utilizing a phonics-based reading curriculum with children who are deaf or hard of hearing. *Journal of Deaf Studies and Deaf Education, 11*, 203–213

Winzer, M. (1993). *The history of special education: From isolation to integration.* Washington, DC: Gallaudet University Press.

Yoshinaga-Itano, C. (2003). From screening to early identification and intervention: Discovering predictors to [*sic*] successful outcomes for children with significant hearing loss. *Journal of Deaf Studies and Deaf Education, 8*, 11–30.

2

See Me Through the Triplicity of My World

Ethical Considerations in Language Choices

MATHEW CALL

Overheard in the teachers' lounge at a large urban middle school: "And now this deaf kid wants to take Spanish as an elective! That's ridiculous . . . he'll never be able to speak Spanish so anyone can understand him!"

Fortunately, some progress has been made since that outburst in the teachers' lounge. In 2007 the American Council on the Teaching of Foreign Languages (ACTFL) approved a document titled "Diversity and Inclusion in Language Programs." Arguably the most influential language teaching organization in the United States, the ACTFL stated that language instruction should "promote awareness and differentiation of language instruction to accommodate students' diverse learning styles; exceptional learning needs; cultural, ethnic and linguistic backgrounds; and personal interests and goals." American Sign Language (ASL) has for many years been approved as one of ACTFL's less commonly taught languages (LCTL).

Even with this forward thinking on the part of the ACTFL, these questions remain: To what extent do teachers and administrators represent barriers to the language aspirations of deaf and hard of hearing students? To what extent do they actually impede the language and cultural acquisition process of these students? This chapter explores a number of barriers that exist in the area of trilingual (ASL-English-Spanish) and tricultural education for the deaf and hard of hearing students who want *and need* immediate access to these languages and cultures.

Introduction

In the United States, nearly one-third of the entire deaf/hard of hearing student population (21 years or younger) is now Hispanic/Latino. In the West, almost half are Hispanic/Latino, and in California, Hispanics and Latinos constitute *more than half* of that population. Spanish is used in about three-fourths of these students' homes nationwide (Gallaudet Research Institute 2006, 2008). The number of deaf/hard of hearing Hispanics/Latinos has been increasing for years and will continue as the general Hispanic/Latino population grows (U.S. Census Bureau, 2008). These demographics will continue to translate into serious implications for the field of Deaf education.

When discussing population trends, it is problematic to group Hispanics and Latinos together because many issues of diversity can be glossed over. In our schools, there are deaf and hard of hearing students with roots in every Spanish-speaking country, representing multiple races, ethnicities, and socioeconomic levels and whose hearing status runs the entire gamut. Some are first-generation immigrants who came to the States as babies, children, or perhaps teenagers. Others are the first generation to be born here and whose hearing parents are monolingual Spanish (or monolingual/bilingual in the case of a native indigenous language). The dominant home language of those with Deaf parents may be the signed language of their country. Still others have parents who have been here for a generation or more, and the dominant language at home may be Spanish, English, or both (or ASL in the case of many Deaf Latino parents). Finally, there are others whose families have been in the United States for many generations, perhaps since the time when the territory belonged to Mexico.

Despite all of this diversity, these deaf and hard of hearing students do indeed share at least one commonality: the triplicity of their worlds (Christensen, 1993; Cohen, 1993). To at least some degree, these children are immersed in ASL and American Deaf culture, English and mainstream American culture, and Spanish and their family's Hispanic/Latino culture. *This is their world by default, not by choice.* The question must be asked, then, Does immersion in three cultures always lead to the successful enculturation of each one? Is it an ethical challenge to educators to ensure that this happens?

Trilingualism and Triculturalism Defined

In this chapter, *trilingual* indicates equal language fluency in ASL, English, and Spanish. By "equally fluent," it is understood that one has little difficulty cognitively or linguistically with respect to input or output in any of these three languages. *Tricultural* here implies being a member of and immersed in three distinct cultural groups (American Deaf, mainstream American, and Hispanic/Latino/Chicano/country of origin). It should be understood that language and speech are by no means synonymous. Having native command of a language does not equate to fluent spoken language. It can equate to literacy. It is important to be aware of this fundamental difference in order to grasp the reasons Deaf education has had relatively little success in fulfilling the true potential of deaf children thus far (Wilbur, 2008).

The Hispanic/Latino deaf student is not by any means the only deaf/hard of hearing student living a multicultural experience with trilingual potential. Although the focus of this chapter is ASL, English, and Spanish, much of the content can apply to any student whose surroundings are trilingual and multicultural. Depending on geographic location, the local multicultural deaf population may vary widely. Trends in immigration, refugee influx (at any point in history), and a myriad other factors impact populations. The same area may be home to a significant number of Russian or Chinese or Navajo individuals who are deaf. However, does the fact that there is perhaps only one Korean or Vietnamese or Persian deaf student in a given school justify withholding a culturally and linguistically fair appropriate public education?

Worthy of mention are the students who have the potential to become quadrilingual and quadricultural, adding to the equation the signed language and Deaf culture of their country of origin. Multicultural Deaf students educated in the social/cultural model of Deafness and what Deaf people can accomplish when society gives them the chance have the potential to return to their countries of origin as Deaf social activists. They can be key to the success of Deaf people in underdeveloped nations where Deafness lags far behind (Muñoz-Baell et al., 2008).

Not to be forgotten are the deaf or hard of hearing students whose dominant home language is English or ASL but whose family *heritage* language differs. If their hearing peers have a right to study the heritage language, it would clearly be considered unethical not to provide equal access to these students as well. What equal access necessitates will change depending on the deaf/hard of hearing students and what they wish to accomplish with the class (e.g., learn to speak/read/write the language; learn the country's national sign language).

Brief History of the Education of Hispanic/Latino Deaf Students

The history of the education of Hispanic/Latino deaf students in the United States is laden with misevaluation, misplacement, and misunderstanding. As early as 1972, empirical evidence showed that hearing Hispanic students, in general, were overrepresented under the label of educable mentally retarded (Mercer, 1972, 1973). This was largely due to low IQ scores on English-based tests that evaluated students' English skills rather than their content knowledge. The same kinds of blunders were occurring within the Hispanic deaf population, and programs to address this situation were just beginning (Jensema, 1975). Kopp (1984b) was at work within the Department of Communicative Disorders at San Diego State University establishing an outreach program for Hispanic deaf students in 1970. Grant (1972) was aware of the need to merge bilingual education and special education and was preparing a range of professionals for early intervention. During the 1979–1980 academic year, Delgado (1984) conducted a national survey, which found that 51% of hearing-impaired students from non-English-speaking families were reported as also having additional handicaps, whereas this same incidence rate for all hearing-impaired students was a much lower 29%. These deficiencies occurred due to a number of factors, including ethnic and racial bias, misunderstanding of the language acquisition process, confusion as to the role of culture in the learning process and curriculum, experience with an essentially monocultural population of deaf students, and the desire to have programs work for every child in the same way (Blackwell & Fischgrund, 1984). In the 1980s and into the 1990s, significant attention was paid to multicultural deaf children. Concerned educators alerted those in the field of the shortcomings, and scattered changes were implemented. Both the national Convention of American Instructors of the Deaf (CAID) and the Conference of Educational Administrators of Schools and Programs for the Deaf (CEASD) initiated multicultural issues special interest groups. "However," as Delgado (2000) succinctly put it, "what evolved was a passing interest. . . . No sustained efforts occurred" (p. 31). He and others attributed this misfortune largely to the fact that educators and funding agencies were promoting ASL-English bilingual education. Overlooked was the fact that Deaf people in this country are not only Deaf but have various ethnic identities, too (Cohen, Fischgrund, & Redding, 1990).

With the turn of the century came another valuable national study of Deaf Hispanic/Latino students (Delgado, 2001), only the second of its kind. Delgado discovered that Deaf Hispanic/Latino students no longer appeared to be disproportionately classified as multihandicapped. They tended to graduate from or complete high school programs in the same number as non-Hispanic/Latino deaf students. A small but growing percentage was going on to college. Although these were noted as positive strides, more remained to be done to ensure equity for Hispanic/Latino deaf and hard of hearing students in the future. For example, programs for Hispanic deaf students still do not include an opportunity for them to develop basic literacy in Spanish. For these students, despite skill in ASL and English, not knowing Spanish can create linguistic and cultural barriers at home and among extended family members and can contribute to estrangement from cultural and family heritages (Suro, 1999; García, 2004). It also has a direct effect on self-identity as was revealed by Page's (1993) and then Foster and Kinuthia's (2003) in-depth interviews with deaf Hispanics/Latinos. Walker-Vann (1998) also wrote about a number of Hispanic Deaf students who felt as though they had to choose one identity or another.

Why ASL-English-Spanish Trilingualism and Triculturalism?

It is anticipated that trilingual-tricultural programs for Hispanic/Latino Deaf students will foster cognitive development and academic success, increase positive self-esteem, decrease the incidence of depression, and raise the high school graduation numbers, thereby decreasing delinquency.

"Considerable research data suggest that for minority groups who experience disproportionate levels of academic failure, the extent to which the students' language and culture are incorporated into the school programme constitutes a significant predictor of academic success" (Cummins, 1988, p. 225). This quote from Cummins is more than 20 years old. Subsequent research in both mainstream hearing and Deaf education has lent even stronger support to his observation. Crawford (1998) summed up the decades of research and debate by explaining that, despite past controversy, because of cumulative empirical evidence, there is now general agreement among applied linguists that native-language instruction does not hinder English acquisition and that non-English native-language proficiency is associated with high levels of academic achievement.

There is an abundance of research from the 1960s onward showing that multilingualism supports cognitive growth. To name a few, Modiano (1966) showed that bilingual students (Tzeltal/Spanish and Tzotzil/Spanish) had higher reading comprehension of the Spanish language than their monolingual Spanish-speaking peers. Forty-one years later, Sneddon (2007) showed the same: Trilingual children (of three spoken languages) had a higher level of reading comprehension than children who spoke only English; moreover, by age 11, these trilingual children were doing better in school than their monolingual peers. Hakuta (1986) showed that well-developed multiple languages do not confuse the mind but instead provide cognitive advantages. Gerner de García (1993b, 1995a) showed that multiple languages do not confuse even

Hispanic/Latino deaf or hard of hearing children. Cazden (1972) found that the ability to know two symbols for one object or action promotes metalinguistic awareness. Lambert (1979) demonstrated that when two languages have equal status, bilingualism enhances rather than diminishes cognitive and educational achievement. Kovács and Mehler (2009), in their study of preverbal 12-month-old children, show that bilingual children tend to learn two languages in the same length of time it takes their monolingual peers to learn one because they are more flexible at learning speech structures at an early age.

In 2009, the American Speech-Language-Hearing Association (ASHA) issued what could be considered an official statement on bilingualism (Marian, Faroqi-Shah, Kaushanskaya, Blumenfeld, & Sheng, 2009). The statement indicates that by summarizing decades of research and incorporating the most recent findings, one can see the advantages of bilingualism over monolingualism emerging in the areas of cognitive development, lexical organization, vocabulary acquisition, cognitive control, and neural organization.

How does self-esteem relate to multilingualism and multiculturalism? Holly (1987) showed that self-esteem is an effect of academic success, not the cause of it. Lang, Muñoz, Bernal, and Sorensen (1982), Berry (1990), and Miranda and Umhoefer (1998) have reported that bicultural Latinos are less likely to be depressed and more likely to demonstrate high social interest than those who lack bicultural identity. Dagenais and Day (1999) and Sneddon (2007) have demonstrated that being a trilingual child elevates self-esteem.

In the fast-paced global marketplace of today, knowing three languages will undoubtedly make a person more marketable, hearing or deaf. In general, the more prevalent the languages are in a given society, the more useful they will be for employment. English and then Spanish are the two most widely used languages in the United States (U.S. Census Bureau, 2003). Sign language is now in contention to be the third or fourth most widely used language in the United States.

An international benefit is the possibility that multilingual, multicultural Deaf students educated in the social/cultural model of Deafness could return to their countries of origin as social and political activists in order to help bring about awareness of Deaf people's rights. Muñoz-Baell et al. (2008) concluded the following:

> The results of this study reveal that social/political changes and a medical/social model of Deaf people's health can promote or limit Deaf people's educational options much more than changes within the education system itself and that a transnational perspective is needed in deciding how best to support Deaf Bilingual-Bicultural education at a national and local level in an increasingly globalised world. (p. 131)

The idea of trilingual-tricultural education is not an extraordinary one. After all, Spanish-English bilingual education has been around for many years and is the norm in many schools around the nation. For several decades ASL-English bilingual-bicultural programs have been in existence and are now the norm at many residential schools for deaf students. If both hearing and deaf peers are allowed to receive a culturally and linguistically appropriate education, should Hispanic/Latino deaf/hard of hearing students be denied the same right? Therein lies an ethical dimension. Decisions are continually made regarding the extent to which a deaf/hard of hearing child may have access to languages other than English in school. Different foreign language classes are offered to hearing students in public schools depending on factors such as grade level, school district, and region. Is it ethical to deny deaf and hard of hearing students equal access to these same classes? Suppose the language is that of the student's own heritage. Does this change the ethical considerations that go into the decision making?

Resistance to ASL-English-Spanish Trilingual-Tricultural Education

Despite the myriad of evidence cited earlier, educators to this day oppose ASL-English-Spanish trilingual-tricultural education (Steinberg, Bain, Li, Montoya, & Ruperto, 2002). The roots of this doubt and opposition are clearly marked. In the 1960s and 1970s, it was assumed that language fluency required input in the form of auditory stimuli and output in the form of speech. There was widespread belief that learning two or more languages was far too much to ask of deaf children, who were sometimes perceived as having *no* language at all when entering school (Dean, 1984; Fischgrund, 1984; Grant, 1984). In reality, the bulk of the world's population is actually multilingual, even across socioeconomic levels (Sneddon, 2007; Tokuhama-Espinosa, 2003). Far too often in this country, monolingual teachers are found in schools teaching students who are conversationally multilingual and who have the potential to become academically multilingual and literate in their other languages. The English-only movement in the United States feeds this ethnocentrism (Crawford, 1998).

Gerner de García (2000) has written that opposition to trilingual education for deaf children may be more political than pedagogical:

> It may be the result of linguicism, as well as . . . the low status of the Spanish language and Spanish speakers . . . this colors the widespread view of Hispanic/Latino deaf children and adults. It is based in the racism that permeates this society that holds some languages and cultures as more valuable. (p. 162)

Is it up to educators to decide for these students which languages and cultures are more valuable than others? If schools were found to be contributing to *linguicism* (i.e., opposition to providing access to language and culture that could enhance a student's self-image, advance academic achievement, and permit communication with family members), would this not be considered unethical?

Barriers to Change

Controversial theories about bilingual and trilingual education, many of which are mere opinions not grounded in research, have stunted growth in the field of Deaf education for years (Jackson-Maldonado, 1993; MacNeil, 1990; Secada, 1984; Struxness, 2000). Programs do not work the same way for every child or even every region. Because of the complexity of the situation, an overarching solution to a national challenge is not the goal of this chapter. What can be presented are questions about specific barriers to trilingual-tricultural education. If all of these obstructions are addressed with ethical decision making in mind, truly successful trilingual-tricultural programs may come within our reach. As I address the most flagrant barriers, note the faithfulness to the "three Cs," which are the foundation of deaf education: cognition, communication, and culture (Christensen, 1993).

BARRIER: MISUNDERSTANDING THE CULTURAL
CONTEXT OF FAMILIES

Before professionals can effectively serve Hispanic/Latino families and their deaf children, they must understand the family in a historical, cultural, and social context (Blackwell & Fischgrund, 1984; Rodríguez & Santiviago, 1991; Struxness, 2000). Professionals who fail to understand what it might be like to have their homeland taken from them by trickery and force, to live in a country where everyone does things differently, to lack health insurance and reliable transportation, or to receive medical and educational instructions in a foreign language will be ill equipped to work successfully with these families. The results of Luetke-Stahlman's (1976) questionnaire to Mexican American parents of "hearing-impaired" children more than 30 years ago revealed how frustrated a mother or father could become when cultural and linguistic barriers stood between the home and the school. Bennett (1987a) explored these barriers in depth and reported that this atmosphere of conflict, misunderstanding, and confusion formed the context out of which the deaf Hispanic child's identity was shaped.

These issues remain extremely pertinent today. Personal experience in recent years has revealed that even in this day and age much progress is still needed in the area of multicultural education. A number of administrators and teachers of deaf students today are quite competent but lack fundamental knowledge of Latino cultures. It is beyond the scope of this chapter to delve further into this problem. Readers are encouraged to read articles such as those by Grant (1984), Jackson-Maldonado (1993), and Ramsey (2000) for in-depth descriptions. One classic example of cultural misunderstanding is worthy of mention, however. Many schools remain puzzled as to why the parents of their deaf Latino students "don't want" to be involved in their child's education. They cite a lack of parental participation and correlate this to poor student achievement. Whether or not parents should be involved in the education of their deaf or hard of hearing child is not the issue. Parental involvement in their deaf/hard of hearing child's school-based education positively contributes to early reading skills and academic performance (Calderon, 2000). (Parental communication skill was an even more significant predictor.) These schools are likely unaware of how respect for authority varies from culture to culture. In much of Latin America, for instance, it is a sign of respect to allow the professionals to do their job since they are the experts. Getting involved might be seen as questioning a teacher's judgment (González Álvarez, 1998). Therefore, instead of flaunting research and expertise to gain trust, professionals in the United States who work with these families should opt in favor of establishing a relationship with parents on a more personal level first (Rodríguez, 1985; Rodríguez & Santiviago, 1991). For example, Spanish-speaking parent groups can help foster involvement with the school (Cohen, 1993). As it turns out, when given an opportunity, Spanish-speaking families are willing to learn signed language as a bridge between the home and school (Christensen, 1986). Both the professionals and the families need to be educated in these areas in order to provide an appropriate education for deaf children from Spanish-speaking families.

BARRIER: VIEWS OF DEAFNESS IN LATIN AMERICA

It comes as no surprise that deafness is not regarded as the most important educational issue in many third-world countries, including those in Latin America. Political crises, for the most part, trump educational objectives. This colors immigrant parents' views of deafness (Gerner de García, 1993a). Despite this:

> The United Nations Convention on the Rights of Persons with Disabilities underlines that people with disabilities have the right to enjoy full human rights. The core factors for the human rights of Deaf people are access to and recognition of sign language including acceptance of and respect for Deaf people's linguistic and cultural identity, bilingual education, sign language interpreting and accessibility. (Haualand & Allen, 2009, p. 6)

The results of the World Federation of the Deaf's Global Survey on the Human Rights of Deaf People (93 countries, including 18 in Latin America) confirms that with regard to signed language access:

> Relatively few countries deny Deaf people access to education, government services or equal citizenship on the basis of deafness alone. But lack of recognition of sign language, lack of bilingual education, limited availability of sign language interpreting services and widespread lack of awareness and knowledge about the situation of Deaf people deprive most Deaf people of access to large sections of society. Thus they are not able to truly enjoy even basic human rights. (Haualand & Allen, 2009, p. 7)

It is no wonder that immigrants arrive here with outdated beliefs that deafness is an ailment, deaf people are mutes, signing is not a language, and the use of sign language will hamper speech abilities.

BARRIER: LATE DETECTION OF HEARING LOSS

The importance of knowing as early as possible that a child has a hearing loss cannot be overemphasized. More than 90% of all currently school-aged deaf individuals in the United States were born to hearing parents, of whom the vast majority had no prior exposure to deafness (Moores, 2001). Before 1993, many parents who were not deaf did not think to have their child tested for a hearing loss. Spanish-speaking parents often face additional barriers when they receive medical attention only in English. Many services and resources are not accessible to them due to language barriers. (Thankfully, the field of spoken language health care interpreting has grown quite rapidly in the last two decades, and national medical interpreter certification in several language pairs is finally being made available.) Spanish-speaking parents must be given information about the possibility of infant hearing loss. Since 1993, hospitals have initiated universal newborn hearing-screening programs to identify hearing loss in infants. Otoacoustic emissions or auditory brainstem response can measure auditory input independently of subjective reaction. In California and other states, the program has an additional goal of linking parents with services by the age of 6 months. Spanish-speaking families must be made aware of these services so that their children can begin to acquire language as soon as possible.

BARRIER: LACK OF CULTURALLY AND LINGUISTICALLY APPROPRIATE EARLY INTERVENTION

The identification of deafness in an infant or child has a profound impact on a hearing family that has little or no prior exposure to deafness. Parents can experience a wide range of emotions, including disbelief, grief, anger, guilt, helplessness, and confusion (Ogden & Lipsett, 1982). Ogden and Lipsett maintain that these are natural stages through which hearing parents must pass. Similar emotions occur for parents who have a Latino cultural background (Goring & Martindale, 1989; Jackson-Maldonado, 1993; Steinberg et al., 2002). For these parents, these emotions may be even more intense (Walker-Vann, 1998).

Universal hearing screening is beneficial with regard to early intervention. However, care should be taken not to limit the knowledge of services and resources offered to families. Extra care should be taken to ensure equality of access, including information about the continuum of options, presented in the language of the family. One study shows that culturally and linguistically appropriate resources and services were indeed sparse for Spanish-speaking Hispanic/Latino parents of deaf children. "Most parents relied on the professionals who were treating their child to provide information, not only about hearing loss itself, but also about available services, medical assistance, and the rights of the child and parents" (Steinberg et al., 2002, p. 21).

Until relatively recently, history presented only one way of viewing deafness: as a deficit or a disease to be prevented or cured. Too often, medical professionals have been educated only in this medical or pathological model of deafness. For Spanish-speaking parents who come from a culture in which, as mentioned, it is considered disrespectful to question the judgment of a professional such as a physician, in whom great trust is placed, audistic and phonocentric attitudes easily get passed on (Steinberg et al., 2002). In fact, in 18 countries, Muñoz-Baell et al. (2008) found this medical model of deafness to be the principal hindering force in the establishment of Deaf bilingual-bicultural education. Hearing parents do not get enough early exposure to the social/cultural model of Deafness. American Deaf culture and Deaf adult role models, including Deaf Latinos, are often not present during the early stages after identification of deafness. Ogden and Lipsett (1982) asserted that for these hearing parents, the primary concern is to find a way to communicate clearly with their child. A substantial portion of Ogden and Lipsett's book has been translated into Spanish and could be useful for literate Spanish-speaking parents and professionals that work with Spanish speakers.

BARRIER: LATE EMERGENCE OF TRILINGUAL INTERPRETING

While both educators and families need to be educated in the differences that may separate them, it is interpreters who are specifically trained to mediate these differences on a daily basis. Trilingual interpreters in this discussion interpret between ASL, spoken English, and spoken Spanish. Gone are the days when interpreters acted strictly as input/output machines (Humphrey & Alcorn, 2001). Professional interpreters have the added complexity of mediating cultural and other differences as well. Professional training ensures that interpreters are educated in their multiple roles and how to weave in and out of them as the situation dictates. Any time a Spanish-speaking family, a deaf student, and school personnel communicate (or any time the family accesses public services, for that matter), two interpreters are needed: one Spanish-English and one ASL-English. However, a single, qualified trilingual interpreter can theoretically offer more accuracy since no message will be required to pass through two languages and two interpreters before arriving at the target language.

The need for a trilingual interpreter often goes unnoticed for several reasons. Personal observation revealed one of these: While Deaf adults in the United States, especially those who lived through the Deaf President Now (DPN) movement, tend to self-advocate for their right to a qualified sign language interpreter, Latino immigrants and deaf children tend not to, despite laws that guarantee them access. Many an IEP meeting boasts a qualified sign language interpreter for communication with the deaf student, while a bilingual aide with no formal training in interpreting will be present for communication with Spanish-speaking parents. Many medical appointments are covered by a Spanish interpreter for the parents, but no sign language interpreter is present for the child who is a minor. In these situations, not all of the parties are represented equally. Expense may also be an issue. The cost of a trilingual interpreter will be more than for a single interpreter but less than for two interpreters. If the deaf/hard of hearing student uses a different sign system, as do many recently arrived immigrants, then either an interpreter proficient in that sign system, a deaf intermediary interpreter, or the family member who best understands the sign system may also need to be present. These are necessary expenses to ensure a fair and appropriate outcome.

The demand for trilingual interpreters is great and will continue to grow (Gerner de García 1993b, 1995b, 2000; MacNeil, 1990; Struxness, 2000). This is especially true since the FCC began approving reimbursement for ASL-Spanish video relay service (VRS) minutes. Trilingual options are offered in interpreter preparation programs at places such as San Antonio College in Texas and Santa Fe Community College in New Mexico. In 1994, a trilingual task force was established by the Texas Commission for the Deaf and Hard of hearing, which later through consolidation became known as the Office for Deaf and Hard-of-Hearing Services (DHHS) within the Department of Assistive and Rehabilitative Services (DARS). The task force verified that the demand for trilingual interpreters was present and growing. Its main concern was to establish a way to verify trilingual interpreter competence. After multiple efforts, DHHS obtained the authority and the funding to train and test ASL-English-Spanish trilingual interpreters. Funded by the U.S. Department of Education, DHHS partnered with the University of Arizona's National Center for Interpretation in a project called the Texas Trilingual Initiative. The initiative yielded the first ever ASL-English-Spanish trilingual certification exam. Although specific to Texas, this certification is having a nationwide impact. The initial seed money of $500,000, provided by the federal government, has resulted in a self-sustaining program with positive national ramifications for the preparation of trilingual interpreters. Perhaps coupled with increased (appropriate) use of video remote interpreting (VRI), the supply of trilingual interpreters can begin to keep pace with the demand.

BARRIER: LACK OF IMMEDIATE AND CONTINUOUS ASL IMMERSION

A sizeable body of literature addresses the most appropriate testing/assessment of deaf Hispanic/Latino students as they first enter school (Bennett, 1987b, 1988; Bowen, 2000; Figueroa, Delgado, & Ruiz, 1984; Gerner de García, 1995a; Jackson-Maldonado, 1993; Secada, 1984; Zieziula, 1982). However, little attention has been focused on the facilitation of ASL-English-Spanish trilingualism before the entrance into formal education.

A naturally acquired language is any language learned during childhood without intervention from professionals (Wilbur, 2008). Spanish, ASL, and English are all examples of natural languages. Each naturally acquired spoken language uses a unique set of sounds. Fascinating research has revealed that hearing infants are born with an innate ability to distinguish all of the sounds, no matter what their place of birth. That ability then begins to fade between the ages of 6 months and 1 year as infants retain only the sounds used in the languages to which they are exposed (Kuhl, Gopnik, & Meltzoff, 1999). Hence, if an opportunity exists, it may be more advantageous for hearing children to simultaneously learn multiple spoken languages early on, especially since children who are learning multiple languages with equal exposure tend to develop them all at the same rate as monolingual children, who are learning only one. They can then build literacy on top of each language they speak. However, it is also possible to become bilingual or multilingual in a sequential fashion. First, a primary language is acquired naturally. Then that language is utilized to scaffold a second language using familiar structures. During the stages before puberty, the languages may not have equal status, but this does not necessarily affect their status later (Wilbur, 2008). Williams (1991) applied this concept as well with a deaf Hispanic adolescent.

If a significant hearing loss is introduced into the picture, the usual milestones for the development of spoken language are altered since they are dependent on comprehensible auditory input. If a natural language is not introduced early, language acquisition is delayed. Systems of signed English were invented in the hopes they would circumvent the hearing loss and instill English in a way that parallels spoken English acquisition. It is now clear that this does not work consistently. Signed English systems are not natural languages because they lack the universal characteristics that natural languages possess (Wilbur & Petersen, 1998). These characteristics are essential for normal communication and serve as a foundation on which literacy and second languages can be effectively built (Schick, 2003). Suppose that ASL is introduced as the natural first language. Since it fulfills all of the requirements of a natural language, it can then be utilized to teach English as a second language. This is how Deaf bilingual-bicultural education works and how thousands of Deaf children have learned English. Trilingual-tricultural education of deaf students can work in a similar manner.

The amount of research showing better overall educational achievement by Deaf students fluent in ASL in comparison with those not fluent in ASL is striking (Hoffmeister, 2000; Padden & Ramsey, 2000; Prinz, 2002; Singleton, Supalla, Litchfield, & Schley, 1998; Strong & Prinz, 1997). Early exposure to signed language can provide deaf infants with a head start toward salient communication. Deaf children of Deaf parents who use ASL achieve linguistic milestones in a manner that parallels the acquisition of spoken language by hearing children of hearing parents (Karmiloff & Karmiloff-Smith, 2001).

Depending on the Hispanic child and the extent of hearing loss, time may be spent on speech output or speech recognition. The point at which speech and auditory training begin to replace academic and extracurricular learning needs to be considered on an individual basis. Incidentally, using early sign language with *hearing* babies and children (more popularly known as "baby signs") has been shown to give them a boost in speech development, IQ, self-confidence, positive emotional development, and trust in their caregivers, all the while reducing frustration and aggressive behaviors (Goodwyn, Acredolo, & Brown, 2000). Introduction and use of a natural signed language such as ASL can ensure full visual access to information regardless of hearing loss.

BARRIER: LACK OF OPPORTUNITY FOR SPANISH-SPEAKING FAMILY MEMBERS TO ACQUIRE ASL

Picture a home in which a hodgepodge of oral English, signed English, ASL, and home signs/gestures is used. Now picture a home where some oral Spanish, some country-of-origin sign language, and more distinct homesigns/gestures are *also* thrown into the mix. If all of these systems are being used at will without rhyme or reason, will confusion ensue? Walker-Vann (1998) observed the answer to be yes among the Hispanic students at the Texas School for the Deaf. Goldin-Meadow and Feldman (1977) found that in the absence of signing, deaf children of hearing parents eventually develop a personal system of invented signs in order to improve communication with each other. Clearly, deaf children intend to communicate, regardless of the hearing status of their parents. While it is true that any attempt at communication should be validated, what is the best way to avoid confusion for the family? Can a child learn multiple distinct languages and still avoid confusion? Saunders (1982) demonstrated that multiple-language acquisition can occur without creating confusion. Gerner de García (1993b, 1995a) established that three languages *acquired naturally and consistently* do not confuse even deaf or hard of hearing children. The main concern is how to provide the best means of developing a deaf child's communicative intent, especially in the case of families who have no familiarity with signed language.

Spanish-speaking parents, like their English-speaking counterparts, can begin learning rudimentary ASL in order to provide early language models as soon as they discover that their child is deaf (Christensen, 2000). They may be apprehensive at first, but not only do those parents who learn ASL discover they can communicate with their children, but their children reap abundant benefits with respect to bilingual and trilingual success in school as well. Mapp and Hudson (1997) reported lower parental stress when children signed either well or fluently. When families see successful Deaf role models and learn of the extent that the law protects access to communication for deaf and hard of hearing individuals, it follows that they will feel more positive about the opportunities available to their deaf child.

English-speaking parents of children with hearing loss have easier access to ASL classes and other ASL resources in English. Deaf teachers of beginning ASL classes also use English as needed to communicate concepts. In order to involve Hispanic/Latino families in the education of their deaf children, many more ASL classes taught in Spanish and other ASL resources in Spanish need to be made available (Christensen, 1986, 1993; Delgado, 1984; Gerner de García, 1993a). There is no research to back up the pedagogical effectiveness of current practice, which is simply to place a Spanish-English interpreter, often not specially trained, beside the Spanish speaker in an ASL class to *chucotage*, or "whisper interpret," the entire course. Successful Spanish-to-ASL didactic methods need to be further developed.

In 1982 Christensen carried out a three-year, trilingual education project. Live sign language instructional programs targeting monolingual, hearing, Spanish-speaking parents of Deaf Hispanic/Latino children were televised once a week and allowed participants to phone in questions. A taped version was televised in two different time slots each week, thus allowing family members who worked on different time shifts to view the program. The series was accompanied by an illustrated manual with direct Spanish and English translations of video scripts. The study found that the parents who faithfully viewed the programs were successful in the acquisition and use of a rudimentary signed language. Additionally, the parents' attitudes toward their children's deafness improved. An unanticipated finding of the study, with extreme potential for utility, was that some parents were pleased to find they were *simultaneously* learning basic English as well (Christensen, 1986). It is a shame that in the last quarter century more researchers and educators have not jumped at this finding and further investigated it in order to develop successful programs around it. On a positive note, however, the California School for the Deaf in Fremont is now piloting a Family ASL Learning Video Project, in which individual ASL tutors teach families of deaf children ASL from the comfort of their homes through high-speed Internet point-to-point video calling. This project shows promise for families of deaf children who speak languages other than English.

It is common for Hispanic/Latino families to have multiple children. The hearing siblings of the deaf child could be urged to develop ASL fluency at a young age. They will also most likely be fluent in Spanish and English, making them trilingual. It is these siblings who could become the greatest pool of potential ASL-English-Spanish trilingual educators and interpreters. However, they must never be made to interpret as children in settings that are required by law to provide trained interpreters (e.g., educational, medical, legal). Besides the dangerous fact that no level of accuracy is guaranteed, the use of young hearing siblings as interpreters has been shown to cause higher levels of family stress, lower levels of parenting effectiveness, and poorer adolescent adjustment in terms of academic functioning, socioemotional health, and substance use (Martínez, McClure, & Eddy, 2009).

BARRIER: ARGUMENTS AGAINST THE TEACHING OF ASL

A common argument against the teaching of ASL as a child's native language is that the child will be unprepared to function as an adult in the larger society. This argument falls fast and hard in the face of the many Deaf persons who have mastered both ASL and English. Imagine a Deaf person who has mastered ASL, English, and Spanish. Imagine a Deaf person who has mastered ASL, English, Spanish, and another signed language.

Once again, it should be understood that having native command of a language does not necessarily equate to fluent speech. The written form of a spoken language can be used very effectively. Unfortunately, society still judges individuals by their speech. By perpetuating the myth of the superiority of speech, the school of thought that stresses speech over language has endured at the expense of Deaf children. Families may not perceive that when professionals are recommending that the deaf or hard of hearing child concentrate on speech, they may purposely be overlooking other, more important cognitive and linguistic goals (Wilbur, 2008). Some professionals may not necessarily argue against the teaching of ASL, but they may advise against additional efforts to improve speech in Spanish in order to avoid confusion with English speech. Yet again the distinction between language and speech is rarely made clear to parents. Overlooked oftentimes is the fact that many of these children are immersed for many hours per day in an environment replete with a variety of model native Spanish speakers. I personally know young students with hearing loss who speak better Spanish than English even though all of their speech therapy is in English. They are exposed to natural language in the home but fractured English in school in order to communicate academic content. Perhaps for some of these students, a minimal amount of professional aid in spoken Spanish would help them make connections, propel them forward, and provide a good foundation on which to learn English and English speech.

Once Deaf individuals have a command of English, they can choose to express themselves in English through a signed system (either to others who know sign or through an interpreter/transliterator). Many adults with hearing loss who use speech utilize English signing in a receptive manner to make voice carry-over (VCO) phone calls through video relay. Hard of hearing Spanish speakers can and do use the same signing systems but layered on top of Spanish word order and mouthing. (Trilingual interpreters must be able to recognize and reproduce this preference of signing and mouthing.)

There was a time when parents were counseled to throw out their Spanish altogether in a misinformed leap of faith that even their poorly modeled English would help their child learn English (Schaeffer-Dresler, 1981). The House Ear Institute's CARE (Children's Auditory Research and Evaluation) Center in Los Angeles used to counsel families to adopt their child's language of instruction at school as the primary language in the home, without regard to the parents' actual proficiency in this language. The center abandoned this practice since the demand was neither sensitive nor realistic (Levi, Boyett-Solano, Nicholson, & Laurie, 2001). The English-only practice is very harmful to parent-child interactions since it can make parents feel inadequate just when they are learning to cope with their child's deafness (Blackwell & Fischgrund, 1984). This impacts interaction at home and may create barriers to communication between family members and the deaf child. In fact, deaf children may be more comfortable communicating with their friends and teachers at school.

Steinberg et al. (2002) found that the medical professionals consulted by Hispanic families frequently had one, narrow philosophy and gave little consideration to alternative approaches. Some Spanish-speaking parents in that study had been told not to speak Spanish to their deaf children, and some were told not to sign to their deaf children. Lane, Hoffmeister, and Bahan (1996) stated the following:

[F]or parents not to communicate with their child in signed language is tantamount to not communicating with the child at all. This advice frequently makes the parents feel guilty (for not providing "the best" language environment), angry (since they cannot live up to the professionals' ideal), and mistrustful (since the advice is counter to their loving desire to communicate). (p. 29)

Certainly an ethical approach to education would include supporting parents to communicate in all languages that are appropriate for their situation.

BARRIER: ORALISM AS THE ONLY METHOD OF COMMUNICATION

Telling Spanish-speaking parents that oralism is the best method of course means oral English. Oral training in Spanish is very hard to locate and likely not covered by insurance. The intrinsic problem is that speechreading is an attempt to "use vision to perceive a language code designed for oral/aural transmission [and] is, at best, difficult" (Kopp 1984a, p. 73). Kopp also stated that "If the auditory stimulus at home is in Spanish and at school is in English, opportunities for input/output confusion are even more probable among the hearing impaired than the hearing (p. 73)." Oralism is fundamentally more difficult for congenitally deaf children, for they have never heard either language and are unfamiliar with the pronunciation of words. For children with oral potential, such as those with significant residual hearing, however, an enrichment program in Spanish *as part of a trilingual program* can improve Spanish speech intelligibility and also help increase expressive English and ASL (Gerner de García, 1989).

Historically, when comparing the two groups of deaf ASL and deaf non-ASL users, speech production and speechreading scores were similar. The ASL users scored better on nearly every other measure of English (Meadow, 1966; Quigley & Frisina, 1961; Stevenson, 1964). Even though these studies are all more than 40 years old, they have not been disproved. More modern research focuses instead on how ASL aids academic success, including speech and literacy (Wilbur, 2008). This dispels any fear that "non-oral" children will not become literate in English.

BARRIER: COCHLEAR IMPLANTS AS A FIX ALL

In the United States, 30.7% of Hispanics are uninsured, the highest rate of any racial/ethnic group in the country (U.S. Census Bureau, 2009). Lack of health insurance is a key barrier that prevents many Latinos from accessing health care services and receiving quality health care (Bierman, Magari, Jette, Splaine & Wasson, 1998). Cochlear implant surgery and follow-up services, especially speech and auditory training, are mandatory for success and very expensive. Proximity to the medical center where services will be rendered makes it difficult for the Spanish-speaking families that live in rural areas. In general, persons who live a great distance from a medical facility and have no medical insurance are at risk for medical complications and unsuccessful implants. The success of a cochlear implant hinges greatly upon the family's efforts but it is also important that the child's school district be supportive. It is unfortunate that a large proportion of Hispanics/Latinos in the United States live in low-income areas, where schools suffer from a severe lack of resources.

Although difficult to achieve in the midst of unfavorable socioeconomic conditions, with appropriate follow-up children with implants from linguistically diverse families do not appear to lag behind their peers in *English* speech-perception skills, although there is some indication that those in total communication programs face greater challenges (Levi et al., 2001). When it comes to children with implants learning multiple spoken languages, so far it appears that only a certain subset of these children are able to attain success. Factors such as the full bilingualism and biculturalism of the parents matter greatly (McConkey Robbins, 2007).

Little research has been accomplished with children who have cochlear implants and manage to become fluent in ASL, English, and Spanish. Individuals with these skills would be truly exceptional and should be studied on a case-by-case basis to reveal the mechanisms for success.

BARRIER: LACK OF EARLY AND ONGOING SPANISH AND ENGLISH LITERACY

Among three-language combinations spoken by individuals throughout the world, the ASL-English-Spanish combination is unique in that two of the languages are aural/oral in nature, accompanied by a written form, while the other is based on a visual medium for which there is no approved written form. Deaf Americans use either ASL in video format or written English for literacy purposes. In the case of deaf Hispanic individuals, written Spanish may be part of the mix. The essential elements of parent-child interaction, which sustain language acquisition in young children, are also present and sustain the early acquisitions of reading and writing (Snow, 1983). Videos produced at Gallaudet University outline principles for parents to follow when reading to deaf children. When confusion is present in a child learning more than one language, the source is most often the child's not knowing when transitions from one language to another occur (Saunders, 1982). A cognitive overload does not necessarily take place. Rather, it must always and consistently be made clear which language is being used at what time.

With regard to literacy and deaf children, Gerner de García (1993b) explains as follows:

> No one has to be taught to read more than once. Once a child knows how to decode print, that child can decode print in other languages by transferring what he or she already knows to the other language. This makes it possible for any child, deaf or hearing, to become biliterate. Hispanic Deaf children also feel empowered as they realize that the language they use at home is also something that they can read. (pp. 84–85)

Once deaf children can read on their own, they should be encouraged to read as much as possible. The activity can be made into an amusing pastime to be enjoyed by family members together. A deep, long-lasting appreciation for reading will do more for the literacy skills of that individual—in any language—than any other single factor. Besides reading from children's and other books, written conversations with extended family members not fluent in ASL can help to teach the informal ways in which Spanish and English are used. Watching captioned television shows and movies is another good way to learn how language is used every day by society in general. English-to-English captions are prevalent. Spanish-to-Spanish captions are less common but becoming more widespread. Ideas such as providing Spanish-to-Spanish captions of the story-telling, value-perpetuating movies of the "golden age" of Mexican cinema by the Described and Captioned Media Program can greatly foster the literacy abilities of Hispanic/Latino children who are deaf. English-to-Spanish and Spanish-to-English subtitles may also be used as appropriate. When literate in Spanish, deaf children can finally overcome the barricade that prohibits them from gaining access to their Latino culture and history, which is rich in oral traditions (García, 2004).

BARRIER: LACK OF AN APPROPRIATE MULTILINGUAL/MULTICULTURAL SCHOOL CLIMATE

One of the goals of a typical bilingual curriculum for hearing children is to provide Spanish-speaking children with a conceptual foundation in order to facilitate their learning of the new culture at school. If this is not done, the children oftentimes know only that something is different between the home and the school. Then, because of unintentional but powerful majority peer influence, the children determine that what is different is inferior (Fischgrund, 1984). This accounts for the high number of Latino hearing children and adolescents who seem to be monolingual Spanish speakers when they begin school but monolingual English speakers when they finish. Somehow they seem to lose their first language. At some point, each language needs to be given equal status. Cognitive development is improved and learning becomes more effective when deaf children can relate home to school experiences. This implies an inclusion of their home culture in the school curriculum (Christensen, 1993; Cohen & Grant, 1981). Even though the population of deaf Hispanic children has been sharply increasing for several decades, only a few programs systematically address their trilingual and multicultural needs (Gerner de García, 1995b). The ones that do exist need to be examined more closely. If the children's multilingual experiences were acknowledged, they could be put to greater use (Sneddon, 2007). A holistic approach to educating the deaf child would likely produce a much better outcome:

> The process of learning two new languages should not mean substituting the new languages for the original language . . . A Spanish literate deaf child should continue to get support and instruction in Spanish while learning English. Such a student may learn a signed language more quickly than hearing children learn conversational English, but his or her academic progress may depend on continued support in Spanish. Competence in ASL doesn't eliminate the importance of reinforcing academic content in Spanish. (Gerner de García 1993a, p. 81)

Several other aspects of an ideal trilingual and multicultural program must not be forgotten, like the inclusion of culturally specific curricula, ethnically diverse teachers of Deaf students, and role models, staff, and other personnel trained in multiculturalism. Literature, traditional stories, and history, told from the Latino/Chicano point of view, must be a part of what Deaf Latino students are learning. None of these are new recommendations (Christensen & Delgado, 1993; Rodríguez & Santiviago, 1991; Sass-Lehrer, Gerner de García, & Rovins, 1997; Wolbers, 2002), but they are still viable.

Discussion

While still president of Gallaudet University, I. King Jordan (February 2, 2005) was a guest on the radio broadcast *Talk of the Nation* on National Public Radio. He had the last comment of the show:

> Deaf people can't hear. That's so fundamental and simple that people seem to forget it. We can't hear. Therefore, we see. What language could be better for vision than sign language, a language that was created to be seen, not a language that was created to be heard and spoken?

American Sign Language comes together with its accompanying culture and history. Being Deaf in the United States means belonging to a unique cultural group with its own language and history. The academic language of the United States is English. Deaf children who attend school in the United States will likely finish school, go on to college, obtain jobs, and raise their own families in the United States. They will encounter hearing mainstream Americans on a daily basis, and this American culture will undoubtedly be a part of their everyday lives. English literacy is imperative. To the degree that these children also learn the Spanish language, they will be able to inherit the rich cultural and family heritage of which they also are a part. They will be able to develop a firm and lasting bond between themselves, their family members, and their ancestors (García, 2004). Unlike second-language learners in an academic setting, Hispanic/Latino deaf/hard of hearing children who are living with Spanish-speaking families are already immersed in a natural context in which to learn Spanish.

It is not hard to see that these children and youth, by default, live in a trilingual, multicultural world. Denying them access to any of the three languages may take away important advantages by removing the very medium through which each culture is passed on. It is curtailing their very identities.

The following quote from a Spanish-speaking mother of a six-year-old Deaf boy speaks eloquently to the issue of ethical decision making in the education of deaf children:

> I want him to be trilingual when he is an adult so that he interacts with his family in Spanish, that he obtains a good job, that he is well paid because he can speak three languages, that if someday he finds himself in a group situation where everyone is deaf, he will be able to communicate with them on an equal basis, that he does not feel apart from the Hispanic group because he is Hispanic, that he does not feel as an outsider with deaf people because he is deaf, and that he does not feel as an outsider with English because he lives here, it is the language of this country and he must be fluent. I think he will have more advantages than other people. And for this reason, I want him to be able to communicate in the three languages. (Steinberg et al., 2002, p. 32; translated from Spanish)

He will live, effectively, in three cultures . . . a world of triplicity. Is this not his right?

References

Bennett, A. (1987a). *Perspectives on identity: The Hispanic deaf child's initiation into formal schooling.* (ERIC Document Reproduction Service No. ED 313825). Retrieved from http://www.eric.ed.gov/.

Bennett, A. (1987b). *Schooling the different: Ethnographic case studies of Hispanic deaf children's initiation into formal schooling.* Final report to the Office of Special Education and Rehabilitation. (ERIC Document Reproduction Service No. ED 300941). Retrieved from http://www.eric.ed.gov/.

Bennett, A. (1988). Gateway to powerlessness: Incorporating Hispanic deaf children and families into formal schooling. *Disability, Handicap, and Society, 3*(2), 119–151.

Berry, J. W. (1990). Comparative studies of acculturative stress. *International Migration Review, 21,* 491–511.

Bierman, A. S., Magari, E. S, Jette, A. M, Splaine, M., & Wasson, J. H. (1998). Assessing access as a first step toward improving the quality of care for very old adults. *Journal of Ambulatory Care Management, 21*(3), 17–26.

Blackwell, P. M., & Fischgrund, J. E. (1984). Issues in the development of culturally responsive programs for deaf students from non-English-speaking homes. In G. L. Delgado (Ed.), *The Hispanic deaf: Issues and challenges for bilingual special education* (pp. 154–166). Washington, DC: Gallaudet College Press.

Bowen, S. (2000). *Hispanic deaf students in rural education settings: Complex issues.* Capitalizing on Leadership in Rural Special Education. (ERIC Document Reproduction Service No. ED 439875). Retrieved from http://www.eric.ed.gov/.

Calderon, R. (2000). Parental involvement in deaf children's education programs as a predictor of child's language, early reading, and social-emotional development. *Journal of Deaf Studies and Deaf Education, 5*(2), 140–155.

Cazden, C. B. (1972). *Child language and education.* New York: Holt, Rinehart, and Winston.

Christensen, K. M. (1985). Conceptual sign language as a bridge between English and Spanish. *American Annals of the Deaf, 130,* 244–249.

Christensen, K. M. (1986). Conceptual sign language acquisition by Spanish-speaking parents of hearing-impaired children. *American Annals of the Deaf, 131,* 285–287.

Christensen, K. M. (1993). A multicultural approach to education of children who are deaf. In K. M. Christensen & G. L. Delgado (Eds.), *Multicultural issues in deafness* (pp. 17–27). New York: Longman.

Christensen, K. M. (2000). Emerging literacy in bilingual/multicultural education of children who are deaf: A communication-based perspective. In K. Christensen (Ed.), *Deaf plus: A multicultural perspective* (pp. 41–58). San Diego: DawnSignPress.

Christensen, K. M., & Delgado, G. L. (Eds.). (1993). *Multicultural issues in deafness.* New York: Longman.

Cohen, O. P. (1993). Educational needs of African American and Hispanic deaf children and youth. In K. M. Christensen & G. L. Delgado (Eds.), *Multicultural issues in deafness* (pp. 45–67). New York: Longman.

Cohen, O. P., Fischgrund, J. E., & Redding, R. (1990). Deaf children from ethnic, linguistic, and racial minority backgrounds: An overview. *American Annals of the Deaf, 135,* 67–73.

Cohen, O. P., & Grant, B. (1981). Ethnic heritage and cultural implications in a school for deaf children. In F. Solano, J. Dodd-Egleston, & E. Costello (Eds.), *Focus on infusion* (pp. 72–78). Rochester, NY: Convention of American Instructors of the Deaf.

Crawford, J. (1998). Issues in U.S. language policy: Bilingual education. Retrieved August 1, 2010 from http://www.languagepolicy.net/archives/biling.htm.

Cummins, J. (1988). From multicultural to anti-racist education: An analysis of programmes and policies in Ontario. (Reprinted in *An introductory reader to the writings of Jim Cummins,* pp. 215–239, by C. Baker & N. H. Hornberger (Eds.), 2001, Buffalo, NY: Multilingual Matters)

Dagenais, D., & Day, E. (1999). Home language practices of trilingual children in French immersion. *Canadian Modern Language Review, 56*(1), 99–123.

Dean, C. C. (1984). The hearing-impaired Hispanic child: Sociolinguistic considerations. In G. L. Delgado (Ed.), *The Hispanic deaf: Issues and challenges for bilingual special education* (pp. 58–68). Washington, DC: Gallaudet College Press.

Delgado, G. L. (1984). Hearing-impaired children from non-native-language homes. In G. L. Delgado (Ed.), *The Hispanic deaf: Issues and challenges for bilingual special education* (pp. 28–37). Washington, DC: Gallaudet College Press.

Delgado, G. L. (2000). How are we doing? In K. Christensen (Ed.), *Deaf plus: A multicultural perspective* (pp. 29–40). San Diego: DawnSignPress.

Delgado, G. L. (2001). *Hispanic/Latino deaf students in our schools: Research report.* University of Tennessee–Knoxville: Postsecondary Education Consortium.

Figueroa, R. A., Delgado, G. L., & Ruiz, N. T. (1984). Assessment of Hispanic children: Implications for Hispanic hearing-impaired children. In G. L. Delgado (Ed.), *The Hispanic deaf: Issues and challenges for bilingual special education* (pp. 124–152). Washington, DC: Gallaudet College Press.

Fischgrund, J. E. (1984). Language intervention for hearing-impaired children from linguistically and culturally diverse backgrounds. In G. L. Delgado (Ed.), *The Hispanic deaf: Issues and challenges for bilingual special education* (pp. 94–105). Washington, DC: Gallaudet College Press.

Foster, S., & Kinuthia, W. (2003). Deaf persons of Asian American, Hispanic American, and African American backgrounds: A study of intraindividual diversity and identity. *Journal of Deaf Studies and Deaf Education 8*(3), 271–290. doi:10.1093/deafed/eng015.

Gallaudet Research Institute. (2006, December). *State summary report of data from the 2006–2007 annual survey of deaf and hard of hearing children and youth.* Washington, DC: Gallaudet University Press.

Gallaudet Research Institute. (2008, November). *Regional and national summary report of data from the 2007–08 annual survey of deaf and hard of hearing children and youth.* Washington, DC: Gallaudet University Press.

García, T. (2004). *La promesa de un tesoro (The promise of a treasure).* Captioned Media Program: National Association of the Deaf.

Gerner de García, B. (1989, June). *Educating Spanish-dominant hearing-impaired children.* Paper presented at the Conference of the American Instructors of the Deaf Convention, San Diego.

Gerner de García, B. (1993a). Addressing the needs of Hispanic Deaf children. In K. M. Christensen & G. L. Delgado (Eds.), *Multicultural issues in deafness* (pp. 65–90). New York: Longman.

Gerner de García, B. (1993b). *Language use in Spanish-speaking families with deaf children.* Unpublished doctoral dissertation, Boston University.

Gerner de García, B. (1995a). Communication and language use in Spanish-speaking children with deaf children. In C. Lucas (Ed.), *Sociolinguistics in deaf communities* (pp. 221–252). Washington, DC: Gallaudet University Press.

Gerner de García, B. (1995b). ESL applications for Hispanic deaf students. *Bilingual Research Journal, 19,* 453–467.

Gerner de García, B. (2000). Meeting the needs of Hispanic/Latino deaf students. In K. Christensen (Ed.), *Deaf plus: A multicultural perspective* (pp. 149–198). San Diego: DawnSignPress.

Goldin-Meadow, S., & Feldman, H. (1977). The development of language-like communication without a language model. *Science, 197,* 401–403.

González Álvarez, L. (1998). A short course in sensitivity training: Working with Hispanic families of children with disabilities. *Teaching Exceptional Children, 31*(1), 73–77.

Goodwyn, S. W., Acredolo, L. P., & Brown, C. A. (2000). Impact of symbolic gesturing on early language development. *Journal of Nonverbal Behavior, 24*, 81–103.

Goring, M. B., & Martindale, M. E. (1989). *Delivery of services to Hispanic families with young hearing-impaired children: One model.* Paper presented at the Conference of the American Speech-Language-Hearing Association. (ERIC Document Reproduction Service No. ED 322657). Retrieved November 4, 2009 from http://www.eric.ed.gov/.

Grant, J. (1972). *Proceedings of a workshop on the preparation of personnel in the education of bilingual hearing-impaired children, ages 0–4.* San Antonio: Trinity University. (ERIC Document Reproduction Service No. ED 113908). Retrieved November 4, 2009, from http://www.eric.ed.gov/.

Grant, J. (1984). Teachers of Hispanic hearing-impaired children: Competencies and preparation. In G. L. Delgado (Ed.), *The Hispanic deaf: Issues and challenges for bilingual special education* (pp. 182–194). Washington, DC: Gallaudet College Press.

Hakuta, K. (1986). Mirror of language: The *debate on bilingualism.* New York: Basic Books.

Haualand, H., & Allen, C. (2009). *Deaf people and human rights.* World Federation of the Deaf and the Swedish National Association of the Deaf.

Hoffmeister, R. (2000). A piece of the puzzle: ASL and reading comprehension in deaf children. In C. Chamberlain, J. P. Morford, & R. I. Mayberry (Eds.), *Language acquisition by eye* (pp. 143–164). Mahwah, NJ: Erlbaum.

Holly, W. J. (1987). Students' self-esteem and academic achievement. Research Round-up, *4*(1), 1–6.

Humphrey, J., & Alcorn, B. (2001). *So you want to be an interpreter?* (3rd ed.). Amarillo, TX: H & H.

Jackson-Maldonado, D. (1993). Mexico and the United States: A cross-cultural perspective on the education of deaf children. In K. M. Christensen & G. L. Delgado (Eds.), *Multicultural issues in deafness* (pp. 91–112). New York: Longman.

Jensema, C. (1975). *The relationship between academic achievement and demographic characteristics of hearing impaired youth.* Washington, DC: Gallaudet College Office of Demographic Studies.

Jordan, I. K. (Guest). (2005, February 2). *An exploration of deaf culture in America* [radio broadcast]. In S. Goodwin (executive producer), *Talk of the Nation.* Washington, DC: National Public Radio.

Karmiloff, K., & Karmiloff-Smith, A. (2001). *Pathways to language: From fetus to adolescent.* Cambridge, MA: Harvard University Press.

Kopp, H. G. (1984a). Bilingual problems of the Hispanic deaf. In G. L. Delgado (Ed.), *The Hispanic deaf: Issues and challenges for bilingual special education* (pp. 69–78). Washington, DC: Gallaudet College Press.

Kopp, H. G. (1984b). Outreach programs for the Hispanic deaf: One model. In G. L. Delgado (Ed.), *The Hispanic deaf: Issues and challenges for bilingual special education* (pp. 195–200). Washington, DC: Gallaudet College Press.

Kovács, A. M., & Mehler, J. (2009). Flexible learning of multiple speech structures in bilingual infants. *Science, 325*(5940), 611–612. doi:10.1126/science.1173947.

Krashen, S. (1996). *Under attack: The case against bilingual education.* Culver City, CA: Language Education Associates.

Kuhl, P., Gopnik, A., & Meltzoff, A. (1999). *The scientist in the crib: Minds, brains, and how children learn.* New York: Morrow.

Lambert, W. E. (1979). Language as a factor in intergroup relations. In H. Giles & R. St. Clair (Eds.), *Language and social psychology* (pp. 186–192). Baltimore: University Park Press.

Lane, H., Hoffmeister, R., & Bahan, B. (1996). *A journey into the deaf-world*. San Diego: Dawn-SignPress.

Lang, J. G., Muñoz, R. F., Bernal, G., & Sorensen, J. L. (1982). Quality of life and psychological well-being in a bicultural Latino community. *Hispanic Journal of Behavior Sciences, 4*, 433–450.

Levi, A. V., Boyett-Solano, J., Nicholson, B., & Laurie, S. (2001, June). Multilingualism and children with cochlear implants. *Hearing Review 8* (6), 44–49.

Luetke-Stahlman, B. (1976). Questionnaire results from Mexican-American parents of hearing-impaired children in the United States. *American Annals of the Deaf, 121*, 565–568.

MacNeil, B. (1990). Educational needs for hearing-impaired students in the public school system. *American Annals of the Deaf, 135*, 75–82.

Mapp, I., & Hudson, R. (1997). Stress and coping among African American and Hispanic parents of deaf children. *American Annals of the Deaf, 142*, 48–56.

Marian, V., Faroqi-Shah, Y., Kaushanskaya, M., Blumenfeld, H., and Sheng, L. (2009, October 13). Bilingualism: Consequences for language, cognition, development, and the brain. *ASHA Leader, 14*(13), 10–13.

Martínez, C. R., Jr., McClure, H. M., & Eddy, J. M. (2009). Language brokering contexts and behavioral and emotional adjustment among Latino parents and adolescents. *Journal of Early Adolescence, 29*(1), 71–98.

McConkey Robbins, A. (2007). Clinical management of bilingual families and children with cochlear implants. *Loud & Clear! 1*, 1–12.

Meadow, K. (1966). *The effects of early manual communication and family climate on the deaf child's early development*. Unpublished doctoral dissertation, University of California–Berkeley.

Mercer, J. R. (1972). IQ: The lethal label. *Psychology Today, 6*(9), 95–97.

Mercer, J. R. (1973). *Labeling the mentally retarded*. Berkeley: University of California Press.

Miranda, A., & Umhoefer, D. (1998). Acculturation, language use, and demographic variables as predictors of the career self-efficacy. *Journal of Multicultural Counseling and Development, 26*(1), 39–52.

Modiano, N. (1966). *A comparative study of two approaches to the teaching of reading in the national language*. Unpublished doctoral dissertation, New York University. Retrieved November 4, 2009, from http://eric.ed.gov/ERICWebPortal/search/detailmini.jsp?_nfpb=true&_&ERICExtSearch_SearchValue_0=ED010049&ERICExtSearch_SearchType_0=no&accno=ED010049.

Moores, D. (2001). *Educating the deaf: Psychology, principles, and practices* (5th ed.). Boston: Houghton Mifflin.

Muñoz-Baell, I. M., Álvarez-Dardet, C., Ruiz, M. T., Ortiz, R., Esteban, M. L., & Ferreiro, E. (2008). Preventing disability through understanding international megatrends in deaf bilingual education. *Journal of Epidemiology and Community Health, 62*, 131–137. doi:10.1136/jech.2006.059378.

Ogden, P., & Lipsett, S. (1982). *The silent garden*. New York: St. Martin's.

Padden, C., & Ramsey, C. (2000). American Sign Language and reading ability in deaf children. In C. Chamberlain, J. P. Morford, & R. I. Mayberry (Eds.), *Language acquisition by eye* (pp. 165–189). Mahwah, NJ: Erlbaum.

Page, J. M. (1993). Ethnic identity in deaf Hispanics of New Mexico. *Sign Language Studies, 80*, 185–221.

Prinz, P. (2002). Crosslinguistic perspectives on sign language and literacy development. In R. Schulmeister & H. Reinitzer (Eds.), *Progress in sign language research: In honor of Siegmund Prillwitz* (pp. 221–233). Hamburg: Signum.

Quigley, S. P., & Frisina, R. (1961). *Institutionalization and psychoeducational development in deaf children.* Washington, DC: Council on Exceptional Children.

Ramsey, C. (2000). On the border: Cultures, families, and schools in a transnational region. In K. Christensen (Ed.), *Deaf plus: A multicultural perspective* (pp. 121–147). San Diego: DawnSignPress.

Rodríguez, O. (1985). *Hispanic families and children.* Paper presented at the Urban Ethnic Minority Deaf Child Conference, Teachers College, Columbia University, New York.

Rodríguez, O., & Santiviago, M. (1991). Hispanic deaf adolescents: A multicultural minority. *Volta Review, 93*(5), 89–97.

Sass-Lehrer, M., Gerner de García, B., & Rovins, M. (1997). *Creating a multicultural school climate.* Washington, DC: Pre-College National Mission Programs, Gallaudet University.

Saunders, G. (1982). *Bilingual children: Guidance for the family.* Clevedon: Multilingual Matters.

Schaeffer-Dresler. (1981). *Hearing-impaired children from Spanish-speaking homes.* Unpublished master's thesis, California State University, Los Angeles.

Schick, B. (2003). The development of American Sign Language and manually coded English systems. In M. Marschark & P. E. Spencer (Eds.), *The Oxford handbook of deaf studies, language, and education* (pp. 219–231). New York: Oxford University Press.

Secada, W. G. (1984). The language of instruction for hearing-impaired students from non-English-speaking homes: A framework for considering alternatives. In G. L. Delgado (Ed.), *The Hispanic deaf: Issues and challenges for bilingual special education* (pp. 80–93). Washington, DC: Gallaudet College Press.

Singleton, J. L., Supalla, S., Litchfield, S., & Schley, S. (1998). From sign to word: Considering modality constraints in ASL/English bilingual education. ASL proficiency and English literacy acquisition: New perspectives. *Topics in Language Disorders, 18*(4), 16–29.

Sneddon, R. (2007). Learning in three languages in home and community. In J. Conteh, P. Martin, & L. H. Robertson (Eds.), *Multilingual learning stories in schools and communities in Britain* (pp. 32–55). Stoke-on-Trent: Trentham.

Snow, C. (1983). Literacy and language: Relationships during the preschool years. *Harvard Education Review, 53*, 165–189.

Steinberg, A., Bain, L., Li, Y., Montoya, L., & Ruperto, V. (2002). *A look at the decisions Hispanic families make after the diagnosis of deafness.* Washington, DC: Laurent Clerc National Deaf Education Center, Gallaudet University.

Stevenson, E. A. (1964). A study of educational achievement of deaf children of deaf parents. *California News, 80*(143), 1–3.

Strong, M., & Prinz, P. (1997). A study of the relationship between ASL and English literacy. *Journal of Deaf Studies and Deaf Education, 2*(1), 37–46.

Struxness, K. (2000). School support services for Hispanic deaf children and families in southern California school settings. In K. Christensen (Ed.), *Deaf plus: A multicultural perspective* (pp. 199–219). San Diego: DawnSignPress.

Suro, R. (1999). *Strangers among us: Latino lives in a changing America.* New York: Vintage.

Tokuhama-Espinosa, T. (2003). *The multilingual mind.* Portsmouth, NH: Greenwood.

U.S. Census Bureau. (2003). Shin, H. B., & Bruno, R., *Language use and English-speaking ability: 2000*, U.S. Department of Commerce, Economics, and Statistics Administration, Washington, D.C.

U.S. Census Bureau. (2008, August 14). Table 4. Projections of the population by sex, race, and Hispanic origin for the United States: 2010 to 2050 (NP2008-T4).

U.S. Census Bureau. (2009). DeNavas-Walt, C., Proctor, B. D., & Smith, J. C., *Current population reports, P60–236, income, poverty, and health insurance coverage in the United States: 2008*, U.S. Government Printing Office, Washington, DC.

Walker-Vann, C. (1998). Profiling Hispanic deaf students: A first step toward solving the greater problems. *American Annals of the Deaf, 143*, 46–54.

Wilbur, R. B. (2008). Success with deaf children: How to prevent educational failure. In K. Lindgren, D. DeLuca, & J. Napoli (Eds.), *Signs & voices: Deaf culture, identity, language, and arts* (pp. 117–138). Washington, DC: Gallaudet University Press.

Wilbur, R. B., & Petersen, L. (1998). Backwards signing and ASL syllable structure. *Language and Speech, 40*(1), 63–90.

Williams, C. (1991). Teaching Hispanic deaf students: Lessons from Luis. *Perspectives in Education and Deafness, 10*(2), 2–5.

Wolbers, K. A. (2002). Cultural factors and the achievement of black and Hispanic deaf students. *Multicultural Education, 10*, 43–48.

Zieziula, F. R. (1982). *Assessment of hearing-impaired people.* Washington, DC: Gallaudet College Press.

3

Ethical Issues Regarding Cochlear Implantation in Children

An International Perspective

KATRIN NEUMANN

Our decision-making processes and actions are guided by ethical positions and judgments even if those are not made explicit. Ethics is a reflecting, theoretical science of morals, conventions, and values. On the one hand ethics are values that tend to be cultural universals and are instigated by ancestral biological programs (Alexander, 1987). These values follow evolutionary strategies to optimize genetic replication. On the other hand ethics are values that are the result of epigenetic processes (e.g., cultural, ethnic, social, environmental, and biographical factors). The former tend to be temporally stable, while the latter may show secular changes, for example, if a society evolves from a feudalistic to a democratic one.

Health professionals around the world distinguish between the terms *impairment* and *disability* or *handicap*. The latter terms are applied when impairments lead to a restriction of people's options for living life as they wish. The values, beliefs, and desires of people with disabilities are influenced by their conditions and also by their perceptions of how other people judge them (Wirth, 2006). Hence, the phenomena of exclusion and stigmatization are relative to a society and a historical period.

Many countries have mandated the basic rights of equality and free development of the individual as guaranteed by ethical principles. In 2001 the World Health Organization (WHO) initiated a shift in the definition of the term *disability*. New definitions have been elaborated in the International Classification of Function, Disability, and Health (ICF; World Health Organization, 2001; children and youth version: World Health Organization, 2007). In addition to the International Statistical Classification of Diseases and Related Health Problems (ICD-10; World Health Organization, 2004), which classifies diseases, the ICF gives definitions of *functioning*, *disability*, and *health*. There, contrasting conditions are formulated, such as participation vs. handicap, activity vs. restricted activity, and functioning vs. impairment. The aim of therapy and rehabilitation is to resolve conflicts with regard to participation,

I am grateful to my friend, partner, and colleague Harald A. Euler for his support in preparing the manuscript for this chapter.

activity, and functioning. This new concept of rehabilitation also has far-reaching consequences for deaf and hard of hearing children. In Germany, for example, it led to the establishment of a new profession—audiotherapy—which supports deaf and hard of hearing people by improving communication, enhancing social skills, and encouraging participation in social life. The introduction of the ICF brought functioning (with its emphasis on quality of daily life) more to the attention of health professionals and the public. Both private and public health insurance companies changed their reimbursement policies accordingly.

This chapter addresses the following questions: Which values guide interactions between hearing and deaf or hard of hearing people? Which attitudes underlie and determine these interactions? Which ethical rules do medical professionals, therapists, and educators follow when they advise deaf people? To what extent do their recommendations accord with the life values of deaf people? This latter, central concern is complicated by the fact that young deaf and hard of hearing children cannot speak for themselves. Decisions have to be made for them by their proxies, typically their parents. All of these concerns are most striking in the case of cochlear implantation, which involves the insertion of an electronic device in the body. Of course, an electronic device can break down or become obsolete. Surgery is invasive and bears risks, in particular in very young children. Another aspect is that future stem-cell therapies of genetically caused hearing losses, which make up about 50% of all infant hearing losses, may not require a cochlear implant. Parents are concerned whether or not such therapy will be still possible for a child who has a cochlear implant.

What is to be expected from the rehabilitation of disabilities in general? A disability should be reduced as much as possible by technical and social aids, as well as by newly learned abilities and strategies so that it no longer constitutes a disability (Wirth, 2006). This does not mean either to deny the disability or to cherish it but rather to overcome it by self-help and help from others, to find compensatory strategies, and to open up new avenues of personal development through new opportunities for participation in social interactions. This is a chance for both sides of the rehabilitation process, the deaf or hard of hearing individual and the caregiver or educator, to find common ground and develop humanity through social acts of giving and taking.

The Deaf Community and Cochlear Implants: Both Sides of the Controversy

The application of electronic implants in the auditory pathway has defined a cultural divide for some people. Childhood implantation in particular has been a focus of concern and debate (Gauntlett, 1996; Gonsoulin, 2001; Harvey, 2001; Hyde & Power, 2006; Levy, 2002; Niparko, 2004; Shultz, 2000; Vonier, 2008). In the discussion of the ethical aspects of cochlear implantation, we have to take into consideration that in secular, pluralistic societies, people have both collective and individual rights. Individual rights are at least as important as any collective view of the common good or any cultural orthodoxy. In our modern Western societies, we have to respect the autonomy and self-determination of other persons. Such individual rights should only in extreme circumstances be overridden by generally accepted social norms or by any minority culture (Nunes, 2001). Ethnic, racial, religious, linguistic, and other minorities have a fundamental right to live their self-determined specific ways of life, and acceptance of this right is obligatory for all others. The Deaf world constitutes such a minority inasmuch as it has its own culture, values, and attitudes. It also has its specific language—sign language. Belonging to the Deaf world means self-identification with Deaf people, with Deaf values, and with a Deaf culture (Nunes, 2001; Solomon, 1994). Although deafness is empirically associated with low educational levels and low family income (Harris, Anderson, & Novak, 1995), deafness and the nonauditive way of communication is not associated with impaired intelligence. This is one main reason that Deaf activists claim that deafness is not a disability (Lane, 2002). They clearly distinguish between the social construction of deafness as a disability and deafness as a cultural and linguistic variation within normality. From a physiological perspective, however, deafness results from a deficient inner ear and auditory pathway. The pathology is characterized by specific changes in the morphological structure of the auditory system and a subsequent functional deficit. This deficit cannot be regarded as a variation within the normal range because nature is efficient, and evolution would not have created and maintained such a delicate hearing structure without a function. Granted, this is a restricted physiological perspective, not a moral or even a necessarily medical one. The English philosopher David Hume has correctly pointed out the pitfall of the naturalistic fallacy, according to which it is not justified to derive the "ought" from the "is." Just because something is natural does not in and of itself mean that it is good. For postlingually deafened adults, the acquired deafness may be felt as a severe disability. Prelingually deaf persons, however, may not miss the experience they could never have.

In the case of cochlear implantation, two systems converge. A new, medically and technically oriented solution for deafness without a social history meets an equally young, self-confident cultural minority with a group identity passionately fought for (Dahm, 1998; Hintermair & Voit, 1990).

About one in a thousand babies is born deaf or with a profound hearing loss. More than half of these conditions are caused mainly by genes. Up to now, at least 120 genes are known to be responsible for nonsyndromic recessive deafness (i.e., deafness with no other associated clinical abnormality) (Nance, 2003). An impairment of the inner ear by ototoxic drugs or a progressive hearing loss caused by genetic factors or by infections such as cytomegalovirus infection may cause deafness or profound hearing loss in infants. Similarly, deafness in adulthood may be caused by skull-base fractures or long-term exposure to excessive noise. Hence, from a medical perspective, deafness is a disease and should be treated appropriately.

Cochlear implantation attempts to overcome deafness as a disease, a disability, and a limiting condition in the hearing world (Nunes, 2001). It is a well-accepted therapy for postlingually deafened adults who do not benefit from hearing aids. However, for children, it was a matter of hot-tempered debates for a long time. Nonetheless, improvements in cochlear-implant technology and surgery, more than two decades of pediatric clinical experience, growing evidence of the efficacy of cochlear implants for young children, and a change in the U.S. Food and Drug Administration's age criteria to include children as young as 1 year of age have all led to increasing numbers of young children receiving cochlear implants (Dettman, Pinder, Briggs, Dowell, & Leigh, 2007). As numerous careful and trustworthy studies indicate, the earlier a child receives a cochlear implant, the better the development of hearing and language in the child. Thus, professionals from the United States, the European Union, and other countries around the world agree that cochlear implantation at a young age is the gold-standard therapy for deaf children and no longer considered an experimental procedure.

This insight is not acknowledged in the same way in the Deaf world. Not long ago it was claimed that "there is not a single published case, after a decade of experimentation with the multichannel implant and more than a thousand implanted children, of a child acquiring oral language with an implant" (Lane, Hoffmeister, & Bahan, 1996). In his book *The Mask of Benevolence: Disabling the Deaf Community*, the Boston psychology and linguistics professor Harlan Lane even spoke of genocide and ethnocide and expressed his belief that auditory (re)habilitation would, in the end, overwhelm and destroy the Deaf culture (Lane, 1992). I am disinclined to enter the debate about this issue, which has had advocates and opponents among Deaf and hearing people for several years (Lane, 2005; Young, 2002). Such an extreme view, where "eugenic practices" like marriage and genetic counseling are considered viable ways "to enhance the possibility that they (deaf parents) will have deaf children" and where it is claimed that "it is unethical for the majority culture to aim to reduce the numbers of children born Deaf because measures intended to prevent births within a cultural group constitute genocide" (Lane & Grodin, 1997), is unacceptable for most people. To intentionally select for human traits that are universally considered as disabilities and handicaps is unethical even in modern pluralistic societies. Rather, the opposite view counters that if pediatric cochlear implantation is regarded as a safe and efficient technology, it might be considered child neglect or even abuse not to implant a deaf child (Nunes, 2001). I endorse neither of these two extreme views, as they tend to stall discussions and do not help us to make wise decisions for individual cases.

A passable way to solve the ethical dilemma of cochlear implantation in infants against the backdrop of the Deaf community is to follow the concepts of personal autonomy and free, informed consent (this concept is elaborated in the following passages). Human dignity is one of the main principles of a democratic society and of health-care ethics. Biomedical ethics is based on this perspective of interpersonal relationship. In an individualistic society, the pluralism of religious, ethnic, and moral views belongs to the realm of personal liberty, and respect for personal autonomy is one of its most important principles. Any approach that disregards the intrinsic value of a subject is to be considered unacceptable (Nunes, 2001). Human dignity and human vulnerability are closely related. A societal consensus exists on the proclaimed rights of people with disabilities, which is derived from the viewpoint that vulnerable conditions must be regarded as unfair. Therefore, disability rights are associated with fundamental rights in democratic societies.

There is a strong public perception that deaf people and in particular deaf children are vulnerable humans and need social solidarity and protection by the social system to achieve an appropriate quality of life. The concepts of human dignity and autonomy recognize fundamental human rights of individuals (Kemp & Rendtorff, 2000). Free and informed consent is one of these rights. Deaf adults are autonomous people and are able to give informed consent for a cochlear implantation. However, who should be allowed to make the decision for a deaf child and based on what grounds?

Consideration of parents as competent, autonomous authorities is indispensable in pediatric care (Nelson & Nelson, 1998). Prima facie, parents or custodians must be considered to make choices in the best interest of their child or ward, within the restraints posed by the values embraced by community in which the child lives (Engelhardt, 1986). Hence, parental decisions in terms of the best interest of a child who is a cochlear implant candidate would be acceptable only within a range of expected benefits for the child. The Deaf community is not closed off from the rest of the society, as are, for instance, the Amish. Most congenitally deaf children are not born into the Deaf world, and, even if they are, they will not live completely in the Deaf world. Therefore, the standard for their best interests should come from a point of view that a reasonable and prudent, probably a hearing person, would choose (Nunes, 2001).

Parents are the legal surrogate decision makers for their child. If they act reasonably and prudently, they must determine the highest possible benefit among all available options in order to promote the child's autonomy and quality of life. Quality of life is a fuzzy concept, depending on the personal perception of well-being at physical, mental, and social levels (Kahneman, Diener, & Schwarz, 1999). The Deaf community judges quality of life by its own standards. According to most Deaf associations, deaf children are not sick or disabled; instead, they are just culturally and linguistically different (D'Silva, Daugherty, & MacDonald, 2004). However, most deaf children live in a hearing world that considers deafness a disability because of its communication limitations. What it means to withhold the opportunity to hear from prelingually deaf children can be experienced when such a child has received a cochlear implant and begins to hear. In my experience, most children appreciate the auditory impressions; they like them, are curious, try to figure out their meaning, and after a while begin to spontaneously ask for their headset. The first listening experience is like playing for the first time with an interesting computer game, and, for diverse reasons, only a small minority of children refuses this experience. The next experience follows soon after; not only can sounds be heard, but communication with the hearing world also becomes possible. In aural-oral communication, the perception and production of oral speech becomes a main goal for social relationships in the hearing world. The Deaf world is a minority culture not only in a linguistic but also in a quasi-ethnic sense because of its specific family bonds. Marriages between deaf people are common, and couples frequently wish to have a deaf child (Anstey, 2002). Some Deaf people even try to make a genetic selection by genetic screening and reproductive technologies. This has been seen as controversial (Benedict & Sass-Lehrer, 2007; Häyry, 2004; Johnston, 2005; Michie & Marteau, 1999). Recently, a couple in the United States deliberately attempted to ensure the birth of a deaf child via artificial insemination (Savulescu, 2002; Spriggs, 2002). However, belonging to the Deaf world is not primarily a matter of the physiological deafness but of acculturation. There is no birthright to be Deaf. Some children are not profoundly deaf congenitally but are born with residual hearing. This residual hearing will disappear after a certain period if these children do not get auditory stimulation. Such children will become members of the Deaf culture only if their parents actively prevent or passively omit appropriate measures.

Lane and Bahan (1998) argue for the right of profoundly deaf children to be referred as Deaf by making cultural analogies to the Native American culture. However, Rui Nunes (2001) counters that if a child has been born Native American and has been adopted transracially by European parents shortly after birth and grows up in a European country, the child will acquire the culture of the adoptive parents and of their surroundings. There are no physical conditions that adjust a baby to a certain culture. The genetic or physical constitution, including deafness, does not necessarily determine cultural membership.

To become a member of the Deaf world requires acculturation (Balkany, Hodges, & Goodman, 1996). Parents from the Deaf community may argue that it is in the best interest of the child to learn sign language or some form of visual-spatial communication. For parents from the hearing world, the aural-oral way of communication and therefore a cochlear implant is preferable and seems to be in the child's best interest. However, because of the right of deaf children to their autonomy, a society should provide the means to fulfill the right to an open future. The existence of this right was proposed by Joel Feinberg (1980) by the concept of "rights-in-trust," which means rights that are to be "saved for the child until he is an adult." Those rights mean that a child's scope of future choices has to be protected (Nunes, 2001).

Consequently, hearing parents may feel that access to auditory rehabilitation, to oral language acquisition, and to the values of the hearing world would be necessary to fulfill a deaf child's right to an open future. This would not prevent life in the Deaf world. It does not prevent children from choosing a life in the Deaf community if they would later find acceptance there. In Western individualistic societies autonomy of the individual is regarded ethically prior to the autonomy of a group (Davis, 1997).

If a society claims a child's right to an open future, it is ethical to demand that it also provide the means to fulfill this goal. In the case of cochlear implantation, which costs at least $40,000, and aural-oral rehabilitation, this is a costly way to accomplish this liberty. Most democratic societies legally guarantee a costly assistance to persons with disabilities, such as devices, special services, and education. It is expected, however, that people so identified are willing to correct their disability (Nunes, 2001). If deafness were not regarded a disability, as suggested by some international Deaf associations, the governments would save considerable expense with regard to provision of special services for deaf and hard of hearing persons (Balkany, Hodges, & Goodman, 1998), services that, by the way, are also demanded by Deaf people.

The Deaf world's arguments against cochlear implants are incompatible with established principles of medical ethics. Physicians' responsibility for individual patients cannot be suspended by the claims of what many consider a subculture. However, we learned from the aforementioned debate that ethical discussions about medical implantation must take into consideration the social and cultural notions of disease and the conditions under which patients both with and without implants will live (Hansson, 2005). A group of persons who have received enhancing interventions, such as a cochlear implantation, may form a new subculture. This enhancement may change majority views of normality. Deaf persons may feel pressured to consider cochlear implantation not only because of the expected benefit but also because the implant may play the role of a positional good, that is, one that contributes to social status. This latter effect, however, may diminish as cochlear implants become common (Hansson, 2005). Irrespective of the controversy between the Deaf and the medical communities, one thing holds true—the cochlear implant has come and is here to stay. There are both advocates and critics of this technology. Historically, most technical revolutions were accompanied by movements that predicted cultural doom. When the new technology was well established, however, people generally did not want the former times back.

What then constitutes good practice for medical professionals who are counseling parents about the opportunities and risks of a cochlear implant? Counselors and physicians must fully respect the parents' values and remain neutral. They should clearly state what they think is in the child's best interest but not impose their own values. The alternatives to a cochlear implant—sign language and a visual way of communication, as well as the values and richness of the Deaf world—must be explained to the parents, who may not be familiar with them. A cochlear implant should not be considered solely as a technically safe and potentially beneficial procedure for a child with a severe or profound hearing loss. Rather, it should also be made clear that the implantation is ethically acceptable only if solid medical evidence suggests a high probability that a particular child will acquire not only auditory perception skills but also oral communicative ability and thus an increased quality of life with regard to the hearing world. These factors must be weighed in each individual case against past and current medical evidence. Health-care professionals should be guided by the family's and the candidate's perception of how best to participate in an environment that will be meaningful, as they define it (Niparko, 2004). To be avoided is thoughtless, routine (over) supply and the allure of financial profit for the medical institution and the implant manufacturer and distributor. For prudent and responsible counseling, the true motivations of the parents and the child must be assessed, if necessary in consultation with a clinical developmental psychologist. It goes without saying that the possibility of unrealistic expectations by the parents needs to be addressed.

Informed consent requires careful information about the potential harm and the potential benefit of the implant, given in an atmosphere of mutual trust. The benefit of a cochlear implant has to be explained seriously to the parents, who might form an unrealistically optimistic expectation of the child's future academic and communicative performance. After all, the hearing loss does remain. Other modalities of communication have to be presented and explained as well. The consent process should follow the principles of personal autonomy and nonmaleficence (Nunes, 2001). Prelingually deaf children usually benefit considerably from cochlear implantation.

Still, technical expertise is not enough to offer cochlear implant programs. Economic, personal, and educational preconditions have to be considered to provide optimal auditory rehabilitation. To be successful, aural-oral rehabilitation requires repeated audiometric testing; regular assessment of speech and language abilities; pedagogical, psychological, and medical evaluation to monitor progress; and parental cooperation (Marschark, 2007). Parental reports and broad outcome measures with respect to oral language have contributed to an improved understanding of the true effectiveness of early implantation (Lin et al., 2008). Since many long-term outcome studies of cochlear implantation in children are now available, the development of the child's self-esteem, independence, overall communicative skills, and quality of life can be predicted—not with absolute certainty but with a realistic probability.

Preschool children using cochlear implants can adequately indicate their own quality of life, as shown in a recent questionnaire-based evaluation (Warner-Czyz, Loy,

Roland, Tong, & Tobey, 2009). Quality of life was rated similarly by both these children and their hearing peers. The longer the cochlear implant was in use and the older the children were, the higher they rated their overall quality of life. However, the parents rated both their children's quality of life in social situations and their self-esteem lower than those of the hearing peers. Hence, the children themselves give us valuable information on their perceptions of the final success of their cochlear implant therapy. Parents afford valuable complementary perspectives on the child's socioemotional and physical well-being.

The Rights of Parents in Cochlear Implant Decisions

Currently, the decision about cochlear implantation for a child is left to the parents. However, economic factors, educational outcomes, and societal attitudes about deafness could increase governmental interest in this choice (Bender, 2004). Although most people believe that parents explicitly have a constitutional right to make decisions on behalf of their children, in most countries, even modern industrialized ones, such rights subsist only in the shadowy areas of the constitution.

Denise G. Bender (2004), a professor of physical therapy, examined the case law related to parental autonomy to determine whether the government could present economic and social reasons to mandate the provision of cochlear implants for all eligible children. Both courts and families in most countries assume that a child belongs to the parents instead of to the state. Cases of child abuse and child neglect, however, demonstrate that parental responsibility does not necessarily imply that parental decisions originate from a natural wisdom and from the intent to do the best for the child. Beyond religious and social reasons, there are also trends and fads in parenting that influence parents' choices. Whereas some of these choices have only little long-term importance, others create a permanent and irreversible impact on the child limiting the child's right to an open future.

In most industrialized countries the law implies that the role of government concerning vulnerable children is applicable only if the parents fail to do their job adequately. The mere existence of a state responsibility, however, does not justify an attempt to override valid parental choices, even when the state disagrees with those choices (Bender, 2004).

Many governments take responsibility in educational matters. Bender (2004) described the case in which Old Order Amish parents brought suit against Wisconsin's requirement that all children must be educated until they turned 16. They felt that mandatory education after the eighth grade had a negative impact on the acceptance of Amish values. The court, however, argued that chances in the job market would improve with an education beyond the eighth grade. With more education, a child could choose between the traditional Amish lifestyle and the secular world, whereas without such an education the choice would be restricted to remaining in the Amish lifestyle.

Parents tend to think (1) that they are better informed about their child than anyone else, (2) that only they know what is best for their child, and (3) that they want the best for their child. That "mom knows best" and "mom wants the best" are not be disputed.

However, I argue that this "best" is only relative (to other decisions made outside the family) and not necessarily optimal (Euler, 2003).

If parents know best what makes the child happy, there should be no disagreement between father and mother or between parents and child. However, such disagreement is more the rule than the exception. Achenbach and coworkers (1987) systematically reviewed 119 independent studies of the degree of consistency in different informants' reports of the behavioral and emotional problems of children of various ages (1½ to 19 years). Informants were parents, teachers, mental health workers, experimental observers, the children's peers, and the children themselves. The average agreement between mother and father about their child's emotional/behavioral problems was only moderate ($r = .59$). Very often the parents disagreed about whether the child even had an emotional/behavioral problem. In general, informants who had similar relations to the children (e.g., teacher/teacher, mental health worker/mental health worker) showed similar agreements. But if the informants had different relations to the children (e.g., teacher/mental health worker), their agreement about whether the child had problems was very low. It is well known in psychology that behavior is to a large extent situation specific. The child behaves differently at home and elsewhere and differently among peers than when at school. Most disturbing is the finding by Achenbach and colleagues (1987) that the agreement between child and parent was a mere $r = .25$, not significantly higher than between child and teacher ($r = .20$) or between child and mental health worker ($r = .27$). Parental wisdom is neither complete nor ideal; it is just particular.

If a gap exists between the parents' judgment and the child's about what makes the child happy, the truth may not lie wholly with the parents but with both child *and* parents. A theory in evolutionary psychology (Buss, 2008) specifies where we can expect discrepancies between the mother's and her offspring's judgment or perspective and in which direction. This theory is called the *parent-offspring conflict* (Trivers, 1974). Parent-offspring conflict can be expected in all species that invest in their progeny, like the investment of feeding the young in birds and mammals. The conflict starts during pregnancy and is most pronounced during the weaning conflict. The conflict centers around the fact that generally the offspring wants more from the mother (e.g., milk, attention, time) than the mother is willing to give. In the human species, with its extraordinarily long period of parental investment, the conflict extends well into adolescence. The conflict occurs because the parents' and the child's interests do not completely coincide. The term *interest* is meant here in a basic sense, namely the basic interest of all living creatures to replicate their genes. Therefore, the bird feeding its nestlings has such an interest as well. The mismatch between parental and offspring interest derives from the fact that parent and offspring have only some genes (more precisely, alleles) in common (namely half of the alleles) if the child is indeed a biological offspring. Therefore, the parents treat the child *also* in their own interest and not only in the child's interest. For example, it is in a child's best interest to get *all* of the cake or at least a much bigger piece than his brother or sister does, whereas the parent's best interest is to have all of the children fed *equally*. Some evolutionary biologists even speak of parental "manipulation," but they mean this term only in a purely descriptive, analytic sense, not a moral one. Such parental influence extends even into adulthood. For example, parents take an active interest in their adult offspring's choice of a mate. They prefer an in-law that suits them (the parents) best. Therefore, arranged marriages, mostly to maintain the family's (parental) wealth, are common in many cultures.

Therefore, parental decisions cannot automatically be qualified as the best option for a child even if they are made in what the parents view as the best interests of their children. The rejection of a cochlear implant for a deaf child of Deaf parents is a possible example of parent-child conflict. If the parents decide in the best interests of their child, they would base their decision on the child's open future; that is, they should protect the child's right of autonomy until the child can express it independently later on.

Courts in modern countries often refuse to authorize parental decisions that would result in the complete elimination of some future options for a child if they cannot be readdressed when the child reaches adulthood. The reasoning in those cases is grounded in the assumption that parents, when they are convinced that their decisions would be the best for the child's future cannot in fact predict that future (Bender, 2004).

If the government decides for a child in educational questions, the processes initiated by such decisions are not life ending, as is, for example, the case with many medical decisions. Such decisions may even be reversible. Deference may be paid to the government that is assuming responsibility for a child in a medical situation. Here, whether a choice leads to a life-or-death decision is a very important factor. This could be the case in an emergency situation, when religious reasons prohibit an intervention. For example, the tenets of the Jehovah's Witnesses forbid blood transfusions or treatment with blood products by its adherents, even in life-threatening situations. Nevertheless, courts have authorized blood transfusions, appendectomies, and other emergency medical care for children regardless of the parents' wishes, thereby enabling the state to act in the perceived best interest of the child (Bender, 2004).

In the United States, another such legal intercession is seen in *Prince v. Massachusetts* (1944, p. 170): "Parents may be free to become martyrs themselves. But it does not follow that they are free . . . to make martyrs of their children." The government may, in such situations, exercise its role of *parens patriae*, which means that the state is authorized to act as the parent of any children who are in need of protection in order to offer these children the best chance to survive into adulthood and to protect future productive citizens. In cases of life-threatening situations in which a treatment is not guaranteed and does not have at least a very high probability of success, courts have deferred to the parents' desires. Bender (2004) mentions a child who had an aggressive and potentially fatal form of pediatric cancer. The parents refused intervention in the form of a chemotherapy protocol that offered a 40% chance of success and instead chose a treatment performed by a Christian Scientist practitioner. The court decided in favor of the parents' desires, implying that the parents knew the child's best interests better than the court. The difference between this case and the earlier one is the questionable benefit offered by the procedure. If a state's interest is the protection of its future citizens, it could not guarantee to preserve the future of the child in the latter case.

In the case of cochlear implantation, the matter is different. Cochlear implantation is an elective therapy. Children may grow up without it and lead a happy and fulfilled life. Moreover, a child will not die because a cochlear implant is withheld, nor will the child's life span be affected. Hence, this decision is no more or less crucial than many other everyday parental decisions that will have an impact on a child's future life. Therefore, great parental deference has to be applied for this intervention. Although numerous scientific studies report that cochlear implantation in children is greatly beneficial for children's linguistic, emotional, cognitive, and social development, a government cannot guarantee that an implant will positively influence the future of a specific child. Conversely, it has no evidence that the parents' rejection of an implantation will place a child in a more vulnerable position. Precedent legal decisions in the United States indicate that courts heavily weigh the life-altering nature, either educational or medical, of an intervention for a child as an important factor when determining whether the government can overrule parents' wishes. These decisions typically defer to the government when a child's future will deteriorate without intervention but defer to the parents in most other situations (Bender, 2004). Apart from a small risk of unwanted surgical outcomes, such as those in other surgical interventions, cochlear implantation cannot be judged only by the immediate postoperative result. It has to be taken into consideration that the procedure has a permanent impact on the auditory pathway and may also cause some permanent changes in the cochlea, such as degeneration of residual hair cells.

When parents are considering a cochlear implant for their child, it is important in a way that they keep in mind that new treatments, such as gene therapies, are being developed. Because these may focus on the regeneration or replacement of hair cells, they may require a cochlea unaffected by an inserted electrode (Kwan, White, & Segil, 2009). One may, however, argue that, in the case of a unilateral cochlear implantation, the other ear remains unaffected. Moreover, the procedures of soft surgery focus on the protection of the cochlear anatomical structures, particularly the residual hair cells. Finally, an implanted electrode does not necessarily make a child unavailable for another, future therapy. An additional risk of a cochlear implant is that a small but significant percentage (3%–8%) of all cochlear implant patients will need a cochlear reimplantation (Zeitler, Budenz, & Roland, 2009). The most common reasons (40%–80%) for this are the so-called hard failures by a complete interruption of auditory input and a nonfunctioning of communication between the internal and external components of a cochlear implant, caused, for instance, by mechanical damage from head trauma. Other common indications include soft failures (device failures without detectable defect while the implant is worn), wound complications, infection, improper initial placement, and electrode extrusions. Although reimplantation is annoying, with thoughtful preparation, individualized patient counseling, and proper surgical technique, most patients can expect successful outcomes.

In addition, the surgical procedure is only the first stage of the cochlear-implantation therapy process. An intensive and long-lasting rehabilitation period is required after the surgery, and the final outcome for an individual child is unknown, although statistically well predictable. If a government would mandate cochlear implantation for a cochlear implant candidate child, it cannot end its involvement after the surgery. It would have to be involved in every new decision of the prolonged rehabilitation process. This, however, is not practicable because the government would require a definition of where the involvement ends.

Bender (2004) reported an Iowa appellate case, a battered and neglected child who was also deaf. Here the state decided on behalf of cochlear implantation and included not only the surgery but the whole rehabilitation process as well. In this case, the court terminated the natural mother's parental rights, citing the need for a demanding rehabilitation after a planned cochlear implantation. Although this was not the only reason to terminate the mother's rights, the mother's failure to learn American Sign Language and her unsuitability to participate in a recommended cochlear implantation program were factors in the court's decision.

One can only speculate whether the court would have made the same decision if no physical abuse of the child had occurred. However, the decision does not mention the abuse when stating that a cochlear implant would be beneficial to the child and that, unless placed in a "stable and structured environment," the child was unlikely to get the extensive rehabilitation needed after the surgery in order to benefit fully from the implant (Bender, 2004).

Despite this case, which demonstrates that the parents' rights to decide for their child are not sacrosanct, it does not seem useful to mandate cochlear implants for severely or profoundly deaf children. Even if the state mandated the surgery, so many factors influence a child's linguistic, social, cognitive, emotional, and educational development that the state cannot guarantee the success of the implantation. Educational outcomes after cochlear implantation depend not only on the quality of the rehabilitation and auditory-oral training process but also on several additional factors, like the availability of assistive devices in classrooms and personal frequency-modulated (FM) systems, good technical services, and regular upgrades of the software and the hardware (e.g., the outer parts of the cochlear implants). This makes aural-oral rehabilitation expensive, and the state would have to agree to absorb all of the costs if it mandated the whole rehabilitation process.

Irrespective of optimal legal solutions, some decisions are better left to the family to make. In my opinion, government should not mandate a cochlear implant for a child. Denise G. Bender suggests that a more suitable role for government is its involvement in the support of educational programs on cochlear implantation. Following the concept that the future of a child is open from birth on, many potential options are available to a child, but only some of them can be realized. The selection of one course of action may make other ways less accessible. Such decisions are made every day. The same is the case in cochlear implantation. Choosing one way or another may makes other options either less or completely unavailable. However, a cochlear implant leaves a child's future much more open with respect to both hearing and deaf social perspectives than an exclusive decision for a life in the Deaf world.

Parents' Decision-Making Process

The trend toward early diagnosis of infant hearing loss as a consequence of newborn hearing screenings requires parents to make an early decision about the best intervention and education for their child. Parents often experience the need to make a quick decision as demanding or even as undue pressure. Immediately after the identification of their child's hearing loss, at a time when they have to accept that their child is deaf, they must evaluate various options of treatment and rehabilitation, with implications for communication and education. During this time and occasionally during the rehabilitation process as well, parents must choose a communication modality, usually categorized into three main approaches: oral-aural habilitation (auditory training, oral training, speechreading, cued speech), visual-spatial communication (e.g., sign language), or a combination of speech and sign language (Li, Bain, & Steinberg, 2003).

Highly developed technological devices such as digital hearing aids and cochlear implants make the parents' decision even more difficult. Parents often have the impression that they do not understand the various options well enough to make a wise choice. This difficulty is more pronounced earlier in life of the child for whom a decision has to be made. During this period, the informed consent and the counseling by health professionals have an outstanding role. This experience is underpinned by several studies that evaluated the factors in the parents' decision making (Christiansen & Leigh, 2004; Li et al., 2003; Steinberg et al., 2000). Li and her colleagues (2003) reported that the extent of the child's hearing loss and the advice parents received from professionals were the most influential factors in their choice of a communication mode. Parents chose an oral approach if they believed that deafness can and should be corrected and if they wanted the child to be able to speak. It is not surprising that the less severe the hearing loss, the more frequently parents chose oral communication. Other studies have shown that preimplant residual hearing in children and adults is one of the best predictors of the cochlear implant outcome (Kiefer et al., 2000; Neumann et al., 2008). The more residual functioning a cochlea has, the more a child will benefit from an implant.

The impact of a diagnosis of deafness and the subsequent decision-making process on the whole family of a deaf child has been described by William McKellin, the father of a hearing-impaired child (McKellin, 1995). He introduced the term *hearing-impaired families*, indicating that a child's hearing loss influences the entire family. McKellin described the interrelationship between the family's values and social relations and the community's cultural values, as well as the various social and educational transformations that occur while the family addresses the child's needs. Each institution the family encounters has its own construction of hearing loss, and parents are expected to master each profession's vocabulary in order to communicate with specialists on behalf of their child. This is a daunting task.

The influence of values and preferences on the decision-making process has become important for health services. In order to quantify the benefits of medical interventions, mathematical models that incorporate the economic, social, and psychological benefits of medical procedures are applied. These models use a variety of methodologies that ask subjects to consider the trade-offs of choosing one particular alternative over another. These analyses derive from mathematical decision theories that examine how a person makes decisions when faced with uncertain outcomes. They incorporate preferences for outcomes and values represented in multiple dimensions. For deafness and its interventions, the dimensions that must be considered include the experience of being unable to hear, its impact on vocational choices, and its impact on psychological well-being (Steinberg et al., 2000).

Annie Steinberg and her colleagues applied such models to the decisions parents made for their deaf children, including the decision about cochlear implantation.

The researchers explored the role of parental values and preferences for their deaf children's communication mode and educational values with respect to academic achievement, social life, communication, and emotional well-being. The results of the study revealed a wide variability in parental preferences. Approximately equal numbers of parents preferred the outcome with an oral approach or with a total communication approach. However, these preferences did not indicate whether a family would indeed choose a cochlear implant. Individual parents obviously value different aspects of their child's well-being. Even among the parents who chose cochlear implantation, there was little agreement about the best outcome in terms of a child's ability to communicate. While some parents clearly seek cochlear implantation as a way to allow their child to communicate freely in the mainstream, other parents believed that their child should also strive for clear communication with other deaf children who communicate primarily through sign language (Steinberg et al., 2000). Hence, professionals should consider individual parental values when counseling parents about their options for intervention. To decide whether to let their child get an electronic device permanently implanted is particularly conflicting for most parents. About 90% of parents who have deaf children are themselves hearing. Most of these hearing parents have had little, if any, contact with deaf persons or understanding of deafness before they learned of their child's deafness. Hence, they find themselves in a situation with minimal experience or knowledge on which to rely when they need to make decisions about how to socialize and educate their child (Christiansen & Leigh, 2004). Parents sometimes feel guilty because of the hearing loss of their child. They may feel responsible for it, or they may feel that they should have noticed their child's deafness earlier than they actually did. Retrospectively, most parents describe the time when they realized they had to learn whether their child had a hearing loss as a difficult one.

John. B. Christiansen and Irene W. Leigh from the Gallaudet University Research Institute (GRI) in Washington, DC, analyzed extensive survey data from families of children with cochlear implants (2004). The study was based on 439 questionnaires from parents of children with cochlear implants and on 56 interviews. A typical child in the GRI study had received an implant at 4 years of age and had worn it for 4 years. Before implantation, about three of four children had used hearing aids all day, and half of the children had used some signing. Only one-third of the parents who participated in the study had suspected deafness in their child before the youngster's first birthday (Christiansen & Leigh, 2004). Reasons for not having detected it earlier were that the parents did not expect to have a deaf child and that they were not sure how much a child is supposed to hear in the first year of life or how a hearing infant typically reacts to sounds. The problem was sometimes aggravated by physicians, audiologists, educators, and others who did not always provide parents with sufficient information. When the parents were asked what they had been told by health professionals, it appeared that the information they received had frequently been either incomplete or only partly understood. More than half of the interviewed parents reported that they had received conflicting information about the preimplant communication mode they should use. The main reason the majority of parents chose a cochlear implant was their desire to facilitate the child's development and use of spoken language, as well as the parents' awareness of safety and environmental issues.

A further result of the GRI study was that parents felt confused if they had to make decisions about special schools, classes, or mainstream placements. Half of the parents had never met a deaf adult, and a few parents had met deaf adults or parents of deaf children whose implants were no longer being used. Some parents had met deaf people, some of whom were supportive, others somewhat or even strictly against a cochlear implant, leaving the parents perplexed and uncomfortable.

After cochlear implantation, about half of the children in the GRI study signed both at home and at school. This means that parents had no strong objection to the use of sign language after implantation. In the schools, nearly half of the children used signs or signs with speech. No data were given about children who used oral-only communication. The GRI study was done in the United States in 1999. Its findings about the communication mode tend to surprise professionals in Europe, where signing after cochlear implantation occurs only rarely. Instead, most children are trained in an aural-oral method after the surgery. A few children use what is called "total communication" in the United States, and a very few use signing alone. This difference between Europe and the United States may be due to scientific and clinical changes during the last 10 years. In our department (Department of Phoniatrics and Pediatric Audiology, the University Medical Center of Frankfurt am Main, Germany) the median age of all 85 children who were implanted between 2005 and 2008 was 23 months. In 2009, it was 11 months. Hence, the vast majority of the implanted children use aural-oral communication as the only or at least predominant communication mode because speech development of children with cochlear implants during the first 2 years of life is deemed more successful than that of children who receive their implants at later ages.

Institutions for child education such as kindergartens or schools for deaf and hard of hearing students vary considerably in style, communication mode, and methods of educating children with cochlear implants. Some institutions prefer a child with an implant to learn oral communication alone, while others prefer bilingual or total communication. Educators often argue for one communication method or another. Oral communication is often acquired almost naturally in early implanted children of hearing parents. An argument for learning bilingual or total communication is that it enables children to use alternative communication modes if they have trouble with their implant, if the oral language outcome is not successful, and/or if they want to communicate with their peers who use sign language.

In the GRI study, the most frequent educational setting, covering nearly two-thirds of children, was either full or partial mainstreaming. In most cases, implanted children were not isolated from both deaf and hearing peers, and parents were mostly comfortable with their children socializing with deaf peers, in addition to hearing classmates. The reports of the GRI study are in line with a German study that shows that nearly half of the children who received a cochlear implant between the ages of 3 and 6 years underwent mainstream schooling, but more than three-quarters did so if implanted before the age of 3 years (Diller, 2006). Both studies indicated a tendency toward more mainstreaming with decreasing age of cochlear implantation, but there is a continuing need for some cochlear-implanted children to receive special education in programs for deaf or hard of hearing students. Also, many children with cochlear implants are multiply disabled and, therefore, need additional special education (Waltzman, Scalchunes, & Cohen, 2000). Some deaf children with multiple disabilities can benefit from cochlear implantation, although their rate of growth in perceptual skills is slower than that of deaf children with no additional disabilities (Waltzman et al., 2000). Therefore, the decision for a cochlear implant is justified in many cases. However, the informed-process has to take into consideration all of the child's medical, physical, psychiatric, emotional, and resource conditions so that a prudent decision can be made together with the child's parents or guardians.

All of the children in the GRI study needed support services. Most of them required sign language interpreting, classroom amplification, and other resources. It should not be forgotten that a cochlear implantation does not result in normal hearing. The child still has a hearing loss and needs continuous technical support, such as FM devices or other assistance. This fact is underlined by the information from the parents in the GRI study. Parents of more than half of the children felt that their child was behind its hearing peers in reading, and more than one-third felt the same for mathematics. Again, however, data collection was done in 1999, and cochlear-implant technology has improved considerably since that time. Nowadays, most early-implanted children have a language developmental outcome comparable with hearing children (Dettman et al., 2007). Moreover, most bilaterally implanted children achieve a satisfactory scholastic performance in mainstream schools, with implant duration as the most important factor determining postimplant outcomes. Some bilaterally implanted children have even been found to reach a higher academic performance than the average of their hearing peers (Motasaddi-Zarandy, Rezai, Mahdavi-Arab, and Golestan, 2009).

It was also learned that, even if the initial decision for cochlear-implant therapy was not an easy one for the parents in the GRI study, most of them were pleased with the outcome, and more than two-thirds were very satisfied. About half of the parents wished that their child had received a cochlear implant earlier. Most of the parents stated that they would be disappointed, but accepting, if their child stopped using the implant in the future. Parental contentedness increased with time, indicating that it obviously takes time to sense the improvement in the child's communicative benefit from the cochlear implant. It is evident that the parents' feeling of satisfaction is also related to what they had initially expected and what they later defined as success with the device (Swanson, 1997). The parents' satisfaction with the outcome of the cochlear-implant therapy, together with the children's high ratings of quality of life (Warner-Czyz et al., 2009), is a convincing ethical justification for the health professionals' initial recommendation of a cochlear implant. For those children who are viable cochlear implant candidates, it is a strong argument for cochlear-implant therapy.

To summarize, parents must begin sorting through the confusion and choices after they have learned that their child is deaf. Their communication with health-care and educational professionals plays a major role in the process of deciding for or against a cochlear implant. Advocates of one approach or another often make it appear that only one option exists, thus making a difficult decision even harder for parents (Christiansen & Leigh, 2004). Clearly, a careful, unbiased, informed process is essential. One other major problem that often confuses parents is the decision about educational settings for their child. In particular, advice from professionals about the communication mode, mainstream or special education in kindergarten, preschool, and schools is crucial, as parents frequently feel that they receive conflicting information. To ensure optimal benefit from a cochlear implant, parents and significant others need to be continually involved in their child's social and educational development.

Cochlear Implantation in Very Young Children

Early detection of infant hearing loss and early intervention have become increasingly important in recent years. In every thousand babies, between one and three are born with a permanent congenital or early acquired hearing loss, depending on what is defined as a hearing loss in a particular country or state (e.g., 30 dB or 40 dB average hearing threshold; bilateral or monolateral hearing loss). This is a high prevalence compared to other congenital diseases for which newborns are screened. Effective therapies such as early hearing-aid fitting and cochlear implantation are available. It has been convincingly shown that children who receive a therapy early in life demonstrate better language development than those who begin therapy later and that children who receive newborn hearing screening benefit more because of early hearing rehabilitation than those who have not been screened and identified (Yoshinaga-Itano, Sedey, Coulter, & Mehl, 1998; Yoshinaga-Itano, Coulter, & Thomson, 2001). This age dependence is due to sensitive periods of the maturation of the auditory pathway. There are time windows for the maturation of the central auditory system that close unless acoustic stimulation occurs within them. For these reasons many countries have implemented newborn hearing screenings.

Currently, the World Health Organization has begun launching universal newborn hearing-screening programs as well. In countries or regions where such programs have been implemented during the last decade, the average age of diagnosis and therapy onset of an infant with hearing loss have decreased considerably (Neumann et al., 2006). Babies who are hard of hearing get hearing aids during the first months of life, and the age of cochlear implantation has decreased to below 1 year for many children. Although the maxim "the earlier, the better" is now accepted by most professionals who make a decision about a cochlear implant for a profoundly deaf child, this viewpoint is not shared equally by parents. Many questions have to be answered first: Is my child too young for such an existential decision? Does a cochlear implant prevent the natural maturation of the auditory system, which would have occurred without the implant? How dangerous is a general anesthesia at that early age, and how dangerous is the operation itself? Is the baby's head much too small for such an implant? What if later therapies (e.g., genetic therapies) are much better than a cochlear implant now? Do I prevent such therapy by electing surgery that cannot guarantee that it does not destroy any of the possible remaining hair cells in the cochlea? Is there real evidence that the plasticity of the auditory system decreases rapidly if a sufficient auditory stimulation is lacking during the first years of life? Are there measurable parameters that may indicate the necessity of switching from hearing aids to a cochlear implant and that could help parents make the best possible decision? Can we verify the age span in which the benefit of a cochlear implant is maximal? During which period would children benefit best from a second cochlear implant, and which children would be suitable candidates? Are there measurable parameters that may indicate the necessity of a cochlear implant? To answer these questions, I now elucidate some important neurobiological findings on the maturation of the auditory system that may help parents in their consideration of a cochlear implant.

Neurobiological Findings

A common finding in neurobiology is that adequate stimulation has to be delivered to a developing sensory system within a narrow time window (sensitive period) to ensure that the system develops normally. Our knowledge about the development of the hierarchically organized central auditory system and in particular of its highest level, the auditory cortex, stems from electrophysiological examinations in hearing and deaf animals and humans. Neuroimaging studies additionally contributed to this knowledge. In 1942, Woolsey and Walzl presented the first report of cortical responses to electrical stimulation of the auditory nerve in hearing cats. They established the cochleotopic organization of the pathways to the primary auditory cortex, which means that each particular point on the cochlea corresponds to a certain region of the primary auditory cortex.

As a consequence of altered input, the central auditory system has a remarkable capacity for plasticity even into adulthood. This plasticity contributes to the continued improvements observed in the speech perception of prelingually deaf children in the period after cochlear implantation. The implantation changes the response properties of nerve cells in the central auditory system. These changes are produced by the continued electrical stimulation of the auditory nerve by stimuli of behavioral relevance and lead to changes in the functional organization of the central auditory system (Fallon, Irvine, & Shepherd, 2008).

The research group of Andrej Kral, professor of auditory neurophysiology at the University of Hannover, showed that, in cats born deaf, the absence of auditory stimulation leads to a dysfunctional intrinsic cortical microcircuitry. The primary auditory cortex, which is the main entrance for auditory information into the cortex, and the primary cortical auditory-processing region consist of six layers. Activity in this region is specific to these layers. If auditory information is lacking from birth on, a delay in activation of some of the layers (the so-called supragranular layers) and a reduction in activity in other (infragranular) layers occur. Such deficits indicate the inability of the primary auditory cortex to properly process the input from the lower levels of the auditory pathway and to generate an adequate output within the infragranular layers and also to incorporate modulations from the higher-order auditory cortex into the processing within the primary auditory cortex. Kral and his group demonstrated that such deficits are the consequence of faulty postnatal development. In deaf animals, the maturation of the primary auditory cortex shows a developmental delay, degenerative changes, and further alterations in the transition of neuronal currents from one nerve cell to another, spread of activation, and alterations of local cortical potentials that can be recorded at the surface of the brain. When hearing is initiated early in life (e.g., by cochlear-implant stimulation), many of these deficits are counterbalanced. However, the plasticity of the auditory cortex decreases with increasing age, so a sensitive period for plastic adaptation can be demonstrated within the second to the sixth month of life in the cat. The results of such animal studies have been compared to electroencephalographic data obtained from cochlear-implanted congenitally deaf children. After cochlear implantation in humans, three phases of plastic adaptation can be observed: a fast one, which takes place within the first few weeks after implantation and shows no sensitive period; a slower one, which takes place within the first months after implantation (a sensitive period up to 4 years of age); and possibly a third (and the longest) one, which is related to increasing activation of higher-order cortical areas (Kral, Tillein, Heid, Klinke, & Hartmann, 2006).

It has also been demonstrated that the auditory pathway can be chronically reactivated with electrical stimuli in deaf cats that received a cochlear implant at 8 weeks of age. The absence of all input from the auditory periphery to the auditory cortex in long-term deafened cats resulted in a complete loss of the normal cochleotopic organization of the primary auditory cortex. This effect was nearly completely reversed by chronic reactivation of the auditory pathway via the cochlear implant. Hence, it seems probable that the maintenance or reestablishment of a cochleotopically organized primary auditory cortex by activation of a limited region of the cochlea contributes to the remarkable clinical performance of deaf children implanted at a young age (Fallon, Irvine, & Shepherd, 2009).

Anu Sharma, now professor in the Department of Speech, Language, and Hearing Sciences at the University of Colorado–Boulder, has studied brain development in children with cochlear implants for more than 10 years. She has, together with her colleagues, performed examinations with congenitally deaf children that determined the existence and the time limits of a sensitive period for the development of central auditory pathways. The researchers recorded cortical auditory evoked potentials that reflect the total activity of the auditory cortex in response to acoustic stimulation and also measured the latency (period between stimulus onset and appearance of a potential), in particular for a certain brain potential, the P1 wave. Because P1 latencies vary with child age, they can be used to reflect the maturational status of auditory pathways in congenitally deaf children who regain hearing after a cochlear implantation (Sharma, Dorman, & Spahr, 2002). The researchers found that central auditory pathways are maximally plastic for a period of about 3.5 years. If the acoustic stimulation was delivered within that period, the latencies reach age-normal values within 3 to 6 months after stimulation. Plasticity remains in some, but not all, children until approximately age 7. After age 7, plasticity is greatly reduced. That is, if stimulation starts after 7 years of age by a late cochlear implantation, after an initial decrease, the latencies remain constant or change only very slowly over months or even years. These findings point to a lack of development of the central auditory system in older children, which is paralleled by poor development of speech and language skills in congenitally deaf children implanted after the age of 7 years (Geers, 2006). As animal studies indicate, the primary auditory cortex of late-implanted children seems to be functionally decoupled from higher-order auditory cortices due to restricted development of inter- and intracortical connections (Kral & Tillein, 2006). This decoupling is likely the reason for the poor oral language development of children who receive an implant after the end of the sensitive period (Sharma & Dorman, 2006). Another aspect of plasticity that works against late-implanted children is the reorganization of the higher-order cortex by other sensory modalities (e.g., vision).

More and more children are undergoing cochlear implantation of both ears. The benefit from binaural hearing includes improved performance in noise, in particular speech performance, localization of sound sources, and some special auditory processing effects. These benefits are well documented in adults and children fitted with a cochlear implant (Scherf, van Deun, & van Wieringen, 2007; van Hoesel, 2004). Bilateral implantation ameliorates the effects of auditory deprivation faster and more comprehensively than unilateral implantation. As to monaural implantation, changes in latency and shape of the P1 also indicate the time window for the benefits of bilateral implantation. After simultaneous, early, bilateral cochlear implantation, the latency of P1 reaches normal limits sooner (within 1 to 3 months) than after implantation in only one ear, where it normalizes after 3 to 6 months (Sharma & Dorman, 2006). A simultaneous stimulation from the two ears obviously creates a converging input to the auditory cortex and lower levels of the auditory pathway, which promotes more normal development.

For many parents, bilateral cochlear implantation of their child during the same operation would be challenging. Typically, bilateral implantation is performed sequentially. If a child is implanted early but sequentially before the age of 3 to 4 years, P1 latencies from the second implanted ear are less delayed than latencies from the first implanted ear and reach normal values sooner than in the first ear. The latency development of the second implanted ear starts close to the upper edge of normal latencies. Children who get their second implant after the age of 5 to 7 years, regardless of the age at which they received their first implant, have delayed and abnormal P1 waves even after 2 to 3 years of experience with the second implant (Sharma & Dorman, 2006). These findings fit well with speech-perception performance in the same children, where the best outcome was achieved when the second ear was implanted at 3 to 5 years of age. Speech-perception performance was intermediate when the second ear was stimulated between 5 and 7 years of age. Children who were implanted in their second ear after age 12 had poor speech perception despite having excellent speech understanding with their first implant (Peters, 2006). These results imply that even early implantation and long-term implant use in one ear cannot preserve the plasticity of the auditory pathways of the other ear.

Comparable to a unilateral cochlear implant, there is a sensitive period for children to develop functioning bilateral central auditory pathways and satisfactory binaural integration (Sharma & Dorman, 2006). Three and a half years of age as the critical period for a first implant is still a big span in the life of a young child. The question arose as to whether finer subdivisions can be made within this period, which are relevant for the designation of the best moment to place a cochlear implant in a congenitally deaf child.

The Earlier, the Better?

Since the advent of pediatric cochlear implantation, age at implantation has decreased, and clinicians report greater benefits the younger the child is at implantation. Infants younger than 1 year of age are still excluded from Food and Drug Administration's clinical trials but are implanted with devices approved by the agency (Holt & Svirsky, 2008).

It was the implementation of universal neonatal hearing screening in many countries that brought about earlier identification, diagnosis, and intervention for infants with a hearing loss. Improvements in cochlear-implant technology, a growing experience with cochlear implants in young children, and the recognition of their efficacy for hearing and oral language development has led to increasing numbers of young children receiving cochlear implants. However, because a delayed maturation of the auditory pathway may occur (with a consequent chance of improvement of hearing loss during the first months of life) as a result of early amplification of the residual hearing; because of the limitations of diagnostic audiometric tools for this population for a very precise measurement of the hearing thresholds; and because of a higher anesthetic and surgical risk for infants younger than 12 months, it is prudent and necessary to carefully evaluate the risks and benefits in the youngest cochlear-implant recipients. Evidence of beneficial provisioning in infants younger than 1 year was derived from physiological studies, from studies of children using hearing aids, and from studies of children older than 1 year of age with implants. For example, the research group of Dettman and colleagues (2007) compared the language development of children who received a cochlear implant on average at 10 months with that of toddlers of 1.6 years on average. The earlier implantation resulted in increased rates of language acquisition, as the children were still in the critical period for their auditory development. Not only did the receptive and expressive language develop faster for children who received implants before 1 year of age compared with children who received implants later, it even exceeded the growth rates of their normally hearing peers. Results of this and other studies imply that cochlear implantation may be performed safely in very young children (younger than 12 months of age), with excellent language outcomes, given that it is done in experienced pediatric implantation centers. Other studies demonstrated that, among children who were implanted under the age of 2 years, between 2 and 3 years, between 3 and 4 years, and between 4 and 5 years, those in the first three age groups performed significantly better in their language development than children implanted after their fourth birthday, according to the findings of the Sharma group (2002). They reached the same levels of speech perception, speech intelligibility, and speech production but not before age 7 or 8. In other words, the earliest-implanted children had a remarkable advantage during their first years of life, years that play an important role in a child's cognitive, emotional, and social development.

Another study examined 96 children who received cochlear implants before 1 to 4 years of age (Holt & Svirsky, 2008). In general, the language development of children who received implants earlier was better than that of children implanted later. Children implanted earlier in life had faster rates of spoken-language acquisition than children implanted later, whereas the rate of speech-recognition development was similar. However, the advantage of implanting children before 1 year of age (compared with an implantation age between 1 and 2 years) was small and evident only in receptive-language development (not in expressive language) or word-recognition development.

How do all of these research findings affect the decision-making process of parents of a profoundly deaf child with regard to a cochlear implant? First, it means that there is no time to lose for therapy onset. If parents decide in favor of a cochlear implant for their deaf child, it is optimal if the implantation happens before the age of 1 year. However, not much time is lost if the implantation takes place between 12 and 24 months of age and should provide enough time for most parents to make a decision. Nevertheless, depending on the age at which the hearing loss has been diagnosed, the time span between this moment and the second birthday may be short. In this case, parents may feel that they are under time pressure and pushed by medical professionals, in particular by physicians. Such a situation can easily lead to the impression that parents and medical doctors are opponents instead of partners in determining what is best for the child. In particular, if a child is very young, hearing parents have to deal first with the diagnosis of having a deaf child. The situation is often complicated by the fact that caregivers such as teachers of deaf students who are involved in the rehabilitation of a deaf child in the child's home (or at least in a more natural environment than in a medical office) have a good understanding of the time parents need to decide on a cochlear implant. This understanding and the close personal relationship between these caregivers, the child, and the child's parents may delay the decision further.

Essentially, the matter is comparable to a broken leg where the healing is better the earlier a treatment starts. Nobody would dispute this. Nobody needs a longer period to get used to the situation because there is no time for such a delay. Deafness in children is not an acute disease that requires an immediate decision. No one is forced to make a decision within a few days. However, a certain habituation to the situation and a decision within a few months should be possible, given that parents receive sufficient support from caregivers. One exception is cochlear implantation in the case of deafness due to meningitis. In this case, the implantation should be done within the first few weeks after the child's recovery because cochlear ossification is highly probable and would either prevent later implantation or make it difficult and less effective. The parents' dilemma is that the more time they take to make a decision regarding cochlear implantation, the less beneficial the implant will be. If parents need a long time to make this decision, they often argue that they want to make the right decision for their child and that they deeply feel their special responsibility for the child's fate. Many of them believe that their child will develop well with hearing aids. This is especially complicated in young children who are fitted with contemporary high-power hearing aids because many of them start to babble or even to speak their first words quite early. This is wonderful on the one hand because these children develop cochlear hearing that has broad dynamics and stimulates maturation—even if rudimentary—of the central auditory pathway in a more natural way than a cochlear implant does. On the other hand, this gain is usually limited, and parents who do not recognize this limitation miss the optimal period in which to switch from the hearing aids to a cochlear implant.

Cochlear Implantation in Both Ears

As described earlier, bilateral and particularly simultaneous cochlear implantation has been shown to be superior in outcome to implantation of only one ear. Bilateral implantation is now state of the art for deaf children who undergo auditory rehabilitation. Speech perception skills in quiet and, in particular, in noise improve when bilateral instead of unilateral implants are worn. Improvements are greatest for children who are implanted with only a short duration of bilateral deafness and a short interval between implantations (Gordon & Papsin, 2009). Although bilateral implantation is thought to produce an optimal auditory outcome, not all patients are suitable for this procedure. Of 46 cochlear implant candidates who were assessed for simultaneous implantation in the Hospital for Sick Children in Toronto between 2005 and 2008, only 37% underwent this procedure. The rest were excluded for several reasons (residual borderline hearing in the second ear, abnormally poor speech development for age, abnormal cochlear anatomy, parental refusal; Ramsden, Papaioannou, Gordon, James, & Papsin, 2009a). No higher complication rates in surgery have been found when children simultaneously received bilateral cochlear implants compared with children getting single implants). The simultaneously implanted children had a shorter cumulative duration of both surgery and hospital stay than is required for sequential bilateral implantation (Ramsden, Papsin, Leung, James, & Gordon, 2009b)

Electricacoustic Stimulation in Children

In recent years, a new cochlear implantation technique has been developed for use with deaf and hard of hearing children—electric-acoustic stimulation (EAS) by hybrid systems. People may have a profound hearing loss only at higher frequencies, whereas hearing of low pitches is still possible. This is the case not only in elderly people but also in children who have this special kind of "ski-slope" hearing loss, which some professionals call partial deafness (Skarzynski, Lorens, Piotrowska, & Anderson, 2007). Such high-frequency hearing loss in children may be caused either by a cytostatic therapy (in the case of a tumor)—such as treatment with certain antibiotics (aminoglycosides)—or by less well-recognized factors, mostly genetic or infectious. These children would benefit best from amplification of their hearing in the low frequencies by conventional hearing aids and from electric stimulation of the auditory pathway by a cochlear implant in the higher-frequency regions, where no or only minimal residual hair cells are left. This kind of therapy combines the advantages of a more natural-sounding "acoustic" or "cochlear" hearing, namely, hearing within a broad dynamic range of sound levels and fine pitch resolution in the low frequencies with those of restituted but "electric" hearing in the higher frequencies.

Manufacturers have recently developed hybrid devices that combine a hearing aid and a cochlear implant. One of the most challenging problems here is the preservation of the residual hearing because the insertion of an electrode into the cochlea may cause trauma with subsequent damage to or later degeneration of the remaining hair cells. To prevent this, special electrodes have been developed, and "soft" surgery must be performed in order to preserve the residual hair cells. In addition, a restricted insertion of the cochlear implant electrode into only the lower part of the cochlea is required. Typically, deep insertion of the electrode was the surgical goal because it resulted in the most comprehesive stimulation and the best benefit due to stimulation of as many cochlear regions as possible. This principle had to be abandoned in the case of hybrid therapy because the hair cells that represent the low frequencies and need to be preserved for acoustic hearing are positioned in the upper, more remote regions of the cochlea. Applying these principles, hybrid therapy resulted in the preservation of residual hearing and excellent speech perception in most adults and children (Skarzynski et al., 2007).

However, some ethical considerations are necessary in the decision for hybrid therapy in children. Such a decision seems even more difficult than the one for pediatric cochlear implantation alone. Sometimes a ski-slope hearing loss is symptomatic of a progressive loss of hearing abilities. However, for hybrid therapy, the hearing loss should be stable over time. Otherwise, partial insertion of an electrode would not produce the best benefit from electric stimulation. A fixed status of hearing loss, however, cannot be guaranteed in children. An impaired cochlea is vulnerable and often deteriorates over time. Another problem is that preservation of the residual hearing, although highly probable, cannot be guaranteed. Although special EAS electrodes have been designed and despite the fact that a 360° insertion of the electrode is sufficient for a good "electric" hearing, parents must be informed that a progressive hearing loss could lead to a suboptimal benefit from hybrid therapy and that the "acoustic" hearing may disappear over time. In most cases, the benefit from the "electric" hearing alone is sufficient and no additional surgery is necessary, although the latter cannot be ruled out completely. Even then, in all probability a child will have benefited so much in the areas of auditory and language development by the quasi-natural "acoustic" hearing that this advantage would largely outweigh the disadvantages of a slow, progressive hearing loss and the possibility of a second surgery.

Weighing the advantages and disadvantages, hybrid therapy in the case of partial deafness may be a recommended treatment method also for children. However, surgery should be conducted only by an experienced surgeon, as always recommendable for cochlear implantation of childen, and parents need to be carefully counseled about the treatment risks and benefits.

Ethical Considerations regarding Technical Implants in General

Vehement discussions about the ethical aspects of the use of biotechnologies have been waged for decades. In science, a specialization called health technology assessment systematically studies the consequences of the introduction or continued use of a technology in a certain context and assesses its value, including nontechnical, socioethical aspects. Ethics should contribute to a better understanding of the complex relationship between individuals, society, medicine, and technology (ten Have, 1995).

By 2008, more than 110,000 deaf adults and children worldwide had received cochlear implants. The implants provide the patients with important auditory cues necessary for auditory development, awareness, and speech perception via electrical stimulation of the auditory nerve (Fallon et al., 2008). Cochlear implantation demonstrates impressively that health technology assessment is not a matter of merely collecting the facts about a technology but also deciding whether such facts are plausible and relevant within a particular framework (van der Wilt, Reuzel, & Banta, 2000). Because health technology assessment aims to enhance the decision-making process with regard to funding and the use of certain health technologies like cochlear implantation, it must deal adequately with existing pluralistic societal values.

The divergence of hearing and deaf people's ethical judgments stems from the fact that deafness and hearing are "world generating states," conditions that not only result in a different understanding of the world but also lead to different life courses and values that make both worlds different (Broesterhuizen, 2008). The conflict between these two views is not resolved by arbitration or the choice of a middle course but by a fruitful discussion between representatives of both worlds. A method of setting up such a discussion is interactive technology assessment (van der Wilt et al., 2000), which consists of a circle of conversation with a complete set of stakeholders. The different frameworks are explicated by encouraging various stakeholders to forward their claims and concerns, including their norms and values. During every conversation, respondents are motivated to explain their perspective. The evaluator, a listener who adopts a critical attitude, creates a picture that is included and adjusted in the next conversation. This process continues until all of the stakeholders have been interviewed. Then the evaluator returns to the first respondent and pursues an additive conversation. Ideally, in the end, the circle reaches a fair agreement, a consensus on the prerequisites for a technology acceptable to all stakeholders. Such a technique should prevent the assessment from being unduly biased toward one particular perspective and provide an option to bridge the different worlds not by reducing their differences but by including and respecting the various perspectives (van der Wilt et al., 2000).

A common approach in health-care ethics is to consider four issues: (a) beneficence (the obligation to provide benefits and balance them against risks), (b) nonmaleficence (the obligation to avoid causing harm), (c) respect for autonomy (the obligation to respect the decision-making capacities of autonomous persons), and (d) justice (obligations of fairness in the distribution of benefits and risks). The European Group on Ethics in Science and New Technologies to the European Commission (2005) has published a European position paper on the ethical aspects of information and communication technologies (ICT) implants, a category to which the cochlear implant belongs. The objective of this position paper was to raise awareness of and questions about the ethical dilemmas created by ICT implants. Its primary goals were to ensure an appropriate and timely impact on the various technological applications and to propose clear ethical boundaries and legal principles, as well as to suggest several steps that should be taken by responsible regulators in Europe. The group summarized ethical principles that must be applied in the decision-making process of funding and supporting ICT implants.

As for the European legal background, specific importance was attached to the EU's Charter of Fundamental Rights, which focuses on the principles of dignity, freedom, equality, solidarity, citizenship, and justice, as well as the integrity and inviolability of the body, with particular regard to informed consent and personal data protection. Specific consideration was given to the Convention on Human Rights and Biomedicine of the Council of Europe (1997) and to UNESCO's Universal Declaration on the Human Genome and Human Rights (1997). The Group on Ethics designated the following principles for the application of ICT (including cochlear) implants: (a) human dignity as an essential component of the human being and a condition of freedom and equality, (b) inviolability of the body and physical and psychological integrity (which should not be referred to whenever body functions are actually reintegrated and/or enhanced),

(c) privacy and data protection, (d) the precautionary principle (aiming at identifying the "acceptable risk" threshold with regard to the values at stake and respect for the human body, which deserve the highest legal protection), (e) data minimization, purpose specification, proportionality principle, and relevance, (f) autonomy of individuals (freedom to choose how to use one's body, freedom of choice as regards one's health, freedom from external controls, and influence; requires consent), (f) informed consent, (g) values conflicts, (h) social aspects (invisibility of implants to an external observer; dependence on market forces; transformation of social and cultural environment), (i) necessity of special caution (if implants cannot be removed easily; for example, limited suitability of magnetic resonance imaging of cochlear implants because of possible dislocation), and (j) ICT implants in minors and legally incapacitated persons. Implantation of ICT devices for health purposes should be governed by the principles that (a) the objective is important (e.g., saving lives, restoring health, improving the quality of life), (b) the implant is necessary to achieve this objective, and (c) there is no other less invasive and more cost-effective method of achieving the objective. All of these principles ensure that special care and attention are applied to this field, maximizing the possibility that cochlear implants in children are safe, appropriate, and reasonable.

Options of Cochlear Implantation

The advent of multielectrode cochlear implantation has dramatically changed the perspectives of profoundly deaf people, in particular of prelingual deaf children. One should imagine what a highly sophisticated prosthesis has made possible. The electrical stimulation of the auditory nerve by a technical device makes auditory information available also to people who have never heard anything because of a completely nonfunctioning inner ear. The cochlear implant has for the first time provided the—at least partial—replacement of a sense organ and created a bionic ear (Dahm, 1998). It is the first neural prosthesis that effectively brings electronic technology into a direct physiological relationship with the central nervous system and human consciousness. It enables speech understanding for tens of thousands of persons with profound deafness and spoken language for children born deaf in more than 80 countries. It constitutes the first major advance in research and technology to help deaf children to communicate since the sign language of the Deaf was developed at the Paris deaf school (L'Institut National de Jeunes Sourds de Paris) more than 200 years ago (Clark, 2008).

The results of cochlear implant therapy for many children are astonishing. An open speech perception (speech perception without additional lipreading), the use of a telephone, and education in mainstream schools and kindergartens have become possible. With the help of a cochlear implant, the brain of a child with congenital deafness learns to perceive and process sounds for the first time. The brain learns to transform the electrical impulses from the auditory pathway into a true hearing impression, that is, one resulting from acoustical stimulation. We know from postlingually deaf adults that hearing with a cochlear implant sounds unnatural during the first weeks and sometimes not very pleasant for people with former hearing experience. After a while, depending on factors such as age, duration of deafness, preoperative hearing, additional diseases, and the quality of the speech processor fitting and of postoperative rehabilitation, listening begins to sound quite natural. We can expect a similar process in children, even more so because of the great plasticity of the infant auditory cortex.

While writing this chapter and searching in MedLine (1985–2009), the commonly used electronic data base for medical publications, the author of this chapter identified 2,847 articles reporting data on the evaluation of cochlear implantation in children. As outcome measures, 980 papers used the term *speech perception* or *speech production*, 129 *oral language*, 84 *sign language*, 774 *communication*, 86 *quality (of) life*, 32 *academic performance*, and 15 *educational needs*. Only a few articles explicitly addressed Deaf communities' concerns and made the attempt to translate these concerns into research questions by assessing outcomes of communication (oral, signing, bilingual, total) and socialization. In a recent systematic review 1,580 publications on cochlear implants were analyzed. All studies that qualified for the final analysis reported that unilateral cochlear implants improved scores on all outcome measures (Bond et al., 2009). Even if there were a potential positive reporting bias (implant studies with positive outcome might have a better chance of getting published), the favorable outcomes of cochlear implantation are undeniable. Biomedical research has revealed strong evidence that cochlear implants are safe and effective. Bilateral implants bring about the benefits of binaural hearing. Future research using nanotechnology should see high-fidelity sound received, which would help deaf persons to better communicate in noise and enjoy music (Clark, 2008). More equity of access for the majority of children who would benefit from a cochlear implant is reached by increased implementation of newborn hearing-screening programs and by funding of cochlear-implant therapy research by government agencies.

Cochlear Implant Therapy in Children of Deaf Parents

Compared with the hearing population, the Deaf community is small. Hence, its internal relationships are close, and anonymity is low. In such small communities members may fear the negative consequences of the exchange of social information and deviation from cultural norms. Hence, Deaf parents of deaf children may fear a loss of social embedding in their community if they let their child undergo cochlear implantation.

Searching the Internet, I found in a blog by Andre (retrieved October 17, 2009, from http://deafarticles.blogspot.com) the statements of John-Michael Stern (2004), who is hard of hearing and at the borderline for a cochlear implant indication:

> Imagine that the hearing and the Deaf represent two separate land masses, and ask if the cochlear implant could bridge the two lands, or become a river between them, flowing on its own. One major barrier between these two lands is that the hearing view deafness as a disability that must be cured. However, the Deaf do not see themselves this way. Rather, they pride themselves with their distinct cultural identity. Many Deaf will argue that the cochlear implant is not a perfect fix, and, therefore, trying to mold into the hearing world is a waste of time. In addition, many Deaf fear that the cochlear implant will bring about the cultural genocide of the Deaf way of life. Third-year student Justin Drezner said, "Implanting is like making black people white or white people black."

This passage coincides with the views of many Deaf parents of deaf children. They show up from time to time in pediatric-audiological counseling during hearing-aid fitting and evaluation of their child's hearing abilities. Many Deaf parents seem to be searching for a way to justify their choice of treatment. They do not want to have their children hearing but want to raise them in their Deaf culture. They may be afraid that otherwise they could not protect and educate their children well enough to succeed as Deaf persons in a predominantly hearing world. They may fear estrangement between themselves and their deaf child after the child has gotten a cochlear implant. They may feel as though they have sent their child into a "foreign country." To such parents I would like to reply that we doctors are not part of an inhumane technical system of a profit-driven, cochlear-implant empire. Instead, many of us are parents like you, who want to make the best decisions for our children even if the decisions are in conflict with other members of society.

It is misleading to assume that Deaf people exist exclusively in the Deaf world. They have hearing friends and family members, hearing teachers, and hearing colleagues. Hence, parents of deaf children do not have to make decisions that will consign their child forever to one world or the other (Miner, 1996). Most of those deaf parents who cross the bridge by choosing a cochlear implant for their deaf child experience relief, knowing that the child will not be estranged from them but will grow up bilingually or use total communication. From the standpoint of a pediatric audiologist who has worked with deaf children for years, I have learned that most of the children I have met want to hear if they have the opportunity. Bonnie Tucker, who is deaf, in her Hastings Center Report (1998), "Deaf Culture, Cochlear Implants, and Elective Disability," has described the wishes of most deaf people to hear their own voices, telephones, music, and spoken dialogue in movies and plays and to participate in group conversations with deaf and hearing people. She asked why anyone would want to deny such pleasures to themselves or their child.

Most prelingually deaf children appreciate auditory impressions. They are curious about and willing to explore the new sensations. After a short time, usually several weeks, most of the children that I have worked with want to wear their devices and ask for them. If, after 6 months, parents feel that the child does not want to wear his or her device one of the following is usually the reason: (a) the fitting has not been done properly, (b) the device is malfunctioning, (c) there are medical problems such as discomfort (which is rare) or ossification of the cochlea after meningitis, which damages good hearing, or (d) the child has additional or multiple handicaps that require a slow habituation to the new sensations.

We should not make more of a cochlear implant than it is—a sophisticated hearing device, nothing more and nothing less. It does not cure deafness. It does not transform Deaf people into hearing people. Hopefully, the Deaf community will accept those who use cochlear implants, just as they have done with hearing aid users (Stern, 2004).

Outlook

In recent years, the Deaf community has somewhat changed its view of pediatric cochlear implantation. There has been a movement from clear disapproval to a more or less tolerant acquiescence to a cautious acceptance. The number of publications debating cochlear implants, with Deaf and hearing communities on opposite sides, has decreased considerably in the second half of this decade. In the United States this development is also expressed in some of the publications of the National Association of the Deaf (NAD). In 1993, its position paper on cochlear implants in children, now withdrawn, stated the following:

> The NAD deplores the decision of the Food and Drug Administration [to approve the commercial distribution of cochlear implants for surgical implantation in children aged 2 through 17], which was unsound scientifically, procedurally, and ethically. . . . Far more serious is the ethical issue raised through decisions to undertake invasive surgery upon defenseless children, when the long-term physical, emotional and social impacts on children from this irreversible procedure—which will alter the lives of these children—have not been scientifically established. . . . The parents who make the decision for the child are often poorly informed about the deaf community, its rich heritage and promising futures. (National Association of the Deaf, 1993)

A later NAD position paper on cochlear implants, issued in October 2000, reads as follows:

> Cochlear implantation is a technology that represents a tool to be used in some forms of communication, and not a cure for deafness. . . . The NAD recognizes all technological advancements with the potential to foster, enhance, and improve the quality of life for all deaf and hard-of-hearing persons. . . . The NAD recognizes the rights of parents to make informed choices for their . . . children, respects their choice to use cochlear implants and all other assistive devices, and strongly supports the development of the whole child and of language and literacy. (National Association of the Deaf, 2000; cited by Christiansen & Leigh, 2004)

Currently, the NAD webpage posts the following message:

> NAD joined nearly 100 other participants at the "Cochlear Implants and Sign Language: Building Foundations for Effective Educational Practices" conference held at Gallaudet University, April 15–17, 2009. The conference was attended by representatives from schools and programs for the deaf and mainstream programs, as well as advocates and other interested parties. The purpose of the conference was to discuss effective practices to meet the needs of children with cochlear implants. Participants considered the challenges of effectively designing programs that include both spoken language and sign language." (National Association of the Deaf, 2009)

The last three paragraphs demonstrate the important way the Deaf community through NAD has undergone a change of perspective. It is desirable that the "cochlear implant community" (if it can be so named) is taking steps toward the Deaf community in order to create an atmosphere of understanding, tolerance, and acceptance on both sides, which are no longer far apart. This process would make it easier for parents to decide whether a cochlear implant is appropriate for their child. The implant does not close the door to the Deaf community. Parents, both hearing and deaf, will feel less torn in their decision for or against a cochlear implant because their children now have more options in both the hearing and the Deaf worlds. Hearing parents do not always feel comfortable about taking advice from deaf persons (Christiansen & Leigh, 2004). Nevertheless, they can benefit from communication with deaf adults about choices for deaf children, acknowledging that only deaf persons know what deafness means.

Another example of change is the establishment of cochlear implant centers, which educate children with implants in a setting that emphasizes both visual and auditory learning. Such a center was established at Gallaudet University in 2000. The following two quotes are from students who responded to a questionnaire about the changing climate at the university: "More parents are choosing to have their deaf kids implanted. That is their right to choose. Gallaudet needs to prepare to meet the needs of a more diverse student body if it wants to continue to exist." "I formerly did not support the cochlear implant as I felt it would destroy the Deaf community. But now I respect individual choice and feel the cochlear implant is part of Deaf culture, anyway. People's perspectives on Deaf culture are different now."

Giving up the either-or point of view will decrease the dilemma of parents who have to make a decision. A both-and attitude gives their children an opportunity to speak or to sign without any moral superstructure, to have friends in the hearing world and in the Deaf world, and to resolve the apparent separation of implanted children from the Deaf community. Finally, it would enrich everyone's life.

Even if cochlear implantation is doubtless beneficial for most deaf children, it nonetheless raises many questions. Ethics usually does not show us clear and simple ways but leaves us alone with difficult decisions which result from a thorough process of exchange. We parents, health professionals, and teachers should engage in dialogue among us that makes use of the most current information and broad knowledge. What does this imply?

Children who are potential cochlear implant candidates have to be diagnosed carefully and repeatedly with a set of objective and subjective pediatric-audiological methods. Detailed and elaborate informed consent and provision of all alternatives for deaf children's lives beyond the focus on the surgery have to be applied for every individual child who is a candidate for a cochlear implant, in order to help parents in their decisions about implantation and subsequent communication and educational conditions of their child. In the case of deaf parents, independent advisors, including a deaf person, should be involved in the informed consent process to provide balanced information. The rights of the child require consultation with the youngster, if possible, and broad information to the parents about risks beyond medical matters, including the information that linguistic, educational, and communicative personal outcomes may vary interindividually and over time (Hyde & Power, 2006). After implantation, long-term rehabilitation of hearing, education tailored to the child's hearing and language abilities, and regular examination of therapy outcomes for personal, emotional, social, and educational development of implanted children must be ensured.

Considering all of the aspects discussed in this chapter, cochlear implant therapy is a highly beneficial option for profoundly deaf children who meet the criteria required for candidacy. It can be viewed as a social good that opens new perspectives for deaf children and their families.

References

Achenbach, T. M., McConaughy, S. H. , & Howell, C. T. (1987). Child/adolescent behavioral and emotional problems: Implications of cross-informant correlations for situational specificity. *Psycholgical Bulletin, 101*, 213–232.

Alexander, R. D. (1987). *The biology of moral systems*. New York: de Gruyter.

Anstey, K. W. (2002). Are attempts to have impaired children justifiable? *Journal of Medical Ethics, 28*, 286–288.

Balkany, T., Hodges, A. V., & Goodman, K. W. (1996). Ethics of cochlear implantation in young children. *Otolaryngology—Head and Neck Surgery, 114*, 748–755.

Balkany, T., Hodges, A., & Goodman, K. W. (1998). Additional comments to "Ethics of cochlear implantation in young children: A review and reply from a Deaf-World perspective." *Otolaryngology—Head and Neck Surgery, 119*, 312–313.

Bender, D. G. (2004). Do Fourteenth Amendment considerations outweigh a potential state interest in mandating cochlear implantation for deaf children? *Journal of Deaf Studies and Deaf Education, 9*, 104–111.

Benedict, B. S., & Sass-Lehrer, M. (2007). Deaf and hearing partnerships: Ethical and communication considerations. *American Annals of the Deaf, 152*, 275–282.

Bond, M., Elston, J., Mealing, S., Anderson, R., Weiner, G., Taylor, R. S., Liu, Z., & Stein, K. (2009). Effectiveness of multi-channel unilateral cochlear implants for profoundly deaf children: A systematic review. *Clinical Otolaryngology, 34*, 199–211.

Broesterhuizen, M. (2008). Worlds of difference: An ethical analysis of choices in the field of deafness. *Ethical Perspectives, 15*, 103–132.

Buss, D. M. (2008). *Evolutionary psychology: The new science of mind* (3rd ed.). Boston: Pearson Education.

Christiansen, J. B., & Leigh, I. W. (2004). Children with cochlear implants changing parent and deaf community perspectives. *Archives of Otolaryngology—Head and Neck Surgery, 130*, 673–677.

Clark, G. M. (2008). Personal reflections on the multichannel cochlear implant and a view of the future. *Journal of Rehabilitation Research and Development, 45*, 651–693.

Dahm, M. C. (1998). Taubheit: Das Recht auf Gehörlosigkeit oder die Chance mit einem "cochlear implant" zu hören? [Deafness: The right to be deaf or the chance of hearing with a "cochlear implant"?] *HNO, 46*, 524–528.

Davis, D. S. (1997). Genetic dilemmas and the child's right to an open future. *Hastings Center Report, 27*, 7–15.

Dettman, S. J., Pinder, B., Briggs, R. J., Dowell, R. C., & Leigh, J. R. (2007). Communication development in children who receive the cochlear implant younger than 12 months: Risks versus benefits. *Ear and Hearing, 28*(2), 11–18.

Diller, G. (2006). Auditive Kommunikationsstörungen im Kindes- und Erwachsenenalter unter besonderer Berücksichtigung von Cochlear Implants [Auditive communication disorders in childhood and adulthood with respect to cochlear implants]. In G. Böhme (Ed.), *Sprach-, Sprech-, Stimm-, und Schluckstörungen* [Language, speech, voice, and swallowing disorders] (pp. 233–252). Munich: Urban Fischer.

D'Silva, M. U., Daugherty, M., & MacDonald, M. (2004). Deaf is dandy: Contrasting the deaf and hearing cultures. *Intercultural Communication Studies, 13*, 111–117.

Engelhardt, T. (1996). *The foundations of bioethics.* New York: Oxford University Press.

Euler, H. A. (2003). A psychologist's look at health-related quality-of-life assessment in children. In G. M. O'Donoghue & S. Archbold (Eds.), *Measuring the immeasurable? Proceedings of a conference on quality of life in deaf children* (pp. 45–53). Oxford, UK: Hughes.

European Group on Ethics in Science and New Technologies to the European Commission, The. (2005). *Opinion on the ethical aspects of ICT implants in the human body.* Luxembourg: Office for Official Publications of the European Communities.

Fallon, J. B., Irvine, D. R., & Shepherd, R. K. (2008). Cochlear implants and brain plasticity. *Hearing Research*, 238, 110–117. [Epub September 1, 2007]

Fallon, J. B., Irvine, D. R., & Shepherd, R. K. (2009). Cochlear implant use following neonatal deafness influences the cochleotopic organization of the primary auditory cortex in cats. *Journal of Comparative Neurology, 512*, 101–114.

Feinberg, J. (1980). The child's right to an open future. In A. William and H. LaFollette (Eds.), *Whose child? Children's rights, parental authority, and state power* (pp. 124–153). Totowa, NJ: Littlefield, Adams.

Gauntlett, R. (1996). Cochlear implantation is controversial among deaf people. *British Medical Journal, 30*, 850.

Geers, A. E. (2006). Factors influencing spoken language outcomes in children following early cochlear implantation. In A. Møller (Ed.), *Cochlear and brainstem implants: Advances in oto-rhino-laryngology* (vol. 64, pp. 50–65). Basel: Karger.

Gonsoulin, T. P. (2001). Cochlear implant/Deaf world dispute: Different bottom elephants. *Otolaryngology—Head and Neck Surgery, 125*, 552–556.

Gordon, K. A., & Papsin, B. C. (2009). Benefits of short interimplant delays in children receiving bilateral cochlear implants. *Otology and Neurotology, 30*, 319–331.

Hansson, S. O. (2005). Implant ethics. *Journal of Medical Ethics, 31*, 519–525.

Harris, J., Anderson, J., & Novak, R. (1995). An outcome study of cochlear implants in deaf patients. *Archives of Otolaryngology Head and Neck Surgery, 121*, 398–404.

Harvey, M. A. (2001). "Does God have a cochlear implant?" *Journal of Deaf Studies and Deaf Education, 6*, 70.

Häyry, M. (2004). There is a difference between selecting a deaf embryo and deafening a hearing child. *Journal of Medical Ethics, 30*, 510–512.

Hintermair, M., & Voit, H. (1990). *Bedeutung, Identität, und Gehörlosigkeit* [Importance identity, and deafness]. Heidelberg: Groos.

Holt, R. F., & Svirsky, M. A. (2008). An exploratory look at pediatric cochlear implantation: Is earliest always best? *Ear and Hearing, 29*, 492–511.

Hyde, M., & Power, D. (2006). Some ethical dimensions of cochlear implantation for deaf children and their families. *Journal of Deaf Studies and Deaf Education, 11*, 102–111.

Johnston, T. (2005). In one's own image: Ethics and the reproduction of deafness. *Journal of Deaf Studies and Deaf Education, 10*, 426–441.

Kahneman, D., Diener, E., & Schwarz, N. (Eds.). (1999). *Well-being: The foundations of hedonic psychology.* New York: Sage Foundation.

Kemp, P., & Rendtorff, J. (2000). *Basic ethical principles in European bioethics and biolaw: Autonomy, dignity, integrity, and vulnerability.* Report to the European Commission of the Biomed II Project, Basic Ethical Principles in Bioethics and Biolaw 1995–1998. Centre for Ethics and Law, Copenhagen.

Kiefer, J., von Ilberg, C., Gall, V., Diller, G., Spelsberg, A., & Neumann, K. (2000). Results from 88 prelingually deaf children with cochlear implants: An analysis of predictive-factors. *Advances in Oto-rhino-laryngology, 57*, 202–208.

Kral, A., & Tillein, J. (2006). Brain plasticity under cochlear implant stimulation. In A. Møller (Ed.), *Cochlear and brainstem implants. Advances in oto-rhino-laryngology* (vol. 64, pp. 89–108). Basel: Karger.

Kral, A., Tillein, J., Heid, S., Klinke, R., & Hartmann, R. (2006). Cochlear implants: Cortical plasticity in congenital deprivation. *Progress in Brain Research, 157*, 283–313.

Kwan, T., White, P. M., & Segil, N. (2009) Development and regeneration of the inner ear. *Annals of the New York Academy of Sciences, 1170*, 28–33.

Lane, H. (1992). *The mask of benevolence: Disabling the deaf community.* New York: Vintage.

Lane, H. (2002). Do deaf people have a disability? *Sign Language Studies, 2,* 356–379.

Lane, H. (2005). Ethnicity, ethics, and the deaf-world. *Journal of Deaf Studies and Deaf Education, 10,* 291–310.

Lane, H., & Bahan, B. (1998). Ethics of cochlear implantation in young children: A review and reply from a Deaf-world perspective. *Otolaryngology—Head and Neck Surgery, 119,* 297–307.

Lane, H., & Grodin, M. (1997). Ethical issues in cochlear implant surgery: An exploration into disease, disability, and the best interest of the child. *Kennedy Institute of Ethics Journal, 7,* 231–251.

Lane, H., Hoffmeister, R., & Bahan, B. (1996). *A journey into the Deaf-world.* San Diego: DawnSignPress.

Levy, N. (2002). Deafness, culture, and choice. *Journal of Medical Ethics, 28,* 284–285.

Li, Y., Bain, L., & Steinberg, A. G. (2003). Parental decision making and the choice of communication modality for the child who is deaf. *Archives of Pediatrics and Adolescent Medicine, 157,* 162–168.

Lin, F. R., Wang, N. Y., Fink, N. E., Quittner, A. L., Eisenberg, L. S., Tobey, E. A., Niparko, J. K., & CDaCI Investigative Team. (2008). Assessing the use of speech and language measures in relation to parental perceptions of development after early cochlear implantation. *Otology and Neurotology, 29,* 208–213.

Marschark, M. (2007). *Raising and educating a deaf child* (2nd ed.) New York: Oxford University Press.

McKellin, W. H. (1995). Hearing-impaired families: The social ecology of hearing loss. *Social Science and Medicine, 40,* 1469–1480.

Michie, S., & Marteau, T. M. (1999). The choice to have a disabled child. *American Journal of Human Genetics, 65,* 1204–1207.

Miner, I. D. (1996). Ethics of cochlear implantation. *Otolaryngology—Head and Neck Surgery, 114,* 748–755.

Motasaddi-Zarandy, M., Rezai, H., Mahdavi-Arab, M., & Golestan, B. (2009). The scholastic achievement of profoundly deaf children with cochlear implants compared to their normal peers. *Archives of Iranian Medicine, 12,* 441–447.

Nance, W. E. (2003). The genetics of deafness. *Mental Retardation and Developmental Disabilities Research Reviews, 9,* 109–119.

National Association of the Deaf (NAD). (1993). *Cochlear implants in children: A position paper of the National Association of the Deaf.* Silver Spring, MD.

National Association of the Deaf (NAD). (2009). *NAD participates in CI and sign language conference.* Retrieved October 11, 2009, from http://www.nad.org/news/2009/4/nad-participates-ci-and-sign-language-conference.

Nelson, H., & Nelson, J. (1998). Family. In W. Reich (Ed.), *Bioethics: Sex, genetics, and human reproduction* (pp. 195–201). Macmillan Compendium. New York: Macmillan Library Reference USA: Simon and Schuster Macmillan.

Neumann, K., Gross, M., Böttcher, P., Euler, H. A., Spormann-Lagodzinski, M., & Polzer, M. (2006). Effectiveness and efficiency of a universal newborn hearing screening in Germany. *Folia Phoniatrica et Logopaedica, 58,* 440–455.

Neumann, K., Preibisch, C., Spreer, J., Raab, P., Hamm, J., Euler, H. A., Lanfermann, H., Helbig, S., & Kiefer, J. (2008). Testing the diagnostic value of electrical ear canal stimulation in cochlear implant candidates by functional magnetic resonance imaging. *Audiology and Neurootology, 13,* 281–292. doi: 10.1159/000124276

Niparko, J. K. (2004). Editor's introduction to J. B. Christiansen & I. W. Leigh, Children with cochlear implants changing parent and deaf community perspectives. *Archives of Otolaryngology—Head and Neck Surgery, 130,* 673.

Nunes, R. (2001). Ethical dimension of paediatric cochlear implantation. *Theoretical Medicine and Bioethics, 22,* 337–349.

Peters, B. R. (2006). *Rationale for bilateral cochlear implantation in children and adults.* White Papers. Melbourne, Australia: Cochlear Corporation.

Ramsden, J. D., Papaioannou, V., Gordon, K. A., James, A. L., & Papsin, B. C. (2009a). Parental and program's decision making in paediatric simultaneous bilateral cochlear implantation: Who says no and why? *International Journal of Pediatric Otorhinolaryngology, 73,* 1325–1328.

Ramsden, J. D., Papsin, B. C., Leung, R., James, A., & Gordon, K. A. (2009b). Bilateral simultaneous cochlear implantation in children: Our first 50 cases. *Laryngoscope.* Retrieved October 16, 2009, from http://www3.interscience.wiley.com/cgi-bin/full-text/122580709/HTMLSTART.

Savulescu, J. (2002). Deaf lesbians, "designer disability," and the future of medicine. *British Medical Journal, 325,* 771–773.

Scherf, F., van Deun, L., & van Wieringen, A. (2007). Hearing benefits of second-side cochlear implantation in two groups of children. *International Journal of Pediatric Otorhinolaryngology, 71,* 1855–1863.

Sharma, A., & Dorman, M. (2006). Central auditory development in children with cochlear implants: Clinical implications. In A. Møller (Ed.), *Cochlear and brainstem implants: Advances in oto-rhino-laryngology* (vol. 64, pp. 66–88). Basel: Karger.

Sharma, A., Dorman, M., & Spahr, T. (2002). A sensitive period for the development of the central auditory system in children with cochlear implants. *Ear and Hearing, 23,* 532–539.

Shultz, K. (2000). Every implanted child a star. *Quarterly Journal of Speech, 86,* 251–275.

Skarzynski, H., Lorens, A., Piotrowska, A., & Anderson, I. (2007). Partial deafness cochlear implantation in children. *International Journal of Pediatric Otorhinolaryngology, 71,* 1407–1413.

Solomon, A. (1994, August 28). Defiantly deaf. *New York Times Magazine,* 38–43.

Spriggs, M. (2002). Lesbian couple create a child who is deaf like them: A deaf lesbian couple who chose to have a deaf child receive a lot of criticism. *Journal of Medical Ethics, 28,* 283.

Steinberg, A., Brainsky, A., Bain, L., Montoya, L., Indenbaum, M., & Potsic, W. (2000). Parental values in the decision about cochlear implantation. *International Journal of Pediatric Otorhinolaryngology, 55,* 99–107.

Stern, J.-M. (2004, January 23). The cochlear implant: Rejection of culture or aid to improve hearing? *Reporter Magazine.* Retrieved October 12, 2009, from http://www.deaftoday.com/news/2004/01/the_cochlear_im.html.

Swanson, L. (1997). Cochlear implants: The head-on collision between medical technology and the right to be deaf. *Canadian Medical Association Journal, 157,* 929–932.

ten Have, H. A. M. J. (1995). Medical technology assessment and ethics: Ambivalent relations. *Hastings Center Report, 25,* 13–19.

Trivers, R. L. (1974). Parent-offspring conflict. *American Zoologist, 14,* 249–264.

Tucker, B. P. (1998). Deaf culture, cochlear implants, and elective disability. *Hastings Center Report, 28,* 6–14.

Van der Wilt, G. J., Reuzel, R., & Banta, H. D. (2000). The ethics of assessing health technologies. *Theoretical Medicine and Bioethics, 21,* 103–115.

Van Hoesel, R. J. (2004). Exploring the benefits of bilateral cochlear implants. *Audiology and Neurootology, 9*, 234–246.

Vonier, A. (2008). *Cochlea-implantierte Kinder gehörloser bzw. hochgradig hörgeschädigter Eltern* [Cochlear implanted children of deaf or profoundly hearing-impaired parents]. Heidelberg: Median.

Waltzman, S. B., Scalchunes, V., & Cohen, N. L. (2000). Performance of multiply handicapped children using cochlear implants. *American Journal of Otology, 21*, 329–335.

Warner-Czyz, A. D., Loy, B., Roland, P. S., Tong, L., & Tobey, E. A. (2009, August 10). Parent versus child assessment of quality of life in children using cochlear implants. *International Journal of Pediatric Otorhinolaryngology*. [Epub ahead of print]

Wirth, W. (2006). Hilfe, Selbsthilfe, Vielfalt: Rette sich, wer kann? Ethische Aspekte der Rehabilitation und Psychotherapie bei erwachsenen Hörgeschädigten [Help, self-help, diversity: Every man for himself? Ethical aspects of the rehabilitation and psychotherapy of hearing-impaired persons]. In M. Hintermair (Ed.), *Ethik und Hörschädigung: Reflexionen über das Gelingen von Leben unter erschwerten Bedingungen in unsicheren Zeiten* [Ethics and hearing impairments: Reflections on succeeding at living under difficult conditions in uncertain times] (pp. 349–368). Heidelberg: Median.

World Health Organization (WHO). (1980). International classification of impairments, disabilities, and handicaps: A manual of classification relating to the consequences of disease: ICIDH. Geneva: WHO Press.

World Health Organization (WHO). (2001). International classification of functioning, disability, and health: ICF short version. Geneva: WHO Press.

World Health Organization (WHO). (2004). ICD-10 international statistical classification of diseases and related health problems, tenth rev. (2nd ed.). Geneva: WHO Press.

World Health Organization (WHO). (2007). International classification of functioning, disability, and health: Children and youth version: ICF-CY. Geneva: WHO Press.

Yoshinaga-Itano, C., Coulter, D., & Thomson, V. (2001). Developmental outcomes of children with hearing loss born in Colorado hospitals with and without universal newborn hearing screening programs. *Seminars in Neonatology, 6*, 521–529.

Yoshinaga-Itano, C., Sedey, A. L., Coulter, D. K., & Mehl, A. L. (1998). Language of early- and later identified children with hearing loss. *Pediatrics, 102*, 1161–1171.

Young, C. (2002). Sound judgment: Does curing deafness really mean cultural genocide? *Reason, 4*. Retrieved October 12, 2009, from http://www.reason.com/news/show/28367. htmlWoolsey, C. N. & Walzl, E. M. (1942). Topical projection of nerve fibres from local regions of the cochlea to the cerebral cortex. *Bulletin of the Johns Hopkins Hospital, 71*, 315–344.

Zeitler, D. M., Budenz, C. L., & Roland, J. T., Jr. (2009). Revision cochlear implantation. *Current Opinion in Otolaryngology and Head and Neck Surgery, 17*, 334–338.

Part Two

Educational Decisions

4

Where Do We Look? What Do We See? A Framework for Ethical Decision Making in the Education of Students Who Are Deaf or Hard of Hearing

KATHEE MANGAN CHRISTENSEN

Be kind, for everyone you meet is engaged in a great struggle.

—Philo, 15 BCE

PJ's Story

When I began looking for subjects for my doctoral dissertation, PJ was 2 years old. I was interested in studying the nonverbal communication of congenitally deaf toddlers from hearing families. PJ's family members were hearing and, at that time, beginning to learn American Sign Language (ASL). They were dedicated to providing the best communication environment for their deaf child in a warm and loving family where everyone spoke English, and some spoke Spanish as well. Thus, PJ was an ideal subject for my study.

I videotaped him in his classroom over a period of three months and transcribed all of his nonverbal communication using the Nonverbal and Verbal Communication Analysis (NaVCA), (Christensen & Regan, 1995 rev.). He was one of 7 subjects and the least overtly expressive of the group. He tended to observe his classmates more than the others, smiling from afar rather than jumping into the center of the action. During the time I was gathering research, his teachers reported that they felt that PJ was cognitively delayed. They were considering a recommendation that he be placed in a deaf special needs class with children who had developmental disabilities, were both deaf and blind, or were deaf with other special needs. When I asked why they were making this referral, the response was simple: "He isn't talking. He isn't signing. He just isn't communicating like the other children in the class. The only thing he does is cry!" It was fortunate for PJ that I had recorded hours of videotape that revealed a plethora of communication, subtle and nonverbal. He used gaze effectively to make choices and requests. He followed the activities of the class by watching the teacher and others for clues

75

and then acting. He independently headed for his chair at group time or snack time along with the others. He watched the clock and, without prompting, stared at the door at exactly the time that his mother was expected to pick him up. He had figured out that when the hands of the clock were straight up, Mom would appear, and she was rarely late.

The only evidence of crying occurred when his mother dropped him off at school in the morning, and even that subsided when something more interesting caught his attention. His nonverbal communication placed him well within the range of normal cognitive and social functioning; he just chose not to use words yet. In the course of the academic year, PJ acquired a large vocabulary of signed language. He used single signs and combinations of signs to understand and make himself understood. Although still a shy observer in the classroom, he was an intelligent and inquisitive 3-year-old. At the age of 8, PJ decided he wanted to learn to speak. His mother enrolled him in speech therapy, where he did very well. By 10 years of age, he could code-switch between ASL and spoken English according to the demands of the situation. He excelled in high school and even gave a presentation to my graduate students when he was 15. He went on to graduate from college, and the last I heard, he was considering law school.

Why tell this story? What would have happened to PJ if he had been labeled a special needs child at the age of 2? What opportunities would have been denied him if his cognitive strengths had not been observed? How often do cases like this happen because decision makers rush to judgment without carefully considering all of the aspects of important decisions that affect the lives of deaf children and their futures? The ethical responsibility of decision makers in the education of deaf children cannot be overstated. This chapter is about PJ, students like him, and the need to make the very best decisions with regard to their education.

A Glance at History

A look back in history will reveal that what is considered to be "true"—what is believed to be humane and ethical—at one point on the time continuum may evolve into quite a different sense of "truth" at a future point. This is true generally, and it is true in the education of deaf students.

Early historians with an eye toward the deaf world introduced stories about El Mudo and Juan Pablo Bonet. These stories, among others, described early communication from an overwhelmingly hearing perspective. Juan Fernandez de Navarrete, known as El Mudo, was a gifted Spanish Renaissance artist who studied with Titian and others in the 16th century (Lang & Meath-Lang, 1995). He learned a form of sign language, was fluent in the Spanish language, and eventually became the court painter to the Spanish king Philip II. Despite these accomplishments, El Mudo is known primarily for his deafness, then considered an overwhelming barrier, rather than for his incredible artistic talent. Bonet, a hearing priest, was considered for sainthood because, in 1620, he illuminated the handshapes of the Roman alphabet so that a small segment of the deaf population, those fortunate enough to be born to nobility, might learn to read. Of course, some changes in attitude have occurred across the centuries. For example, in 16th-century Europe, deaf persons could not inherit property.

Today that law is considered both wrong and unethical.Truth as defined in the 18th-century chronicles of the education of deaf people begins with the stalwart opinions of Abbé Charles-Michel de l'Épée and Thomas Braidwood as self-proclaimed leaders. De l'Épée observed natural sign language used among deaf people in Paris and used it to teach deaf children primarily for the purpose of saving their souls. Without language, he believed, deaf people would be denied entry to heaven. Braidwood, in England, developed an oral approach to teaching deaf children from wealthy families. He used a form of sign language as a means to the desired goal of oral communication. Without speech, he believed, deaf people could not be successful in life. Given Braidwood's inclination toward oral education, it is interesting to note that his signs were the eventual basis for British Sign Language, which was recognized officially as a language in 2003. In any event, both men were more interested in their own goals and less interested in the aspirations of deaf people who were, metaphorically and actually, voiceless. As we reflect on history, it is possible to identify an evolving focus on rights in the education of deaf children in recent decades. In the 1940s, the focus was on the "right to speak" and the advent of private oral schools, along with the "right to work" and development of vocational programs at public residential schools for deaf students. The 1970s promoted the "right to use signed language" in education. Signed systems were developed and disseminated. American Sign Language research ensued, and in the 1990s we saw a trend toward the "right to a bilingual ASL-English education." More recently, Siegel (2008) has raised the issue of equal protection under the law. "Deaf and hard of hearing children have a right to access and develop communication and language in school, and the failure to provide both is a violation of the constitutional right to be treated equally under the Fourteenth Amendment to the U.S. Constitution" (p. 95). Each of these rights can be viewed as branches emanating from the same societal trunk. Some positive outcomes, along with controversy, have resulted from these independent branches. However, negative perceptions persisted into the late 20th century and in some instances remain today. Certain research reports that are still cited would lead us to believe that deaf children are locked into the fourth grade with regard to literacy (Moores, 2001). This conclusion, reached in the 1970s and 1980s, has been used in the literature to defend what amounts to poor teaching practices. Discussions of low scores on achievement tests rarely took into consideration alternative ways of approaching the task of literacy. Examples of nonverbal problem-solving abilities or "thinking without language" among young deaf children were typically not included. American Sign Language–English bilingualism was yet to be respected by those who promoted English-only education, stymied by the false debate over which blade of the scissors was more important. Reading programs were concocted based on lowered expectations for literacy (Quigley & King, 1981–1984), and deaf children were measured on standardized tests in English designed for hearing children. It is unnerving to note that in 2007 only 8% of deaf students and 15% of hard of hearing students were able to score at the levels of "proficient" or "advanced" on the California Standards Test for English-language arts. Teacher-preparation programs and the teachers they graduate must be held accountable for this situation. To paraphrase a tongue-in-cheek comment of the late Sen. Daniel Moynihan, there are a lot of mistakes that you have to have a PhD to make. The years of underestimating the literacy potential of deaf students is a case in point. Fortunately, the work of Furth and Youniss (1971), Johnson (1989), and others provided evidence that helped to unlock the deaf education curriculum and gave reasons to throw away the "rusty" Fitzgerald Key. Perceptions and behaviors can change, however slowly, over time, and what was believed in 1940, because of experience, can be tempered with new ideas in 2010. At the International Congress on Education of the Deaf in Vancouver in July, 2010, history was re-examined and amended when the participants voted to "reject all resolutions passed at the Milan Congress (1880) that denied the inclusion of sign language in educational programs for Deaf students." Furthermore, all nations were called upon "to ensure that educational programs for the Deaf [*sic*] accept and respect all languages and forms of communication" (ICED press release, July 20, 2010). ICED 2010 effectively endorsed a "both-and" approach to education. At a time when controversy and division are the norm, the action of ICED 2010 offers hope for collaboration and progress in education of children who are deaf and hard of hearing.

This has not always been the case in the past. When I attended graduate school in the mid-1960s, signed language was not an integral part of approved Deaf and Hard of Hearing (DHH) credential programs in the United States. In fact, it was not taught at all in most programs. Deaf teachers, often without credentials, were relegated to teach in "manual units" at residential schools for deaf students. Parents were told to speak English to their deaf children, unilaterally, and non-English-speaking parents were asked to refrain from speaking their native language in the presence of their deaf children. Culture and language were seen as separate entities, and English was considered the language of choice. It is notable that, in some recent situations, these narrow views have expanded to include a more balanced multicultural-multilingual viewpoint. In the mid-1990s, linguistic anthropologist Michael Agar popularized the term *languaculture* and the idea that an automatic tie exists between language and culture. Agar surmised that culture erases the circles that linguists draw around language components (e.g., syntax, phonology). He considered overlapping, expanding circles to be a more logical model when studying spoken language in diverse groups of hearing subjects. Research with hearing children in the area of bilingual education has shown how fluency in a first, natural language supports the acquisition of second-language ability (Lambert & Tucker, 1972; Genesee, 1987; Krashen,1991). Cummins's (1984) dual iceberg theory reminds us of the overlapping circles of languaculture. There are, of course, many other examples of research with hearing individuals that point toward the positive benefits of fluency in more than one language. However, these models have been confounded when applied to the education of deaf children. English-based systems have been invented by late-deafened individuals in consort with hearing individuals, all of whom have the benefit of English fluency. In addition, confusion exists when persons outside the Deaf culture see someone signing and speaking simultaneously and assume that ASL is just a visual form of English. Further confusion develops when the traditional medical view of deafness is challenged. The Deaf President Now movement at Gallaudet University in 1988, as well as the media coverage of that event, brought some insight into this complex situation, so entrenched with hearing hegemony. However, stereotypes and myths continue to nudge reality.

The community of fluent ASL users, deaf and hearing, is relatively small, and no matter how eloquent the "voice," it often is disregarded by the majority. The "language of the person" is deemed less important than the "language of the majority." With this mind-set, the work of pioneers in languaculture falls prey to the ethnocentricity of the majority, and the notion that diverse cultures influence and enrich one another is given a nod and a pass. English, the language of the majority, is deemed the sole vehicle for academic advancement for all students regardless of the language of the family or the ability to hear. Current research on the linguistic and cognitive development of deaf children supports the notion that a narrow, monolingual English view has a negative effect on young deaf children who need an early ASL/English bilingual-education approach in order to maximize educational potential (Mayberry, 2007; MacSweeney et al., 2008).

The work of Ladd (2003) in exploring the concept of "Deafhood" as a state of actualization and heightened identity of Deaf individuals was a step forward. Deafhood rejects a pathological view of deafness and proclaims a positive self-identity for persons who are deaf. Ladd's work is proactive rather than reactive. As a result, we see a movement away from a dualistic view of "deaf or hearing" and a movement toward distinction between rights of birth and the limitations of labels assigned by society. Childhood, sisterhood, neighborhood, adulthood—all of these designations connote groups or collectives, the members of which share conditions or states of being. An element of choice is involved to some extent. An individual might deny membership in a neighborhood, for example, and live as a recluse. The fact remains, however, that by virtue of that person's existence in a particular place, the option for membership exists. In opposition to naturally occurring cultural constructs are those that are assigned to or imposed upon groups of people. Among these assignations are "disability" and "ability," terms that are losing significance in the current discussion of deafness. Deafhood implies a way of seeing the world and of being in the world, one that constitutes a visually oriented, shared cultural and linguistic collective.

Vision as a Metaphor and a Tool

Educators can and should intuit the need to present information visually to deaf children. Deaf children use vision to make sense of a complicated world. However, a question that often is overlooked or undervalued when educators make life-molding decisions for deaf students is the following: How do we, deaf and hearing participants in the educational dialogue, value the use of eyes? What is our vision for deaf children? How do we employ vision in our decision-making process? Do we simply see the surface behavior and make quick interpretations of motivation and potential? Is it possible to develop a bivisual ability to look *at and into* a situation, using our experience to see more than what is readily apparent? According to Arnheim (1969, p. 13), "The cognitive operations called thinking are not the privilege of mental processes above and beyond perception but the essential ingredients of perception itself . . . an active concern of the mind." What we see is fundamental to what we think. We are challenged to pay close attention and to develop what is deemed in chapter 5 and elsewhere in this book a "both-and" mentality. Much has been said about the importance of visual-spatial intelligence in the education of both deaf and hearing learners (Gardner, 1983; Christensen, 1988). Visual strength, so crucial to members of the Deaf culture, is frequently ignored in an auditory-dominant mainstream environment. Today, more and more deaf children are being educated in mainstream settings (Mitchell & Karchmer, 2006). On closer examination, the term *mainstream* implies the presence of a majority culture in the class-room, therefore relegating the mainstreamed child to a lower status. When deaf and hard of hearing students are incorporated into the mainstream, little is done to ensure that visual-spatial access is available *at all levels.* Traditionally, schools attempt to insert culture into education instead of inserting education into culture (Ladson-Billings, 1995).The overlapping circles of ASL, English, Deaf culture, mainstream American culture, and other cultures in the classroom demand attention to all human dimensions, including auditory and visual ones. To understand this notion better, we can view the sensory dimensions through the lens of science. Inner dimensions, in Greek called *autopoiesis* or self-creation, ensure power to each entity and strengthen the capacity for self-manifestation (Taussig, 2008). Biologists apply this term to living systems and allude to the stability of an interconnected entity in which all of the parts maintain the whole in a continuous dynamic despite the continuous flow of energy through the system. This term has been adapted for use in sociology and has, in my opinion, implications for use in education. We could view our decision-making teams as interconnected entities and recognize that all of the members contribute to and maintain the whole decision in a dynamic rather than a rigid state. Along with the concept of *autopoiesis* is the tenet from physical and biological sciences that "nothing is itself without everything else" (Swimme & Berry, 1992). Each condition has multiple sides, and all of the sides are powerful in their own right. If one sense is less powerful, the remaining entities work together to strengthen perception. In a situation where an individual has limited hearing, vision can strengthen the person's capacity for perception of distant stimuli. Is this multisensory view apparent in all educational settings for deaf and hard of hearing learners? Ethically speaking, it should be a major component in decision making.

Ethics

A general definition of situation ethics was presented in the introductory chapter to this book. For the purpose of this chapter, I further define *"situation ethics" as behavioral standards that guide the process of making decisions in a variety of situations aligned with legal, religious, medical, or cultural norms.* In decision making, those who solely follow the medical model (deficit theory) keep culture at a distance. An individual or a group is described according to what is lacking. The group is effectively relegated to a lower position. In the case of a deaf baby, parents who interact only with medical professionals and not a balanced team of persons knowledgeable about deafness run the risk of thinking that their child is defective or "less than" the child should be. On the other hand, an over-arching focus on culture might alienate those who are not a part of the culture (e.g., Deaf culture) and cause discord.

Strict adherence to the special education law is fraught with difficulty as well. In a broad interpretation of the law, the unique qualities and needs of an individual deaf child are frequently overlooked, especially in the area of communication. An ethical approach to decision making recognizes the pitfalls in a limited view of the case at hand. A broad, in-depth understanding of diverse factors is necessary so that decisions can be based on credible evidence. The term *evidence* does not equate with *anecdotes.* To present valid evidence requires the ability to see behavior clearly and report findings objectively. After all, life experiences are personal and subjective. Each person brings opinions based on life experiences to interactions with others. It takes time and an open-minded approach to sort this out and reach consensus. The alternative is to engage in what David Brooks of the *Wall Street Journal* has called a "squabble culture," which does not lead to a dignified outcome in any circumstance (Brooks, 2010).

Programs that prepare teachers, administrators, and other significant personnel bear a great responsibility to ensure that ethical decision making undergirds all individual educational plan (IEP) outcomes. Persons in leadership roles should be prepared, at their level of involvement, to identify the dimensions of a situation and approach decision making with sensitivity and consideration of the impact that their determinations will make on deaf individuals and their immediate and future circumstances. For example, how effective is it to provide a cochlear implant for a deaf Mexican baby from an impoverished family who will return to their village with no possibility of therapeutic and monetary support? Is it right to withhold a cochlear implant from a deaf child who is exhibiting a strong inclination toward speechreading and speech and whose family is committed to follow-up therapy? Should an individual family service plan (IFSP) team deny access to signed language for a deaf child whose hearing peers are learning signs in a preschool Baby Signs program in order to enhance their prelinguistic communication abilities? Is it fair to risk marginalization and recommend a placement in a school setting where a child is the only deaf child enrolled? What support systems do we have for individuals who experience a change in their hearing during their school years? Little guidance is available to help decision makers in these and other highly controversial and emotionally charged situations. As alluded to earlier, change in belief does not happen in a vacuum. It takes time and incredible effort. We can look to history for proof of that. For example, almost 100 years elapsed between the Emancipation Proclamation in 1863 and the Supreme Court's decision to desegregate public schools in 1954 (*Brown vs. Board of Education*). Change is the result of many eyes focused on a new vision, viewing an issue from a variety of perspectives, personal experiences, and positions and weighing success and failure objectively. It is at the point of personal awareness that something does or does not make sense. Shared personal experiences can create a sense of interconnectedness and shared vocabulary if those who disagree come together around issues of mutual concern and seek to understand a variety of perspectives. It is time to reevaluate our professional "truths" from a new perspective, to differentiate among stereotypes, myths, and reality, and to recognize what we have gained from research and experience that is useful to the contemporary education of deaf children. An ethical approach to educational decision making carries with it responsibility for the present and implications for the future. Much is at stake.

Situations

At the beginning of this chapter, you met PJ. We can learn so much from stories of children like him. The more we consider the unique perspective that a deaf child brings to a situation, the greater the chance that we will make the best decisions for that child. When we get to know a child and his or her familiar environment well, surprises are in order. According to Bateson (2000), "Wherever lives overlap and flow together, there are depths of unknowing. Parents and children, partners, siblings, and friends repeatedly surprise us, revealing the need to learn where we are most at home.

We even surprise ourselves in our own becoming, moving through the cycles of our lives. There is strangeness hidden in the familiar" (p. 3).

There are many examples of situations in which a decision cannot be made quickly or easily and where depths of unknowing remain to be examined. In the next section, two stories are presented from real life. I invite you to imagine that you are part of an IEP team that will consider the future of the deaf children featured in their own unique stories. What would you do to ensure the very best options for Jamie and Tony?

SITUATION I

Jamie scampered off the school bus, eager to tell her mother the news. "MOM MOM," she signed, "SUSIE HAS IMPLANT. ME NEXT!" The expression on her mother's face revealed her shock and anxiety. "WHO SAID YOU IMPLANT ? WHO?" "MUST! ME ONLY DEAF LEFT MY CLASS!" Jamie's reply was a clear indication of her ability to observe a situation and draw conclusions on her own. Her mother reached for Jamie's hand, and, as they walked up the steps into their comfortable home, she thought, " DESTROY OUR CULTURE . . . WHY?"

Meanwhile, in the audiologist's office, we overhear the following phone conversation between Jamie's audiologist and the otologist who is known for cochlear implant surgery: "Yes, my testing indicates that Jamie is a good candidate for a cochlear implant. I will recommend that at her next IEP meeting. The problem, of course, is her parents. They are both deaf, you know, and are stubbornly opposed to implants. We'll have to deal with their resistance."

Jamie's teacher, Casey, has another point of view. Casey grew up in the Deaf community, although she is a hearing woman. She learned sign language as a young child and uses it fluently. She understands the position of Jamie's mother and values and respects Deaf culture. She considers Jamie to be bicultural with an opportunity to move between the hearing and Deaf cultures successfully. Casey wonders to what extent Jamie's quality of life would be enhanced with digital hearing aids, a cochlear implant, or some other technology that might allow her to use her residual hearing effectively. What can an IEP team do in order to make the best decision for Jamie?

SITUATION II

Tony was a geography buff. As a student in the fourth grade at a state residential school for deaf students, he spent as much time as possible studying maps and world globes on his own. He could find the capital of each state of the United States in seconds. He was fascinated by maps of other countries and spent time in the school library, looking at pictures in *National Geographic* magazine and matching them to the appropriate location on the globe. Reading was not his strength, and neither was math. His preferred mode of communication was ASL.

One afternoon Tony decided to study the map of the state where he lived. He found the city where his school was located, his hometown, and the town where his grandparents lived. On the map they looked very close together. In fact, his hometown was just a couple of inches from school . . . how far could that be? Why did it take so long to get there on the school bus? There must be a shortcut, and he decided to find it. He hopped on a bicycle and headed down Main Street for the freeway.

The highway patrol found Tony pedaling frantically along the emergency lane against traffic. They hauled him and his bike into the station, where hours later it was determined that he was deaf and a student at the local residential school. When he was returned to the school, he was restricted to the dorm, his parents were summoned, and, as punishment, all of his maps, globes, and magazines were taken away. Tony was branded as a runaway. What does this situation tell us about Tony and his educational environment?

A Flexible Framework for Ethical Decision Making

Situation ethics, that is, an ethical system based on regard for the individual in a specific situation, is the foundation of this framework. The notion of situation ethics is modified in light of specific social situations appropriate for deaf learners. Two fundamental premises of situation ethics are, first, that the morality of an act is a function of the state of the system at the time it is performed and, second, that the ultimate goal is care, concern, and high expectations. Questions posed in this framework attempt to discern the level of care, concern, and high expectations present in situational decisions about learners who are deaf. Deafness is viewed as a cultural category with medical considerations rather than a medical condition with cultural ramifications.

The framework that follows is suggested as a means of organizing the decision-making process so that ethically based decisions can be made when controversy, snap judgment, budgetary limitations, and other roadblocks interfere with the goal of reaching common ground for the *good* of the individual. Obviously, a framework of this nature will be effective only with the commitment of the administration, along with the members of the decision-making team, all of whom are working together with a large portion of common sense. If the prevailing attitude is that no two deaf students are alike, then it follows that all IEP decisions will lead to truly *individual* educational programs.

1. Identify the ethical dimensions of a decision to be made.

    a. Are the members of the decision-making team diverse and experienced?

    b. Could the decision damage someone or a group? Who is involved?

    c. Is there more than one possible positive outcome?

    d. Are legal, religious, medical, or cultural standards confounding the discussion?

2. Gather data.

    a. Examine the facts on all sides of the question.

    b. What else do we need to know?

    c. Who has the most important stake in the outcome?

    d. Have all of the relevant persons been consulted?

    e. Are there factors apart from human dignity that influence or interfere with the decision?

       i. Budget: Is there a question of limited funds?

       ii. Bias: Are all personal biases identified?

       iii. Misunderstanding and/or lack of information: Have all points of view been heard and respected?

       iv. Time: Has enough time been allocated to reach a fair and appropriate decision?

    f. What role do the children and their desires play in the process?

3. Determine options.

    a. Identify all options.

    b. Recognize that the options may involve competing alternatives.

    c. Determine which options respect the rights of those involved.

    d. Determine which option provides the most positive opportunities for those involved.

    e. Reach consensus.

4. Make ethical decisions.

    a. Make decisions by negotiation and agreement.

    b. The parties involved may "agree to disagree" and reconvene at a later date to evaluate the situation from the vantage of the stakeholder.

    c. Put decisions into practice.

    d. Review all decisions regularly and revise as needed.

In sum, an ethical framework for decision making will reflect the following:

- sound, unbiased evidence
- personal preferences based on accurate information rather than emotion intellectual honesty (i.e., knowing one's limits as an "expert" and teaming with informed others)
- respectful, open dialogue (e.g., start with positive comments and lead into concerns)

One of the most daunting challenges for teachers of children who are deaf is the mandate to discover the unique individual strengths and needs of their students and to design comprehensive IEPs that capitalize on the strengths and meet the needs of each child effectively. A deaf child's basic needs (development of clear communication, independence, and self-esteem) manifest themselves outside of the classroom and must be addressed as part of an effective classroom program. Teacher preparation programs traditionally concentrate on isolated, classroom strategies that occur within the confines of a classroom. Effective teachers and other professionals must look beyond the classroom to assess and understand the strengths and needs of learners who are deaf. For example, there is logic behind the 8:1 student-teacher ratio in many classrooms for deaf and hard of hearing students; however, the typical teacher may function in a traditional manner and follow the regimen of general education, albeit with fewer students. This defeats the purpose of the smaller, more individually focused classroom structure and may, in large part, lead to negative attitudes among the general education staff. A common complaint among general education teachers in public school settings is that classes of deaf and hard of hearing children are small, usually 8 to 10 students or fewer. General education teachers see a teacher of deaf children presenting a parallel curriculum in a signed language to a small group, often with interpreters, teacher's aides, and others to help and wonder why general education classes serve 25 students or more without support personnel. Diversified small-group, one-on-one, communication-based teaching methodology is not readily apparent in classrooms of children who are deaf or hard of hearing.

We have made some progress in recent decades with regard to the education of deaf students. However, a number of probing questions remain to be addressed by those who are given the responsibility of ensuring fair and appropriate educational opportunities for children who are deaf. What does it mean to be a visual learner? How can educators and others think through the eyes of a visual learner? How do visual-spatial thinking and learning affect all aspects of a deaf learner's educational situation? How can educational programs be reformed to meet the unique social and educational situation of the deaf individual? What are the ethical considerations in educational reform? Robert Panara, the renowned Deaf professor and poet wrote poignantly, "You have to be deaf to understand." Yet, I wonder if there are bridges to understanding that can and should be built among the various communities, hearing and deaf, that are involved in the task of educating deaf children effectively? Can professionals, parents, and others mobilize to work toward effective, ethical educational reform? Can we all truly understand the challenge? The answers to these questions now will shape the futures of deaf students in decades to come.

References

Agar, M. (1996). *Language shock.* New York: Harper Collins.

Anderson, C, (July 20, 2010). Press release. International Congress on Education of the Deaf. Vancouver, British Columbia.

Arnheim, R. (1969). *Visual thinking,* 35th anniversary ed. Berkeley: University of California Press.

Bateson, M. C. (2000). *Full circles, overlapping lives: Culture and generation in transition.* New York: Random House.

Bonet, J. (1620). *Reduccion de las letras y arte para ensenar a hablar a los mudos.* Madrid: Francisco Abarca de Angulo.

Brooks, D. (July 25, 2010). *Meet the Press,* NBC-TV.

California Department of Education. (2007). Retrieved from http:www.cde.ca.gov/eo/in/se/agdeaf.asp.

Christensen, K. (1988). I see what you mean: Nonverbal communication strategies of young deaf children. *American Annals of the Deaf, 131,* 285–287.

———, & Regan, J. (1995 rev.). Nonverbal and verbal communication acts. Retrieved from http:www.christensenconsults.com.

Cummins, J. (1984). *Bilingualism and special education: Issues in assessment and pedagogy.* San Diego: College Hill.

Furth, H., & Youniss, J. (1971). Formal operations and language: A comparison of deaf and hearing adolescents. *International Journal of Psychology, 6,* 49–54.

Gardner, H. (1983). *Frames of mind.* New York: Basic Books.

Genesee, F. (1987). *Learning through two languages: Studies of immersion and bilingual education.* Cambridge, MA: Newbury.

Johnson, R. (1989). *Unlocking the curriculum: Principles for achieving access in deaf education.* Working paper 89-3. Washington, DC: Gallaudet Research Institute.

Krashen, S. (1991). *Bilingual education: A focus on current research.* Washington, DC: National Clearinghouse for Bilingual Education.

Ladd, P. (2003). *Understanding deaf culture: In search of deafhood.* Buffalo, NY: Multilingual Matters.

Ladson-Billings, G. (1995). But that's just good teaching: The case for culturally relevant pedagogy. *Theory into Practice, 34,* 159–165.

Lambert, W., & Tucker, R. (1972). *Bilingual education of children: The St. Lambert experiment.* Rowley, MA: Newbury.

Lang, H., & Meath-Lang, B. (1995). *Deaf persons in the arts and sciences.* Westport, CT: Greenwood.

MacSweeney, M., Capek, C., Campbell, R., & Wolf, B. (2008). The signing brain: The neurobiology of sign language. *Trends in Cognitive Sciences, 12,* 432–440.

Mayberry, R. (2007). When timing is everything: Age of first language acquisition effects on second language learning. *Applied Psycholinguistics, 28,* 537–549.

Mitchell, R., & Karchmer, M. (2006). Demographics of deaf education: More students in more places. *American Annals of the Deaf, 151,* 95–104.

Moores, D. (2001). *Educating the deaf: Psychology, principles, and practice.* Boston: Houghton Mifflin.

Quigley, S., & King, C. (1981–1984). *Reading milestones.* Beaverton, OR: Dormac.

Siegel, L. (2008). *The human right to language: Communication access for deaf children.* Washington, DC: Gallaudet University Press.

Swimme, B., & Berry, T. (1992). *The universe story: From the primordial flaring forth to the ecozoic era.* New York: Harper Collins.

Taussig, H. (2008). Disparate presence. In C. Hedrick (Ed.), *When faith meets reason: Religion scholars reflect on their spiritual journeys.* pp. 149–160. Santa Rosa, CA: Polebridge.

5

Educating Students Who Become Hard of Hearing or Deaf in School: Insights from Disability Studies

WENDY S. HARBOUR

I begin this chapter by sharing my personal and professional experiences with audiological changes that happen postlingually. I do this for two reasons: to situate myself as author of this chapter and to reveal some of my own biases and hermeneutical positions from the start. In this chapter I encourage readers to look at their own personal biases and those of the field; I cannot write with integrity unless I am also willing to do the same. Furthermore, my background is not in the field of ethics. Most of the questions and suppositions I pose have roots in the field of education—in my work with people who became hard of hearing or deaf[1] while they were in school.

This chapter has four parts: a summary of the influences on my writing, a discussion of the difficulty in identifying students with changes in their hearing, an overview of how academic literature describes students' experiences in school after their hearing changes, and reflections on the application of ethical principles in deaf education to students who become hard of hearing or deaf in school. I conclude by discussing limitations on current ethical frameworks in deaf education and suggest that disability studies may offer new ground for the field.

My Personal and Professional Background

As a child, with the exception of studying American Sign Language (ASL) fingerspelling at camp one summer, I had no exposure to ASL or deaf people. Throughout my childhood, my parents noticed I was a daydreamer, not remembering directions when they had just been explained to me and off in my own little world even in the midst of conversation or chaos. A routine hearing screening at school detected a mild-to-moderate hearing loss, which my doctor disregarded as an error because I was getting good grades in math and English (apparently believing that good grades in those subjects were more reliable than hearing tests). When I was in eighth grade, further failed hearing tests at school and thorough testing by audiologists, however, confirmed that I needed hearing aids. During high school my hearing levels changed several more times, necessitating more powerful hearing aids each time and eventually an FM system just before I entered college. The etiology of my progressive hearing loss is unknown.

It is difficult to describe how devastating these changes were, coinciding with all of the usual angst, upheaval, and drama of high school. By my senior year, after a great deal of agonizing, I decided to give up my dreams of a career in music and to take advantage of a small liberal arts college curriculum. I hoped the small campus, which prided itself on personal attention, would give me flexibility as I tried out increasingly powerful hearing aids and newly purchased gadgets like flashing alarm clocks and an FM system. I planned to try out a number of academic fields until I found something that suited me. For a while, I felt like any other college student and didn't worry much about my hearing or my future. During my third year of college, however, my hearing changed again, and this time I was unable to understand my friends, follow discussion in classes, use my FM system, or talk on the phone. My grief reappeared, and I dreaded a life as a deaf person.

An undergraduate course called "The Psychology of Handicapping Conditions" took my class on a field trip to the Indiana School for the Deaf, where the National Theatre of the Deaf performed the "Odyssey." The title of the show proved prescient on a personal level. I had resisted learning sign language, which seemed like elaborate miming. Convinced that deafness and sign language would mean never driving, having children, going to college, or living a happy life, I was shocked to see Deaf people at the Indiana School for the Deaf driving with their children, arriving after their professional jobs, and smiling and joking with each other. I was stunned to see someone in the first row of the auditorium signing with someone in an upper balcony—I had difficulty understanding someone right in front of me! After that, I started my own odyssey, eventually learning sign language, working with sign language interpreters, and becoming active in Deaf culture. This also led to my interest in on-campus groups for students with disabilities, and I eventually became an activist in disability communities as well. I continued my education, switching my focus to study disability and deafness in education. I now speak and speechread and am also fluent in ASL; I work with sign language interpreters on a regular basis and occasionally use CART (Communication Access Realtime Translation). On a daily basis, I negotiate hearing, hard of hearing, late-deaf, and Deaf labels, as well as deaf politics, academics, identities, and communities.

Professionally, I have worked in both K–12 and higher education settings and have often met students who became hard of hearing or deaf while they were in school. I often had difficulty separating my personal experiences and opinions from the students' individual situations. I also occasionally struggled with students whose choices or paths differed considerably from mine (e.g., students who resisted learning sign language, those who relied on cochlear implants or cued speech, students with a profound hatred of themselves as hard of hearing or deaf people). During the early years of my career, as a self-proclaimed activist, I frequently divided deaf and hard of hearing people into three categories: proud of themselves, not proud and buying into internalized self-oppression, and not yet proud but getting there. Pride in myself, claiming my rights under the law, and understanding deafness and disability were hard-won battles in my own life; it was difficult to avoid projecting my own goals onto others.

Now, after nearly twenty years in the field and a great deal of life experience, I am more willing to embrace paradoxes, complications, and incongruities in myself, others, and the fields of deaf education, special education, and inclusive education. Even my own goals have evolved into a journey of individual steps along the way instead of endpoints. However, I still wonder what has happened to some of the students I have met through the years. Did that young boy ever get the cochlear implant he wanted so desperately? Did that teenager ever break up with the boyfriend who told her hearing aids were ugly? Did those parents ever learn sign language as their daughter became deaf and visually impaired? Did that teacher ever follow up with the troublemaking daydreamer with a possible hearing loss?

I also question my own decisions with students. To what degree did a particular decision reflect my beliefs in what is best for deaf people as a whole? To what extent did I acknowledge ways that a student's situation might be influenced by that person's values and culture, socioeconomic status, ethnicity, or recent immigration to the United States? Am I truly open to other ways of being, worldviews, and outcomes, and if not, how do I acknowledge my biases and mental blocks? With these questions in mind, in this chapter I explore how best to educate students with postlingual hearing changes during their K–12 schooling.

Students Who Become Hard of Hearing or Deaf in School

One of my own concerns in writing this chapter involved the title itself: How should I describe the group of students under discussion? When students become hard of hearing or deaf in school, a variety of terms can be used to describe the experience. Students may simply be "hard of hearing" or "deaf." They may have a "progressive hearing loss" if their hearing level is expected to change in the future. "Postlingual" or "prelingual" are useful definitions, but they focus on language and fail to capture many important details about audiological or sociocultural aspects of being hearing, deaf, or something inbetween. "Hearing impaired" has fallen out of favor with many people in the Deaf community because it focuses on hearing loss as a problem, with hearing as the "norm" and nonhearing as "impaired" (see, e.g., Brueggemann, 1999; Lane, 2000), although the term is still common among professionals in all fields. "Late deafened" or "late deaf" usually refers to adults over age 18 who became deaf as adults; the term does not apply to young people or those with mild changes in their hearing. Even "acquired hearing loss" is inadequate because it places emphasis on medical (and negative) aspects of changes in hearing levels as "loss." Indeed, some Deaf studies scholars question whether these students are losing their hearing or gaining their deafness.

For the purposes of this chapter, however, "acquired hearing loss" or "a change in hearing levels" appear to be the most comprehensive terms since they are applicable to students with mild hearing changes and to those with profound deafness. These terms work for those with one-time changes in hearing, progressive changes, and unilateral or bilateral changes (i.e., changes in one or both ears). They also apply to those who choose to use their residual hearing with speech, those who learn ASL, and those who choose a myriad of other communication options, including cochlear implants. Students described as having "hearing losses" or "changes in hearing" may include those who were hard of hearing or deaf at birth, as well as those who had a change in hearing at any point after that. In this chapter, I alternate between "acquired hearing loss," "changes in hearing," and "becoming hard of hearing or deaf" partly for stylistic purposes and also because no single term perfectly captures the complexities of this group.

Other terms I use include "hard of hearing," "deaf," and "Deaf," following conventions currently used in deaf education and Deaf studies (see discussion in, e.g., Brueggemann, 1999; Padden and Humphries, 2005). Students who are hard of hearing may have mild to severe hearing losses, rely on their hearing for communication, and do not identify with members of the broader deaf community. The deaf community (lowercase *d*) includes culturally Deaf people who use ASL and also interpreters, late-deafened adults, and hearing children whose parents are culturally Deaf signers. Students who become deaf (lowercase *d*) have mild to profound changes in their hearing but do not use ASL and may not identify as members of a larger deaf community. Culturally Deaf students (written with a capital *D*) identify themselves as part of a broader Deaf culture with its own language of ASL, cultural norms, arts, history, and community. Thus, changes in hearing can be described not only in audiological and medical terms but also in terms of identity and communication preferences (for further discussion see, e.g., Brueggemann, 1999; Lane, 2000; Moore, 2001; Trychin, 2002).

According to the National Health Survey, hearing loss is the second most prevalent public health condition in the United States, ranking second only behind rheumatism and arthritis (Trychin, 2002). Likewise, the Census Bureau has estimated that 21 to 28 million Americans have some type of hearing loss (Moore, 2001). Although the frequency and severity of hearing loss increases with age (Code, Müller, Hogan, & Herrmann, 1999), more than 1 million children under age 18 have a hearing loss (Mathos & Broussard, 2005). These figures suggest that statistically, every classroom in the United States is likely to have at least one child with a hearing loss of some kind (Richburg & Goldberg, 2005).

Changes in hearing may be abrupt or progressive, from very minimal losses (defined by audiologists as losses of less than 25 decibels) to profound hearing changes that result in complete deafness with no residual hearing (Richburg & Goldberg, 2005). These changes may or may not be detected immediately even though routine hearing screenings occur in most schools. Symptoms and signs of hearing loss can be easy to miss or seem like other conditions. These symptoms may include everything from frequently pulling on ears to inattention, behavior issues, or poor academic performance (especially in reading and math). Signs of a hearing loss may be mistaken for frequent colds and upper respiratory illnesses, fatigue, speech delays or difficulties, or a lack of social skills (Kaderavek & Pakulski, 2002; Richburg & Goldberg, 2005). Identification may be complicated if students also have learning disabilities or other disabilities. In a study by English and Church (1999) of 406 children with hearing losses, 13 percent had learning disabilities, and 9 percent had other disabilities, including visual impairments and attention deficit disorders (ADD or ADHD). For 15 percent of the children in the study, problematic behaviors were also a concern for family members or school staff.

Students may acquire a hearing loss in a variety of ways, including genetics, viruses, injuries, infections, and noise (Barlow, Turner, Hammond, & Gailey, 2007; Kaderavek & Pakulski, 2002). Concomitant symptoms may include vertigo or dizziness, tumors, and tinnitus (severe ringing or noise in the ear) (Trychin, 2002; Barlow et al., 2007). Even chemotherapies and other medical treatments may cause changes in hearing (Goren, 2009). Research, however, has suggested that up to 60 percent of children under 18 will experience hearing changes for unknown reasons (English & Church, 1999), and 95 percent of hard of hearing and deaf children will have hearing parents who do not sign (Eleweke, Gilbert, Bays, & Austin, 2008)—two factors that are significant for those who work with these students and their families.

Educational Experiences of Students with Changes in Hearing Levels

While it is difficult (and perhaps unethical) to make generalizations about such a diverse group, research and commentary suggest that students with postlingual changes in their hearing do have some similar experiences in school. They experience a period of adjustment to hearing loss, which can be brief or prolonged or recurring if a hearing loss is progressive (Barlow et al., 2007; Trychin, 2002). Students and their families have to deal with emotional, social, and educational consequences of changes in their hearing (Barlow et al., 2007). For some, recognition of a hearing loss may occur gradually. Tidwell (2004), a professor, described his experience of becoming hard of hearing as one of slow realization, beginning with fatigue, increased stress, and a feeling of being worn down. He initially blamed his students for not communicating well until he realized that they were communicating but he was not hearing them. In one study, adults in the United Kingdom described the sudden onset of deafness as being in a "twilight zone between worlds . . . [which] had robbed them of their identity"; not being hearing and not being part of the signing deaf community left them "between worlds" (Barlow et al., 2007, p. 442).

From an educational perspective, these highly individualized experiences of hearing loss require highly individualized approaches. Students' responses will vary a great deal, depending on their cognitive, social, and emotional functioning. Academic demands may also contribute to students' responses. Goren (2009) recalls a familiar axiom of education: First-grade students learn to read, fourth-grade students read to learn, middle-school students learn to organize, and high-school students learn to work independently so that they can master tasks on their own in college. Thus, an acquired hearing loss in first grade may affect literacy development, and a hearing loss in high school may affect skills in time management, studying, and public speaking (see Goren, 2009).

Also of consideration for educators is the fact that family members and parents may experience changes in their child's hearing as a significant personal loss. They may be concerned not only about how the student is functioning at school but also about how the student is doing in family settings and the larger community. Will the child be safe? Have friends? Be independent? A change in their child's hearing may even mean a loss of intimacy as communication becomes more difficult or requires new ways of thinking, speaking, or signing (Trychin, 2002). These changes have typically been viewed as problematic because they typically require intervention or adjustments by professionals. However, Eleweke et al. (2008) note that these responses are in fact normal and healthy and are indicative of a changing worldview, including what is normal for a child and family, how students must learn, and the foundations of good communication. Communication becomes key as "hearing losses" often have "as much to do with a loss of voice as they do with a loss of hearing" (Boswell, 2001, p. 47).

The literature on acquired hearing loss focuses largely on interventions and services for children and their parents. Recommendations include the following (compiled from Archbold, Sach, O'Neill, Lutman, & Gregory, 2008; Barlow et al., 2007; English & Church, 1999; Goren, 2009; Kaderavek & Pakulski, 2002; Trychin, 2002):

- changes in instruction, including increased use of technology and facing students while speaking
- technological access, including closed captioning, FM loops in classroom, and accessible fire and smoke alarms

- improved signage in halls and classrooms
- adjustments in the classroom to reduce reverberation or give preferred placement to the student who is deaf or hard of hearing
- amplification to utilize residual hearing, including hearing aids and cochlear implants
- speech and language services to assist with speech development, speechreading, strategies for various settings in schools, and utilization of assistive technology, hearing aids, or cochlear implants
- information and training about hearing loss for staff, teachers, students, and family members
- other services, including mental health care, interpreting services, and reading and math support.

Students may also utilize strategies that are less deliberate and conscious, such as acting out, resisting or defying professionals and family members, dominating conversations, or refusing to participate in extracurricular activities (Tidwell, 2004). These, too, are normal responses to the many linguistic, cognitive, social, and acoustic demands on students who have experienced a change in their hearing (Archbold et al., 2008). Students may also perceive subtle or overt oppression in school or in their families in reaction to changes in hearing or to the ways in which hearing loss interacts with other aspects of their identity, for example—being a young, black, and deaf boy, a female hard of hearing adolescent, or a gay and deaf teenager (Boswell, 2001; Tidwell, 2004). Literally and metaphorically, they may struggle with hearing *and* being heard (Tidwell, 2004).

Research suggests that students with hearing loss are at risk academically (in terms of both grades and literacy) (Eleweke et al., 2008; English & Church, 1999; Kaderavek & Pakulski, 2002), in terms of potential substance abuse (Titus, Schiller, & Guthmann, 2008), for psychological well-being (Goren, 2009), and for lower rates of postsecondary education and competitive employment (Moore, 2001). Of course, research in this vein is often difficult to critique since studies may combine students and adults, focus on hard of hearing and deaf children, or combine prelingually and postlingually deaf children. In addition, much of the research in deaf education has focused on medical (i.e., pathological) aspects of hearing, changes in hearing, communication, sign language, and deafness—a significant bias (Benedict & Sass-Lehrer, 2007; Lane, 2000; Marschark, Rhoten, & Fabich, 2007).

Deaf Education and Ethical Decision Making for Students with Acquired Hearing Loss

Ethics is essentially a search for principles or theories to guide behaviors and determine right from wrong on the basis of society's values and beliefs about morality (Beattie, 2002; Marschark et al., 2007). A first step is to identify the ultimate goal of such actions by asking broad questions like "What is the measure of a good life?" (Beckner, 2004). To this end I submit that a goal of deaf education is to provide a good education to all students who are hard of hearing or deaf. Of course, a "good" education may be defined differently by individuals in a variety of times and places and according to diverse experiences and perspectives. This dilemma was addressed in chapter 1 of this book.

To again root my writing in my own biases, it is important to acknowledge that I am not a scholar of ethics, although I have studied ethics and philosophy. I also admit to being a constructivist and postmodernist when it comes to ethics inasmuch as I see ethical decisions as being contingent on who is making them, as well as when and how the decisions are made. When making my own ethical decisions, I draw on whatever resources, vocabularies, moralities, or opinions are available to me at that moment—what is often called *ethical bricolage* (Beckner, 2004; Nash, 2002). Many interdisciplinary teams in education (e.g., a K–12 special education team formed to create an Individualized Education Plan [IEP] or a group of postsecondary disability services providers consulting on a student situation) are also doing ethical bricolage in that they draw upon the multidisciplinary backgrounds, codes of ethics, norms, and skills at their disposal. While discussion of various ethical approaches is beyond the scope of this chapter, those who wish to learn more about such models may want to read Howe and Miramontes (1992), Nash (2002), or Stewart and Ritter (2008) for further information about ethics in education as a whole.

Professionals in deaf education usually have very little training in ethics and ethical concepts such as nonmaleficence, beneficence, justice, free and informed consent, privacy and confidentiality, respect for persons, and exploitation (Beattie, 2002). Furthermore, teachers in deaf education may be well versed in educational or instructional options but are likely to be less familiar with research about what works with specific groups of students, including those with changes in hearing levels (Stewart, 2008).

The literature on students with acquired hearing loss tends to respond to this gap in teacher preparation by offering concrete solutions. Advice includes not telling parents and students what to do but instead explaining all of the options (Harvey, 2001). Professionals are told to work in teams to reduce bias and empower students and families (Eleweke et al., 2008). Teachers are told to investigate empirical research about best practices (Marschark et al., 2007). Parents of hard of hearing and deaf children should be referred to other parents in similar situations for information and support (Eleweke et al., 2008). All of this information must be provided in an unbiased manner (Eleweke et al., 2008) that avoids a biomedical orientation, which is dominating deaf education today (Beattie, 2002; Marschark et al., 2007). At the same time, the literature acknowledges that moving past biases may be difficult work inasmuch as it involves challenging ethical decisions (Harvey, 2001; Marschark et al., 2007). Such hard-and-fast advice and rules may be helpful for concrete thinkers looking for external guidance on how to make decisions, but they do not necessarily lead to reflective awareness that can guide educators who must make ethical decisions in the moment (Beckner, 2004; Nash, 2002).

Furthermore, many teachers in deaf education learn that ethical decision making is a choice between dichotomies that affect students' social and cultural lives, instruction, communication, educational placement, and support services (Beattie, 2002; Harvey, 2001; Marschark et al., 2007; Stewart, 2008). In addition, educational professionals may be taught (implicitly or explicitly) that ethical decisions should be based on collectivistic ethics about what is good for deaf and hard of hearing persons as a group rather than what is good for individuals in unique situations (Enerstvedt, 1999). Stewart (2008, pp. 180–181) created a list of statements to show that many deaf educators frame their positions as moral or ethical choices at one end (or the other) of a dichotomy. Here are some examples:

- "If you sign to deaf children, they will not learn to speak well."
- "This is a hearing world; therefore, every deaf child must learn to speak."
- "Deaf children will eventually become members of the Deaf community; therefore, teach them to sign."
- "Don't give deaf children hearing aids because you are trying to make them hearing, which is something they will never be."
- "Giving a child a cochlear implant is denying their deafness."
- "Don't send a deaf child to a mainstream school because he will grow up isolated and develop poor social skills."
- "Deaf children who go to a school for the deaf learn to live in a Deaf ghetto and never learn how to interact in a hearing world."

Based on my own personal and professional experiences, I would add that professionals in deaf education also see postlingually hard of hearing and deaf children in terms of dichotomies. The following are some examples of statements that demonstrate this kind of thinking:

- "Children who become postlingually deaf are deaf and must learn to sign."
- "Children who become postlingually deaf should not learn to sign because they will never learn to use their residual hearing and be able to maintain their speech."
- "Children with an acquired hearing loss must get cochlear implants because they will never be a part of the Deaf world."
- "If children become deaf while they are in school, they must stay in a mainstream setting because Deaf people will never accept them."
- "If students become deaf or hard of hearing after they begin attending school, they will never accept their hearing loss; it will always be a source of grief."

These extreme viewpoints, which use terms like "always" and "never," and polarizing opinions all combine professional opinions with moral ones. Unlike Stewart (2008), however, I see these statements not only in terms of the either/or thinking about what to do with deaf and hard of hearing children but also in terms of the dichotomy of deaf/hearing. My examples also (purposely) used "D/deaf" and "hearing" as frames of reference, with nothing in between. Students with acquired hearing loss, therefore, seem to be the "in-between" subjects of our field, and ethics for this population has possible ramifications for the field of deaf education as a whole.

Originally, I had hoped this chapter would be a literature review of articles and books related to acquired hearing loss and ethical considerations for educators. However, one of the central difficulties was finding anything in the literature where "deaf," "deaf and hard of hearing," and "hearing" were not the central descriptors for research participants. When reading research articles, I usually found it impossible to learn whether any of the research participants had postlingual changes in their hearing. In academic commentary, even articles about excluded deaf populations or oppression often further excluded people who do not neatly fit into the categories of Deaf, deaf, or hearing. For example, in a 2007 article, Benedict and Sass-Lehrer advocated D/deaf-hearing partnerships to address imbalances in power since hearing people influence most of the field of deaf education. Yet there was no mention of people who identified with neither deaf nor hearing groups or of people moving between the two categories. Marschark et al. (2007) and Hintermair and Albertini (2005) have written articles about ethics in deaf education, and both argue against the use of "either/or" thinking in the field of deaf education even while using the dichotomy of either deaf/hearing or deaf and hard of hearing/hearing. Research on late deafness focuses primarily on adults (see, e.g., Moore, 2001) and thus is rarely applicable to K–12 deaf education (note that even the term *deaf education* excludes those with changes in hearing levels and hard of hearing students).

Hintermair and Albertini (2005), like many ethicists, return to the central idea of students, parents, and educators working at an individual level when dealing with ethical decisions for students who are deaf, hard of hearing, hearing, or moving between these groups: "[P]arents and professionals alike must know what they [students] want and how they want to live" in order to "influence decisions that affect their lives and the conditions under which they live" (p. 189). This "individualizing ethic" (pp. 246–247) also emphasizes the importance of dialectical thinking, where complexities, contradictions, and paradoxes are embraced, and "either/or" thinking is rejected. Enerstvedt agrees, using cochlear implants as an example: "It is not the cochlear implant that threatens the Deaf. It is the either/or mode of thinking . . . that threaten[s] sign language, Deaf culture, the school for the Deaf, deaf instruction, and deaf children's future" (1999, p. 249).

"Both/and" thinking is an ethical and moral approach that eschews objectivistic and traditional limitations in the field of deaf education. Purporting that one approach is better than another is, in itself, a matter of ethical debate. One advantage of "both/and" individualistic thinking is that it honors more traditional, concrete "either/or" thinking. When educators approach decision making from a social constructivist perspective, they provide the deaf child with opportunities to learn the social and cultural meanings of deafness, while at the same time honoring the child's (and family members') internal constructions and understandings of the experience of hearing loss, language, and communication. More concrete "either/or" thinking can be easily incorporated as part of an overarching paradigm but not as a limiting factor. A child who is provided with "both/and" options will see an expanded social network and understand the cultural dynamics therein; in other words, the child will see options, both concrete and constructed. This perspective is consistent with the research findings of educational theorists such as Piaget, Vygotsky, and Kegan.

Another advantage of using "both/and" individualistic thinking is that it deliberately addresses all of the confusion and contradictions in professional, medical, and educational information (Eleweke et al., 2008). Marschark et al. (2007) acknowledge that some parents may long to be told what to do or to have complicated decisions overly simplified; these authors' response is, "Well, raising and educating a deaf child is complicated" (p. 59). I would add that raising a child with acquired hearing loss may be equally complicated or *repeatedly* complicated as hearing levels and academic levels continue to change.

Yet another advantage to the "both/and" approach is that it takes unique circumstances into account. Just as an individualizing ethic does not sacrifice individual needs for the good of deaf education as a whole, so it also does not assume that all children fit a certain stereotype. Thus, bias or oppression is reduced for children who are deaf or hard of hearing with other disabilities, who may constitute up to 41 percent of the population of deaf and hard of hearing students (McCracken, 2008). An individualistic ethic may also prove useful when educators are dealing with behavioral issues or students from families dealing with divorce, chronic illness, criminal behavior, or other difficult home situations (English & Church, 1999). Finally, this ethical approach may raise the general awareness of cultural factors that relate not only to students who are deaf but also to students of color or immigrants (see, e.g., Steinberg, Bain, Li, Montoya, & Ruperto, 2002; Partington & Galloway, 2005). Rarely are teachers prepared to work with these groups of students or to present parents with all of the available options when making decisions about educational placement, instructional practices, and other services (English & Church, 1999; McCracken, 2008; Mauk & Mauk, 1992; O'Connell & Casale, 2004).

With a raised awareness of the issues and the stakes, as well as of the ways deaf education has failed to address ethical considerations for students with acquired hearing loss, we next consider how to move forward.

Critiques and Moving Forward: Intersections of Deaf Studies and Disability Studies

The individualizing ethic is not without critics. For example, dialectical thinking and individualizing ethics can seem to lack a strong moral foundation. As discussed earlier, its focus on subjectivity, context, and decisions-in-the-moment may be difficult for someone who prefers objectivity, neutrality, or, in contrast, axiomatic approaches that incorporate religious or specific values (e.g., caring, justice, individualism) as guiding principals (Beckner, 2004).

Another critique is that an individualizing ethic does little to recognize the way "deaf," "hearing impaired," "hard of hearing," "hearing loss," and other terms are socially constructed. As an adult, Boswell (2001), for instance, identifies herself as being "hearing impaired" or having a "hearing disability" while also recognizing that these categories are "arbitrary and constructed" (pp. 50–51). She believes that without recognizing how society constructs these categories, professionals and teachers cannot move toward social justice in the field of education. Likewise, Stratton's (2007) anthropological research with people identified as "hard of hearing" in Sweden suggests that when a hearing loss is identified, people are redefined as "hard of hearing." This group is then expected to learn ways they should *be* "successful" hard of hearing people who use hearing aids, cooperate with professionals, and accept the loss as a limitation. If schools are places to create future members of society, then in what ways are schools creating deaf and hard of hearing people for membership in society? And what do students learn when their experiences of changing hearing levels cannot even be categorized or easily defined?

While many deaf people identify as members of Deaf culture and resist being identified as "disabled" or having "disabilities" (Brueggemann, 1999; Lane, 2000; Padden & Humphries, 2005), people with acquired hearing loss are somewhat different. As discussed previously in this chapter, the first reaction to a change in hearing is typically a feeling of loss, grief, and even a loss of identity on the part of the student and the students' family and friends. An acquired disability seems like a disability in the traditional, medical, and pathological sense—a physical condition that is inherently negative. At the same time, hearing loss and disability are both social constructions. Activists who are hard of hearing, deaf, and Deaf have shown that hearing loss does not need to be a negative condition and can even be a rallying point for community, identity, and pride. Activists in disability studies have shown that disability can be viewed the same way. Because people with changes in their hearing may experience the hearing loss as a disability, a complement to the individualizing deaf education ethic may be a disability studies approach.

Disability studies is a multidisciplinary field that examines the ways disability has traditionally been viewed as pathology and seeks new ways of viewing disability that are less oppressive, neutral, or even celebratory (see., e.g., Linton, 1998). Disability studies has typically not been associated with deaf studies or deaf education, but that is changing (Padden, 2005). For example, in recent years, hard of hearing, deaf, late-deaf, and Deaf people (as well as those identifying at other points in the spectrum) have made presentations at disability studies conferences. Many scholars are also making connections between deaf studies and disability (e.g., H-Dirksen L. Bauman, Brenda Brueggemann, Lennard J. Davis, Christopher Krentz, and Carol A. Padden).

In discussing ethics and students with acquired hearing loss, connections between deaf education and disability studies can be beneficial at both theoretical and pragmatic levels. Theoretically, disability studies offers an opportunity to look at the similarities and differences in the ways that acquired hearing loss, deafness, and disability are constructed. Disability studies can also demonstrate how oppression and the biases of hearing and deaf people may affect ethical decision making in education. The field also goes a step beyond the dialectical and individualizing ethics recommended in deaf education by forcing both fields to look at broad moral stances (e.g., deaf and hearing dualisms) that have been ignored thus far.

At the pragmatic level, disability studies acknowledges that students with acquired hearing loss may be experiencing their condition as a disability. At the same time, it also refutes medical and pathological views of disability and acquired hearing loss and suggests that even if students do not identify as members of Deaf culture, they can still have affiliations with communities, cultures, and identities of their choice, as well as pride in who they are. This may offer hope to students, parents, and educators—hope where very little currently exists. Incorporating a disability studies framework with deaf education ethics also follows the recommendations of ethicists in deaf education (Marschark et al., 2007) to consider ethics in research by expanding theoretical frameworks beyond traditional pedagogy, politics, bioethics, and the history of deaf education, making them more inclusive.

Conclusion and Recommendations

Because the goal of this chapter was not to provide a "how-to" series of steps but instead to provide prompts for ethical reflection, I began by sharing my personal experiences and biases as an adult who started becoming deaf as a child, now negotiating daily between hearing, late-deaf, hard of hearing, and culturally Deaf labels, communities, and identities. I reviewed the difficulty in defining individual experiences of changing hearing and deafness, as well as the field's bias toward focusing on negative experiences and outcomes for children with "acquired hearing loss" in school and after graduation. Ethicists in deaf education have suggested that a dialectical and individualizing ethic can provide a framework for working with students, as well as their parents and families. While essentially agreeing that this ethic can be useful with students who have changes in their hearing, I also note that it does not necessarily address the social construction of categories within deafness and hearing loss; nor does it examine the dualism of deaf/hearing, which pervades much of the literature in deaf education. To address these gaps, I suggest that deaf studies and deaf education turn to disability studies.

In conclusion, I have hope and cautious enthusiasm about what the future may bring for my own ethical decision making and that of my colleagues and future students. As the field of deaf education and ethics deals with increasingly diverse students and families struggling to choose from expanding options in education and communication, I close with a quote from Marschark et al. (2007): "Hopefully, we will have the flexibility, foresight and hindsight to recognize that the ethical perspectives of yesterday may not explain the right and wrong of tomorrow" (p. 49).

Note

1. The publication manual for the American Psychological Association (APA) recommends reducing bias in writing by using person-first language (e.g., saying "students who are deaf" instead of "the deaf" or "deaf students") (American Psychological Association, 2001). This chapter alternates between person-first language and other forms in order to enhance flow and readability. Disability-first language has also been utilized by those who identify as culturally Deaf or as having disability as part of their identity (see further discussion in, e.g., Brueggemann, 1999; Lane, 2000; Linton, 1998; Padden & Humphries, 2005); alternating between forms may reflect these sensibilities where appropriate in the text.

References

American Psychological Association. (2001). *Publication manual of the American Psychological Association* (5th ed.). Washington, DC: American Psychological Association.

Archbold, S., Sach, T., O'Neill, C., Lutman, M., & Gregory, S. (2008). Outcomes from cochlear implantation for child and family: Parental perspectives. *Deafness and Education International, 10*(3), 120–142.

Barlow, J. H., Turner, A. P., Hammond, C. L., & Gailey, L. (2007). Living with late deafness: Insight from between worlds. *International Journal of Audiology, 46*, 442–448.

Beattie, R. G. (2002, April 29). Ethics in deaf education. *Audiology Online*. Retrieved May 20, 2009, from http://www.audiologyonline.com/articles/article_detail.asp?article_id=343

Beckner, W. (2004). *Ethics for educational leaders*. Boston: Pearson Education.

Benedict, B. S., & Sass-Lehrer, M. (2007). Deaf and hearing partnerships: Ethical and communication considerations. *American Annals of the Deaf, 152*(3), 275–282.

Boswell, M. (2001). Sexism, ageism, and "disability": (Re)constructing agency through (re) writing personal narrative. *Women and Language, 24*(2), 47–51.

Brueggemann, B. J. (1999). *Lend me your ear: Rhetorical constructions of deafness*. Washington, DC: Gallaudet University Press.

Code, C., Müller, D. J., Hogan, A., & Herrmann, M. (1999). Perceptions of psychosocial adjustment to acquired communication disorders: Applications of the Code-Müller protocols. *International Journal of Language and Communication Disorders, 34*(2), 193–207.

Eleweke, C. J., Gilbert, S., Bays, D., & Austin, E. (2008). Information about support services for families of young children with hearing loss: A review of some useful outcomes and challenges. *Deafness and Education International, 10*(4), 190–212.

Enerstvedt, R. T. (1999). New medical technology: To what does it lead? *American Annals of the Deaf, 144*(3), 242–249.

English, K., & Church, G. (1999, January). Unilateral hearing loss in children: An update for the 1990s. *Language, Speech, and Hearing Services in Schools, 30*, 26–31.

Goren, S. S. (2009). Implications of childhood cancer survivors in the classroom and the school. *Health Education, 109*(1), 25–48.

Harvey, M. A. (2001). "Does God have a cochlear implant?" *Journal of Deaf Studies and Deaf Education, 6*(1), 70–81.

Hintermair, M., & Albertini, J. A. (2005). Ethics, deafness, and new medical technologies. *Journal of Deaf Studies and Deaf Education, 10*(2), 184–192.

Howe, K. R., & Miramontes, O. B. (1992). *The ethics of special education*. New York: Teachers College Press.

Kaderavek, J. N., & Pakulski, L. A. (2002). Minimal hearing loss is not minimal. *Teaching Exceptional Children, 34*(6), 14–18.

Lane, H. (2000). *The mask of benevolence: Disabling the deaf community*. San Diego: DawnSignPress.

Linton, S. (1998). *Claiming disability: Knowledge and identity*. New York: New York University Press.

Marschark, M., Rhoten, C., & Fabich, M. (2007). On ethics and deafness: Research, pedagogy, and politics. *Deafness and Education International, 9*(1), 45–61.

Mathos, K. K., & Broussard, E. R. (2005). Outlining the concerns of children who have hearing loss and their families. *Journal of the American Academy of Child and Adolescent Psychiatry, 44*(1), 96–100.

Mauk, G. W., & Mauk, P. P. (1992). Somewhere, out there: Preschool children with hearing impairment and learning disabilities. *Topics in Early Childhood Special Education, 12*(2), 174–195.

McCracken, W. (2008). Educational placement. In R. G. Beattie (Ed.), *Ethics in deaf education: The first six years* (pp. 119–142). Bingley, UK: Emerald Group.

Moore, C. L. (2001). Disparities in job placement outcomes among deaf, late-deafened, and hard-of-hearing consumers. *Rehabilitation Counseling Bulletin, 44*(3), 144–150.

Nash, R. J. (2002). *"Real world" ethics: Frameworks for educators and human service professionals*. New York: Teachers College Press.

O'Connell, J., & Casale, K. (2004). Attention deficits and hearing loss: Meeting the challenge. *Volta Review, 104*(4), 257–271.

Padden, C. A. (2005). Talking culture: Deaf people and disability studies. *PMLA, 120*(2), 508–513.

Padden, C., & Humphries, T. (2005). *Inside deaf culture.* Cambridge, MA: Harvard University Press.

Partington, G., & Galloway, A. (2005). Effective practices in teaching indigenous students with conductive hearing loss. *Childhood Education, 82*(2), 101–106.

Richburg, C. M., & Goldberg, L. R. (2005). Teachers' perceptions about minimal hearing loss: A role for educational audiologists. *Communication Disorders Quarterly, 27*(1), 4–19.

Steinberg, A., Bain, L., Li, Y., Montoya, L., & Ruperto, V. (2002). *A look at the decisions Hispanic families make after the diagnosis of deafness (Un studio sobre las decisions que toman las familias hispanas despues de un diagnóstico de sordera).* Washington, DC: Laurent Clerc National Deaf Education Center, Gallaudet University. (ERIC Document Reproduction Service No. ED472086)

Stewart, D. A. (2008). Ethics and the preparation of teachers of the deaf. In R. G. Beattie (Ed.), *Ethics in deaf education: The first six years* (pp. 167–184). Bingley, UK: Emerald Group.

Stewart, E., & Ritter, K. (2008). Ethics of assessment. In R. G. Beattie (Ed.), *Ethics in deaf education: The first six years* (pp. 67–87). Bingley, UK: Emerald Group.

Stratton, A. (2007). Hard of hearing in Sweden: Educating about and for pathology. *Teachers College Record, 109*(7), 1775–1776.

Tidwell, R. (2004). The "invisible" faculty member: The university professor with a hearing disability. *Higher Education, 47,* 197–210.

Titus, J. C., Schiller, J. A., & Guthmann, D. (2008). Characteristics of youths with hearing loss admitted to substance abuse treatment. *Journal of Deaf Studies and Deaf Education, 13*(3), 336–350.

Trychin, S. (Ed.). (2002). *Guidelines for providing mental health services to people who are hard of hearing.* San Diego: Rehabilitation Research and Training Center, California School of Professional Psychology–San Diego. (ERIC Document Reproduction Service No. ED466082)

6

Ethical Assessment Approaches

A View of What We Have and What We Need

MELISSA HERZIG AND KARY KRUMDICK

We shape our tools and then our tools shape us.

—Marshall McLuhan

Scenario

The Deaf and hard of hearing students are seated at their desks in the classroom with pencils poised. Their eyes are fixed on an interpreter in the middle of the room who is listening attentively to the audiotape of the exam questions. The interpreter proceeds to sign the audionarrative. The questions and the multiple-choice answers are all recorded with a monotone voice. This procedure was a modification added to the individual education plan (IEP) for of the students to increase their chance of understanding the test items clearly. The students nervously bubble in the answers on their scantrons. They are taking the "dreaded" California High School Exit Exam (CHSEE), and passing this test is one of the conditions they must satisfy to receive a high school diploma. Parents, teachers, administrators, and the State Department of Education place a significant weight on this exam. Students are expected to pass; if they don't, no diploma! This is a scenario that is repeated statewide. Teachers know that the progress made by Deaf and hard of hearing students during their years in school is not reflected in the CHSEE. The CHSEE and other state-mandated exams were normed and designed to measure the progress of English-speaking students with normal hearing. This places the Deaf and hard of hearing students at a significant disadvantage.

Introduction

In this day and age, the ever-increasing reliance on students' performance on standardized tests holds educators and schools accountable for demonstrating the yearly progress of their students based on the accountability requirements of the No Child Left Behind (NCLB) Act of 2001. The reliability of such tests is of concern to educators of Deaf and hard of hearing high school students. How accurately do these tests in English reflect the knowledge of the Deaf students, who are English-language learners? Do they help educators identify areas that are in need of improvement? Are they authentic exams that give us a holistic view of the Deaf and hard of hearing students' progress?

As educators of Deaf and hard of hearing students, we face challenges in finding appropriate performance assessments that accurately reflect our students' abilities and help us measure their performance. We have found that other teachers we work with are facing the same challenges with their hearing Latino students, who are English-language learners. Our school is situated a few miles from the Mexican border. There are approximately 2,900 students at this high school, and 80% of them, hearing and deaf combined, are Hispanic.

In this chapter we draw from our experiences as graduate students in Deaf education, as educators of Deaf students, and as Deaf individuals ourselves to address questions about critical issues surrounding the validity and the ethical administration of assessments for Deaf and hard of hearing students, particularly in view of the fact that these tests have been standardized on a hearing population. Several issues need to be considered before using standardized achievement tests that were designed for a primarily hearing, English-speaking population to make high-stakes decisions for Deaf and hard of hearing students. We also propose alternative assessment tools.

Validity Issues

It is imperative that, if high-stakes decisions are based on the results of standardized assessments, equitable and fair procedures for Deaf and hard of hearing students must be developed. Lam (1995) described a fair assessment as one in which students are given equitable opportunities to demonstrate what they know. This means that students must be assessed using methods and procedures that appropriately reflect their prior knowledge, cultural experiences, and cognitive style.

One of the disturbing trends in education today is the use of standardized multiple-choice tests written in the English language as the primary factor in high-stakes decision making for Deaf and hard of hearing students. Decisions such as eligibility for high school graduation or a certificate of some kind or for successful completion of a course are based on these test results. According to the American Educational Research Association (AERA) and the National Council on Measurement in Education (NCME) (1985), there are issues of validity for students (including Deaf students) who are not proficient in the language of the test. Students' performance may be affected by their understanding of test questions presented in a language other than their native or natural language.

The National Research Council (1997) indicates the following additional concerns about validity: (1) a *norming* bias (the samples include few Deaf students or English-language learners); (2) a *content* bias (the test items reflect the dominant language, knowledge, and behavior); and (3) a *linguistic and cultural* bias that affects students' formal test performance (timed testing, difficulty with English vocabulary, and difficulty in knowing what the students know about other languages and the cultures in which those languages are spoken). The assessments may, in actuality, test the students' knowledge of English instead of their true knowledge of content. Although the language of the test may be translated by an interpreter and additional accommodations given to Deaf students and English-language learners, the test results will still not represent a holistic picture of the academic capability of these students.

The primary purpose of assessments should be to inform teachers, students, and parents of students' needs and strengths relative to their performance. However, the results of standardized tests have been widely misused. Maria del Rosario Basterra (1998), director of National Origin/Language Minority Programs at the Mid-Atlantic Equity Center in Chevy Chase, MD, has reported that large-scale tests are rarely used to improve instruction. In fact, the results of the tests are not valid because they do not properly reflect students' knowledge. Instead, most standardized tests are used to determine students' eligibility for promotion or graduation. They serve a gatekeeper rather than an academic function.

The problems that are associated with large-scale assessments can influence the validity of the results (Eccarius, 1997). In addition to the appropriateness of the assessments for students who are Deaf or English-language learners, the level of expertise of the diagnosticians can also be problematic. Diagnosticians, especially those in mainstream settings, may not have credentials for or experience in dealing with the deaf population. Having a degree in psychology, deaf education, or speech-language pathology does not mean that the examiner has acquired the skills necessary to evaluate Deaf children. In some cases, the diagnosticians do not have the skills to even communicate with Deaf children. The communication modalities and skill levels that students use may vary with signed systems, ASL, or cued speech. In cases we have seen at our mainstream school, an interpreter is needed for communication between students and the diagnosticians. As we see elsewhere in this book, the interpreters' qualifications are in question as well (see the chapter by Peterson & Monikowski). Interpreters' skills vary anywhere from novice to expert. In some instances, one is left to wonder what exactly is being tested. Is it the student's knowledge in a content area, or is it the student's ability to make sense of a vague communication environment?

Standardized tests are not uniformly provided by the school district. In some states, such as Massachusetts, Deaf and hard of hearing students are excluded from high-stakes testing. This calls into question just who is to be held accountable for the progress of Deaf and hard of hearing students in school. In California, the California Standards Test (CST), for which no norms have been established, is used with Deaf children in both alternative and standard forms. Some school districts choose not to test the Deaf and hard of hearing students using standardized tests but instead use the California Modified Assessment (for middle school students) or the Alternative Performance Assessment (for high school students). Typically, these instruments are used to test students who have cognitive or behavioral challenges. Although some states do include Deaf and hard of hearing students in large-scale assessments with accommodations such as interpreting the test items into ASL, this does not necessarily solve the problem of making the tests equitable for Deaf and hard of hearing students. In 2007, State Superintendent of Public Instruction Jack O'Connell (California Department of Education Address, 2007) reported that only 8% of California's Deaf students and 15% of the state's hard-of hearing students scored at the "proficient" or "advanced" level on the CST for English-language arts. In math, only 10% of the Deaf students and 18%

of the hard of hearing students scored at either of these levels. Both Deaf and hard of hearing students suffer in a standardized assessment environment when they perform at a level below their ability as judged by classroom teachers. A dilemma facing these teachers is how to provide assessment opportunities that meet state requirements and also allow Deaf and hard of hearing students to demonstrate their understanding of content to the very best of their abilities.

A more comprehensive system is needed that ensures that students are evaluated with appropriate, valid, performance-based assessments that are norm referenced using the Deaf and hard of hearing student population. It is important to give students different ways to demonstrate what they know (Gardner, 1983).

Benefits of Assessment

Not all assessments are inappropriate for Deaf students, we do see the benefits of unbiased assessment of Deaf students. If used in the right way, assessment results can inform parents, teachers, and students of the students' progress in reading, writing, and mathematics, for example. This may help teachers identify strengths, as well as areas in which the students need additional support. Students can benefit by knowing the areas in which they excel. Appropriate assessments can also provide documentation to support the development of goals during students' IEP meetings and beyond.

The benefits of assessments are limited by the skills of the evaluators who interpret the results, the interpreters who administer the test, and the individuals who design the tests. Since the Deaf and hard of hearing students' environmental experiences differ from those of hearing students, who have full auditory access to English from birth, the assessments may not accurately compare these disparate groups even though they may be at the same age and grade level. Even when a test is administered in ASL, the results may be biased according to the age at which children acquired ASL, whether their language models were fluent users of the language, and whether the interpreters and teachers can capture the nuances of young children's signed utterances.

Language Use for Deaf Students

According to Erting (1994), deaf children are born into an environment that takes hearing and speaking for granted. As a result, society, as it is today, often does not take deafness into consideration with regard to services being provided to others. Deaf people often have no other choice but to act according to a set of rules that does not take their cultural and linguistic backgrounds into consideration. The majority of deaf children are born to parents with normal hearing. A deaf child is brought into this world without auditory input, and it may be years before an accurate diagnosis of hearing loss is identified. During the early "critical period" of language acquisition, many deaf children are not provided with the tools that will enable them to make visual/linguistic connections. This disconnect continues until these children are brought into contact with an environment that takes their exceptionality into account. When deaf children begin school, however, they enter an educational system that has failed over the years to meet the needs of deaf learners (Erting, 1994). To continue to condone this failure is both misguided and unethical.

Because many Deaf students have limited proficiency in their primary and most accessible language (Cummins, 2006; Strong, 1988; Wilbur, 2000), language development is crucial. A solid first-language base is essential for the development and mastery of literacy. There is a need to focus on developing and validating effective instructional interventions, particularly in language, and appropriate assessment tools (Francis, 2003). Unfortunately, the high-stakes assessments we currently use do not inform us as to how to support students' bilingual development in ASL and English. It is our view that early development of competence in a natural, visual language, ASL, is a critical component in the education of Deaf children.

Language Acquisition and Learning

Prelingually deaf children do not have the same language acquisition experience as children with normal hearing. In the United States, approximately 90% of deaf children are born to hearing parents who do not use ASL or any form of visual-spatial communication (Mitchell & Karchmer, 2004). By the time hearing children are learning how to read, they have conversational competence in their first language. At this time, they can be exposed to a curriculum in which they can apply their understanding of idiomatic spoken language to develop literacy in English. Children's deafness is a barrier to their ability to acquire spoken English naturally since they are not able to process linguistic input through auditory means (Van Hattum, 1980). Unless visually salient language is introduced early, deaf children in hearing families grow up in an environment that deprives them of opportunities to practice and use language for effective communication (Naiman, 1982).

Furthermore, ASL is considered a natural or primary language for congenitally deaf children because its visual modality makes it eminently accessible to them. Also, ASL has a community of users, a long history, and a vibrant literature. Babies can learn ASL from birth and acquire it in almost the same stages and patterns as children acquiring spoken languages (Wilbur, 2000). In discussing biases prevalent in a monolingual educational setting, Cummins (1996) stated that "One of the misconceptions entails drawing inferences about children's ability to think logically on the basis of their familiarity with and command of Standard English" (p. 51). Disregard of a child's first or most natural language, as well as an emphasis on facility in standard English, presents a dilemma with regard to assessment. Children are at a disadvantage when asked, at a tender age, to code-switch to an unfamiliar or a less familiar language in order to meet assessment standards.

Because approximately 90% of deaf children come from hearing families, most of whose members do not use ASL either fluently or at all, the situation for deaf students' acquisition of English is unique. The natural, visual language of ASL does not align with the hearing family's language, but the second language, English, often does. Development is different from that of hearing students who are learning English as second language because the majority of these hearing students have already acquired their primary language at home before coming to school. Most deaf students come to school without a strong background in any language, and their only language models for ASL and/or English are at school. Their lack of ASL or English skills is not due to their inability to learn but to the fact that they are "language deprived" (Kuntze, 1998).

Correlations between ASL and English

The body of research on deaf students' ASL and English skills exhibits a number of common findings. Chamberlain and Mayberry (2008), Singleton, Suppala, Litchfield, and Schley (1998), Padden and Ramsey (1998), and Strong and Prinz (1997) all show that a greater mastery of ASL as a first language correlates with higher English proficiency in Deaf students. Wolkomir (1992) has reported that it is critical to learn a first language during the first few years of life, when the brain is most ready for that task. Chamberlain and Mayberry (2008) find that Deaf students' phonological awareness, in and of itself, does not influence reading skills. How does the development of ASL help with acquisition of English language skills? Krashen and Biber (1988) discuss the importance of background knowledge of a first language when acquiring a second language. When students gain knowledge about the world, as well as about subject matter, in their primary language, the same information, when presented in the second language, becomes comprehensible. Students then apply the knowledge they acquired in their first language (ASL) in order to understand what they are reading in English, their second language.

BICS and CALP

Cummins (1996) pointed to a misconception that occurs when "conversational skills are interpreted as a valid index of overall proficiency in the language" (p. 52). Basic interpersonal communication skills (BICS) are equivalent to playground language, which differs from academic language, which teachers use in the classroom. In academic settings, students need to develop cognitive and communication skills, such as evaluating and inferring, in all areas of the curriculum (Cummins, 1996). Those who already have some conversational skills in ASL may still have a hard time acquiring academic English skills because they do not have cognitive academic language proficiency (CALP) in ASL to support the transition to academic English.

Teaching advanced English language skills before students have sufficient experience in using ASL as an interpersonal, social language makes it difficult for the students to access and use academic English. Normally, BICS are quickly acquired in the first few years of life, and CALP develops during a child's years in school (Cummins, 1996). This is another problem for deaf students when learning to read and write. Wilbur (2000) describes "inadequate language skills, compounded by distorted amplified input due to the hearing loss" (p. 83), as barriers to academic success. Furthermore, in Wilbur's opinion, limited and/or distorted input is a major hindrance to the full development of English competence in deaf children. They receive language fragments rather than complete language input. Part of the problem is that ASL fluency is usually not regarded as an important foundation for learning English as a second language.

It is important for teachers to model language that is clear and comprehensible but goes beyond what learners themselves can produce (Cummins, 1996). This helps to promote students' academic language development through activities in which teachers model ASL skills that challenge students. From our observation, the problem is that teachers have few guidelines to help them identify and improve students' ASL skills. Therefore, there is a need for an ASL assessment scale to help ASL specialists and classroom teachers identify the skills the students have already acquired and the additional ones that need further development. An assessment of this nature will be valuable in determining IEP goals for communication in a bilingual ASL-English setting.

Bilingual Approach

Deaf individuals recognize themselves as a unique cultural group, bilingual by necessity in both ASL and English (Lane, Hoffmeister, & Bahan, 1996). Some educators, however, have expressed the view that ASL may hinder the development of English. When ASL is viewed as a problem and not a resource, ASL skills are usually not recognized as a valid tool for helping Deaf and hard of hearing students learn English. Development of fluent, articulate ASL is overlooked in the curriculum of English-only programs for visually oriented Deaf and hard of hearing learners (Nover, 2000). This viewpoint contradicts current research in bilingual education.

Although deaf students have the need to use two languages, ASL and English, one must to be cautious before teaching and assessing visually oriented Deaf and hard of hearing students who are using the strategies developed solely for English-language learners. These practices may not prove to be effective scaffolds unless carefully adapted for use in Deaf education programs. Deaf students face issues that are different from hearing students who are English-language learners, such as Spanish speakers. Spanish speakers are able to draw on the natural experiences attained from birth in using the native language of their families. Moreover, Spanish has both a spoken and a written form, whereas ASL does not have a written form. In addition, Deaf and hard of hearing children are often born into a family that does not use ASL as their first language; thus, most Deaf and hard of hearing children do not grow up in a rich communication environment where they can acquire language from native users. In this instance, Deaf and hard of hearing students do not have an opportunity to draw on natural experience through language. Issues of access to both natural-language and fluent-language models are critical to a discussion of ethical assessment.

In an educational setting, the use of two languages as the medium of instruction is known as *bilingual education* (Crawford, 1999). Many programs recognize ASL as a viable, accessible language for deaf learners because it can be seen completely. English, a less transparent language for Deaf learners, is necessary in order to achieve literacy in the written language. Therefore, a bilingual ASL-English program would be ideal for many deaf students; it would allow them to advance socially and academically to their fullest potential.

In the bilingual approach, deaf children are instructed in the use of both ASL and English (Livingston, 1997). In developmental bilingual programs, students are expected to become proficient in both ASL and English. This is a model in which deaf students may develop and maintain their native or first language (ASL) and become exposed through a curriculum to the eventual mastery of the target language (English) (Crawford, 1999). With this approach, ASL and English are treated equally. Students would, in the end, become proficient in both languages. Some programs include hearing children of ASL-using deaf parents as English-language models. The overarching goal of bilingual programs of this nature is meaning-centered instruction (Cummins, 1994).

In addition to the pedagogical aspects of bilingual education, the sociocultural aspect incorporates students' daily lives and language into the classroom. By developing English and ASL in tandem, deaf children would be able to value their well-being and look at their deafness as a cultural phenomenon instead of as something that needs to be "fixed." Cummins (2006) suggests that "developing a strong first language foundation in the early years is important not just for the child's cognitive growth but also as a passport to membership in a social community that affirms the child's intelligence and identity" (p. 6). In Cummins's perspective, the ability to identify oneself with Deaf culture and heritage exists, enabling deaf children to develop cognitively and identify themselves as a members of the Deaf community. This also enables the deaf child to absorb the cultures of families representing other ethnicities and cultures and thereby develop a positive self-identity. Encouraging parents to refrain from using a language other than English with their children at home seems counterintuitive in the light of recent research:

> Supported by empirical evidence, pupils obtain better academic results when their low-status L1 [primary language] is valorized and fully used than when L1 is neglected in the home. The school results and language proficiency in both languages improve also when their primary language is valorized and used in the school system. (Dube & Herbert, 1975, as cited in Hamers, 1998, p. 63)

Members of the hearing community often see deafness as a pathological condition and, by extension, undervalue American Sign Language as "less than" English. In contrast, Deaf people view themselves as having a unique community united by a common language, American Sign Language (Padden & Humphries, 1988). The acceptance of language and culture in a bilingual environment can contribute to an improved sense of self-esteem (Lane, 1992). Elevated levels of self-esteem have a positive effect on school achievement. "In order to function successfully, deaf children, like all children, have to develop a positive self-esteem" (Beattie, 2001). Confounding the process of measuring self-esteem, so critical to school success, is the problem of assessment:

> A critical limitation of these studies [of self-esteem] has been the difficulty the students experienced with the linguistic demands of the measures (developed for hearing students) and the inability of those administrating the measures to effectively communicate with the participants. (Van Gurp, 2001, p. 56)

Effective communication is key to effective assessment, effective education, and, apparently, the growth of self-esteem. All of these components are closely linked and mutually influential.

Current Findings

Krumdick's (2006) research on communication, language policies, and assessments in Deaf education resulted in significant findings. A high percentage (90%) of schools for deaf students contacted in the study recognized the students' need for communication accessibility. The extent of recognition of this need shows that schools and the states that fund them are well aware of the role that communication plays in the dismal academic achievement records of deaf and hard of hearing students. Several schools in the study indicated that they used a variety of ASL assessments. Most of these were conducted through individual interviews using checklists. Many have yet to be standardized. Most schools realized a need for deaf children to have access to salient communication; however, few schools provided a means of measuring and ensuring a consistent, comprehensible communication environment. Krumdick reported that, despite this awareness, standardized policies, documented expectations, or proficiency levels and unbiased assessment tools have yet to be designed.

Apparently, there is a national need for consistency in the evaluation of signed language proficiency for teachers, administrators, parents, students, and others in the communication environment. The majority of schools do not name a specific tool for measuring ASL proficiency. In spoken-language assessments, there are valid measures that are used nationwide, such as the Oral Proficiency Interview (OPI), whose standards are set by the Educational Testing Service (ETS) and the American Council on the Teaching of Foreign Languages (ACTFL). Additionally, there are speech-language professionals to assist students who fall short of English competence.

The existing literature on deaf students shows that they are clearly at risk of being categorized as language delayed, if not functionally illiterate, by the time they reach adulthood (Allen, 1986; Marschark, 1997; Traxler, 2000). Krumdick's (2006) review of literature details the educational and communicative modalities available to programs for Deaf and hard of hearing students and emphasizes the interrelationship between language and cognition. The history of language policies in deaf education documents the suppression of signed language and the failure of attempts to design systems that increase deaf students' facility in communicating in English. With respect to language and communication policies, the literature has an apparent lack of standardized definitions of communicative modalities. Also lacking are uniform systems for and expectations of sign language competence in employees at state-funded residential schools for the deaf in the United States (Krumdick, 2006). Again, is this practice ethical?

Authentic Assessment of Biliteracy Development

On the basis of research on the importance of ASL development and its link to literacy, language, and cognitive and cultural development, a clear need exists to assess Deaf children's biliteracy development. A plethora of assessments have been designed to provide information about students' literacy development, but they are standardized on a hearing population. How is ASL development assessed?

Standardized assessments have been used for many years to report the academic achievement, or lack of achievement, of Deaf students. The SAT-HI is probably the most popular instrument, perhaps because it remains one of few tools available that has been standardized on a deaf population. Although normed with Deaf students, the SAT-HI is not designed for Deaf children. A national report based on this test showed that deaf students graduate with an average reading level of third to fourth grade (Commission on Education of the Deaf, 1988). As suggested elsewhere in this book (Christensen), this interpretation of test scores may fall short of complete accuracy. Since the majority of deaf children score in the normal range on nonverbal assessments, low scores on literacy tests clearly show the need for better biliteracy curricula for Deaf children. The NCLB-mandated tests do little to inform teachers or to guide the teaching/learning process in general. Scores reported on standardized assessments often mask the academic progress of students because prior experiences and problem-solving situations are discounted. Data collection that can inform school accountability is difficult to carry out. In fact, "the constraints imposed on data collection are more exacting and, in the case of schools, more onerous. If we are to produce 'scientifically based research' in order to demonstrate 'what works' in deaf education, the burden of, and for, proof is great" (Mitchell & Karchmer, 2006, p. 102).

Authentic Assessment: The Learning Record

Since it is not our intent to simply point out the apparent weaknesses of so-called standardized assessment, we would like to offer some possible alternatives to what we consider an unsatisfactory situation. Authentic assessment, such as that provided by the Learning Record (LR) Portfolio Assessment System (Barr, Craig, Fissette, & Syverson, 1999), can be coupled with standardized assessment to provide in-depth portraits of students' biliteracy development. The LR has been touted as a powerful assessment process by the National Center for Fair and Open Testing (2007). With the evidence of students' growth, the LR provides information that teachers need in order to make helpful instructional plans and decisions. The LR correlates highly with SAT scores for hearing students in reading comprehension and vocabulary (Hallam, 2000). Thus, it is plausible that similar correlations between the LR and standardized assessment scores can be determined for deaf children (Allen & Herzig, 2005). The ASL Scale of Development (Herzig, 2002) has a positive correlation with the LR reading scales (Humphries & Allen, 2008).

The LR's underlying principles reflect the benefits of using authentic assessment by emphasizing the following: (1) thoughtfulness over rote learning, (2) performance over assumptions of deficit, (3) individual development meshed with grade-level expectations, and (4) the strengths of being bilingual and of understanding cultures beyond one's own (Barr et al., 1999, p. 2). Teachers who have used the LR to assess student learning and academic progress have found that it: (1) values students' experiences and knowledge, (2) encourages teachers to observe and document tasks in which students can apply new knowledge and strategies, and (3) determines what needs to be learned and the ways the students can learn best (Barr et al., 1999).

The LR has reading and writing scales that guided observations and data collection of student work in English, but it did not provide a scale to determine the level of deaf children's ASL development. The ASL Scale of Development (Herzig, 2002) was designed and field-tested with graduate students and cooperating teachers from the Educational Studies Program at the University of California–San Diego over a 2-year timespan (2002 to 2004). The ASL Scale of Development is a chart that depicts the progression of skills at five levels. It is used as a guide, not a checklist. It should not be used in an artificial setting (e.g., a traditional one-on-one testing situation). The scale provides teachers with a holistic view of language development in a natural setting. Teachers document growth over time with anecdotal observations across various learning and social contexts (e.g., lunchtime; classroom; recess; one-on-one with an adult, with a friend, in a circle, in front of the class; different subject areas). This scale of development includes aspects of ASL such as phonology, morphology, syntax, signing space, classifiers, motion/location verbs, topic/comment structure, conditional structure, conversational rules, fingerspelling, cultural behaviors, and the use of academic (CALP) and social (BICS) language. Students' achievement levels on the ASL Scale of Development was positively correlated with the LR reading scales for both years, corroborating previous research findings that linked fluency in ASL and reading achievement.

Documented ASL development, using the ASL Scale of Development, helped student teachers and cooperating teachers to provide specific examples of ASL skills and how they related to ASL and English literacy. The ASL scale allowed teachers to view the students' ASL skills in terms of strengths and areas to be further developed. It prompted teachers to focus on specific ASL skills, as well as other abilities that were improving and may have been overlooked in the past. The ASL scale facilitated parents' understanding of language development (specifically bilingualism) and helped to develop goals in the students' IEPs. By using the results of the ASL scale, the teachers became more aware of the importance of developing both languages within the classroom and how language, in general, is connected to literacy. During the two years of field testing, a positive correlation was found between the reading scale placement and the ASL development scales. This indicated that ASL fluency might provide access to English and serve as a foundation for advancing the literacy of Deaf and hard of hearing children (Humphries and Allen, 2007).

Through the study of the use of LR in the classrooms, Allen and Herzig (2005) conclude that using only one measure of assessment to determine deaf children's accomplishments does not provide teachers the information that is needed to inform their teaching practices or to assist them in fostering deaf children's biliteracy development. Teachers and preservice teachers need ongoing support and training in how to use authentic assessment tools and implement effective teaching practices that promote deaf children's academic achievements and eventually lead to an ethical model of classroom assessment.

Note: For more information on use of the ASL scales, contact the authors.

References

Akamatsu, C. T., & Armour, V. A. (1987). Developing written literacy in deaf children through analyzing sign language. *American Annals of the Deaf, 132*(1), 46–51.

Allen, B. M., & Herzig, M. (2005, July). Assessing deaf children's biliteracy development. *TESOL's Bilingual Education Interest Section, 7*(1). Retrieved June 23, 2010, from http://www.tesol.org/s_tesol/docs/4100/4033.html?nid=3077.

Allen, T. E. (1986). Patterns of academic achievement among hearing-impaired students: 1974–1983. In A. N. Schildroth and M. A. Karchmer (Eds.), *Deaf children in America* (pp. 161–206). San Diego: College Hill.

American Educational Research Association and National Council on Measurement in Education. (1985). *Standards of educational and psychological testing.* Washington, DC: American Psychological Association.

Barr, M. A., Craig, D. A., Fisette, D., & Syverson, M. A. (1999). *Assessing literacy with the learning record: A handbook for teachers, grades K–6.* Portsmouth, NH: Heinemann.

Beattie, R. (2001). *Ethics in deaf education: The first six years.* San Diego: Academic.

California Department of Education Address. (2007). *Closing the achievement gap for students who are deaf or hard of hearing.* Retrieved May 1, 2009, from http://www.cde.ca.gov/eo/in/se/agdeaf/asp.

Chamberlain, C., & Mayberry, R. (2008). American Sign Language syntactic and narrative comprehension in skilled and less skilled readers: Bilingual and bimodal evidence for the linguistic basis of reading. *Applied Psycholinguistics, 29,* 367–388.

Commission on Education of the Deaf. (1988). *Toward equality.* Washington, DC: U.S. Government Printing Office.

Crawford, J. (1999). *Bilingual education: History, politics, theory, and practice* (4th ed.). Los Angeles: Bilingual Educational Services.

Cummins, J. (1994). Knowledge, power, and identity in teaching English as a second language. In F. Genesee (Ed.), *Educating second language children: The whole child, the whole curriculum, the whole community* (pp. 33–58). New York: Cambridge University Press.

Cummins, J. (1996). *Negotiating identities: Education for empowerment in a diverse society.* Ontario: California Association for Bilingual Education.

Cummins, J. (2006). *The relationship between ASL proficiency and English academic development: A review of the research* [1]. Retrieved August 20, 2006, from http://www.mhb.jp/mhb_files/CumminsDeaf.rtf.

Del Rosario Basterra, M. (1998, Winter–1999, Spring). *Using standardized tests to make high-stake decisions on English-language learners: Dilemmas and critical issues.* Retrieved March 10, 2009, from http://www.maec.org/ereview1/html.

Dube, N. C., & Herbert, G. (1975). St. John Valley Bilingual Education Project. Report prepared for the U.S. Department of Health, Education, and Welfare, contract no. OEC-0-74-9331.

Eccarius, M. (1997, August). *Educating children who are deaf or hard of hearing: Assessment.* Retrieved September 27, 2005, from the ERIC Clearinghouse on Disabilities and Gifted Education, http://ericec.org/digests/e550.html.

Erting, C. (1994). *Deafness, communication, social identity: Ethnography in a preschool for deaf children.* Burtonsville, MD: Linstok.

Francis, N. (2003). Schooling and bilingualism in Latin America: Perspectives for bridging the language-literacy divide. In P. Ryan & R. Terborg (Eds.), *Language: Issues of inequality* (pp. 77–94). Mexico City: Universidad Nacional Autónoma de México.

Gallaudet Research Institute. (2005). *Stanford Achievement Test,* 10th ed., form A, norms booklet for deaf and hard-of-hearing students. Washington, DC: Gallaudet University.

Gardner, H. (1983). *Frames of mind: The theory of multiple intelligences.* New York: Basic Books.

Hallam, P. J. (2000). *Reliability and validity of teacher-based reading assessment: Application of "Quality Assurance for Teacher-based Assessment" (QATA) to California Learning Record moderations.* Unpublished doctoral dissertation, University of California, Berkeley.

Hamers, J. (1998). Cognitive and language development of bilingual children. In J. Parasnis (Ed.), *Cultural and language diversity and the deaf experience* (pp. 51–75). New York: Cambridge University Press.

Herzig, M. (2002). *Creating the narrative stories: The development of the students' ASL and English literacy skills.* Unpublished master's thesis, University of California, San Diego.

Humphries, T., & Allen, B. M. (2007). Reorganizing teacher preparation in deaf education. *Sign Language Studies, 8*(2), 160–180.

Krashen, S., & Biber, D. (1988). *On course: Bilingual education's success in California.* Sacramento: California Association for Bilingual Education.

Krumdick, K. D. (2006). *A survey of communication and language policies at state-funded residential schools for the deaf in the United States.* Unpublished master's thesis, San Diego State University.

Kuntze, M. (1998). Literacy and deaf children: The language question. *Topics in Language Disorders, 18*(4), 1–15.

Lam, T. C. M. (1995). *Fairness in performance assessment.* ERIC Digest. http://ericae.net/db/edo/ED391982.htm (ERIC Document Reproduction Service No. ED 391 982).

Lane, H. (1992). *Mask of benevolence: Disabling the Deaf community.* New York: Knopf.

Lane, H., Hoffmeister, R., and Bahan, B. (1996). *A journey into the Deaf-world.* San Diego: DawnSignPress.

Livingston, S. (1997). *Rethinking the education of the deaf students.* Portsmouth, NH: Heinemann.

Marschark, M. (1997). *Raising and educating a deaf child.* New York: Oxford University Press.

Mitchell, R., & Karchmer, M. (2004). When parents are deaf versus hard-of-hearing: Patterns of sign use and school placement of deaf and hard-of-hearing children. *Journal of Deaf Studies and Deaf Education, 9*(2), 133–152.

Mitchell, R., & Karchmer, M. (2006). Demographics of deaf education: More students in more places. *American Annals of the Deaf, 151,* 95–104.

Naiman, D. (1982). *Identification and instruction.* In D. Tweedie & E. G. Shroyer (Eds.), *The multihandicapped hearing impaired.* Springfield, IL: Thomas.

National Center for Fair and Open Testing. (2007). Retrieved May 1, 2009, from http://www.fairtest.org/learning-record.

National Research Council. (1997). *Improving schooling for language minority children,* ed. D. August and K. Hakuta. Board of Children, Youth, and Families. Washington, DC: National Academy Press.

Nover, S. (2000). History of language planning in deaf education in the 19th century. (Doctoral dissertation, University of Arizona). UMI No. 9972098.

Padden, C., & Humphries, T. (1988). *Deaf in America: Voices from a culture.* Cambridge, MA: Harvard University Press.

Padden, C., & Ramsey, C. (1998). Reading ability in signing deaf children. *Topics in Language Disorders, 18*(4), 30–46.

Singleton, J., Suppala, S., Litchfield, S., & Schley, S. (1998). From sign to word: Considering modality constraints in ASL/English bilingual education. *Topics in Language Disorders, 18*(4), 16–29.

Strong, M. (1988). A bilingual approach to the education of young deaf children: ASL and English. In M. Strong (Ed.), *Language learning and deafness* (pp. 113–129). New York: Cambridge University Press.

Strong, M., & Prinz, P. (1997, March 7–10). The relationship between ASL skill and English literacy. In J. Egleston-Dodd (Ed.), *Monograph of collected papers from the 23rd Annual Conference of the Association of College Educators of Deaf and Hard-of-Hearing Students.* Santa Fe, NM.

Traxler, C. (2000). *Stanford Achievement Test,* 9th edition: National norming and performance standards for deaf and hard-of-hearing students. *Journal of Deaf Studies and Deaf Education, 5,* 337–348.

Van Gurp, S. (2001). Self-concept of deaf secondary school students in different educational settings. *Journal of Deaf Studies and Deaf Education, 6,* 54–69.

Van Hattum, R. J. (1980). *Communication disorders: An introduction.* New York: Macmillan.

Wilbur, R. B. (2000). The use of ASL to support the development of English and literacy. *Journal of Deaf Studies and Deaf Education, 5*(1), 81–104.

Wolkomir, R. (1992). American Sign Language: It's not mouth stuff—it's brain stuff. *Smithsonian, 23,* 30–41.

7

Vision Quest

Ethical Leadership in the Education of People Who Are Deaf

JAMES J. DECARO AND PATRICIA A. MUDGETT-DECARO

Scenario

I had a dream. I came to a river and needed to cross a bridge to get to the other side . . . it was one of those arched bridges like you see in Chinese paintings. I arrived at the base of the bridge, and there stood my parents. They told me what I must do to cross, and I kept on going. On the next level of the bridge was the principal of my school for the deaf, and he told me what I must do and what I could not do . . . and I kept on going. At the next level of the bridge was my audiologist, who told me what I must do . . . and I still kept going. At the next level of the bridge was my teacher of the deaf, who also told me what I could not do and what I must do. Depressed, I turned around and ran back to where I started. I then gathered all my strength and walked back up to the bridge. When my parents started to tell me what to do, I threw them off the bridge. I did that in turn with each person on the bridge. I made it to the other side and became the author of my own life story . . . I got on with MY life!

(Paraphrase of a dream related by a successful deaf professional who has entered society and the workplace and is making contributions on a par with her peers who hear . . . a well-adjusted member of the communities of people who are deaf and those who are hearing.)

Introduction

We have spent more than 80 years between us working in the field of education . . . almost all of those years in the education of people who are deaf. In addition, Pat comes from a long line of educators who are deaf and taught at the Illinois School for the Deaf, California School for the Deaf, Texas School for the Deaf, and Gallaudet College (now Gallaudet University).

Throughout our careers and around family dinner tables in New York, California, Washington, D.C., Illinois, and Texas, we have participated in many discussions about ethical leadership as it relates to educating youngsters and young adults who are deaf.

In this chapter we relate what we have learned and the implications of that knowledge for education.

However, before we go any further, we proffer a vision of what we mean by "ethical leadership" as it pertains to those of us who have been entrusted with the education of people who are deaf:

> Ethical leadership is facilitating, as a collaborating author, the development of the life stories of those who are deaf so that they become the primary authors of their own life stories.

The story at the beginning of this chapter provides a context for our discussions about ethical leadership. Clearly as manifest in her dream, our friend's life story was being authored by many significant others who surrounded her. It was not until she was able to pass them by that she became the author of her own life.

Many of us (parents, teachers, administrators), acting with very good intentions, make decisions that lead us to author the life story of a youngster who is deaf without giving the child an opportunity to fully participate in developing that story. Doing this can often make daily existence easier for us and even for the student. However, in the long run, it delays the ability of the student to assume responsibility for his or her own life story. Parenthetically, it can be argued that we are never really able to fully author our own life story because of the environmental conditions that impinge upon life. However, people who are deaf should be as much an author of their lives as are their peers who hear.

Decisions and Leadership

All of the major players in the life of a deaf child or young adult help to make, or make, decisions about the formulation of the child's life story. These people include parents, doctors, audiologists, social workers, school administrators, teachers, committees concerned with disabilities (committees on special education), career/guidance counselors, and employers. All of these significant others, and many more, exercise some form of leadership/authority in deaf people's lives and contribute in direct or indirect ways to decisions about their life stories.

Some decisions must be made early in a deaf person's life, usually by others. Other decisions are made well into the deaf person's life, often by others or shaped by others. What sorts of decisions? Here are some examples:

1. decisions about hearing itself, that is, testing and diagnosis; forms of intervention; cochlear implants; hearing aids; and, in earlier times, treatments such as shock therapy
2. decisions about types and facilitation of language use; an oral/aural approach; American Sign Language; Signed English approaches, including SEE, cued speech, and bilingual approaches
3. decisions about school placement programs; various forms of mainstream placements from full inclusion to separate classes and separate schools for deaf students, including oral, bilingual, and signed language programs; decisions made at national or local levels have strong effects, such as the deinstitutionalization movement in the 1980s, which had a significant impact upon placement decisions in favor of mainstreaming

4. decisions about access to education and society; use of interpreters, computers, videophones, captions for news, films, and television, C-Print, video streaming, to mention a few
5. decisions about career goals and attainment (e.g., encouragement of deaf persons to pursue a certain career because "deaf people are visually strong" rather than for reasons of talent or passion)
6. decisions about friendships and even marriage; encouragement and programming for interaction with hearing and/or deaf playmates or acquaintances or encouragement and support for widely diverse interactions

Decisions are made every day that influence the life story of people who are deaf. Here is one example:

> On 9/11/2001, students and faculty all over my university campus were watching the nearest available television. Seeing the collapse of the Twin Towers but not knowing what it was about, I ran all over campus from one end to the other to find a television that had captions. I finally ran to the Office of Special Student Services, where I found one.
>
> (Paraphrase of a story related by a student studying in a mainstream setting)

The decision by others as to where on campus captioning should be provided, despite the knowledge that deaf students were all over campus, had a strongly negative effect upon this young woman. Access to information was thereby limited. Similarly, decisions about where to place interpreters or considerations of whether security preparations are accessible to deaf individuals are too often made by persons who are not directly affected—that is, hearing individuals who have not consulted with deaf individuals.

On the other hand, the status quo can strongly influence decisions made by deaf persons. Because something has never been done previously by an individual who is deaf, a person who is deaf may not consider attempting to do so. It is very difficult to find the energy to overcome the momentum of the status quo:

> I am a profoundly deaf man who went to the University of Illinois, with no support services, to obtain my master's degree. At the end of my program of study my advisor strongly urged me to pursue a PhD. I would have been the first or second profoundly deaf person with a PhD. However, I declined, saying, "What is the point? I will never be an administrator because I am deaf."
>
> (Paraphrase of a story related by an elderly, profoundly deaf man)

It would be some years before that glass ceiling began to crack.

Underlying decisions such as these are beliefs held by significant others that influence deaf persons' own beliefs and eventual ability to become the author of their own life . . . beliefs about the following:

1. the degree of responsibility that deaf persons should exercise; responsibility for their academic work rather than allowing excuses based upon deafness
2. the degree of control a deaf person should have; coauthored decisions about school placement and programs, language use, and the like, based upon individuals' desires and their perceived needs rather than upon the authority's belief that they know what is best

3. contributions to society that should be expected of a person who is deaf; maintaining high expectations in daily life, including encouraging contribution to society rather than allowing pity and low expectations to guide decisions and actions

4. respect for deaf people and their language and culture; demonstrating respect for deaf individuals' opinions and decisions by listening to and discussing their ideas, thereby also facilitating positive self-esteem and self-confidence, which are essential for growth and development; respecting the language choices made by individual deaf persons and respecting the significant creative, cultural contributions they make

5. the role of hearing people in the deaf person's life; demonstrating through action the hearing person's role as facilitator, coauthor, and consultant rather than decision maker.

In March 1988, deaf students at Gallaudet University, along with supporters from around the country, made the momentous decision to demand a voice in a critical decision that affected their lives: the selection of a new president of the university. They declared that deaf individuals needed to be recognized as able and ready to lead a university. This movement, Deaf President Now (DPN), challenged centuries-old beliefs about the abilities and rights of persons who are deaf.

Later that year at the National Technical Institute for the Deaf (NTID), a convocation titled Vision Quest was convened by Jim DeCaro on the occasion of the 20th anniversary of NTID. Jim was then dean of the college. The purpose of the convocation was to provide faculty and staff with an opportunity to focus upon teaching and learning and offer counsel to their colleagues of 2018. Reflecting upon the DPN events and the concomitant events at NTID, Jim said, "Some hearing people have claimed, throughout the centuries, to speak for deaf people. . . . Many deaf people feel that they have been treated, to a great extent, as children, who are not capable of speaking for themselves or of expressing their needs . . . the events [at Gallaudet and around the United States] were a manifest demonstration of the leadership skills and capabilities of people who are deaf" (DeCaro, 1988).

Barriers to decision making and positions of responsibility were being openly challenged. The community of people who are deaf was seeking the removal of "barriers to access."

Barriers to Access

Two general classes of barriers can act to limit deaf people's access to education, a career, society, and the workplace: attitudinal and environmental barriers (DeCaro & Egleston-Dodd, 1982). Attitudinal barriers are constructed both by people who are deaf and by significant others in their lives. More often they are based in assumptions about deafness that are part of the fabric of a society. For example, there may be no other barrier to a deaf person's embarking on a career or taking a job than the attitude of an employer or educator that "deaf people have never done that before" (attitudes are treated in more depth in the next section of this chapter). Environmental barriers, on the other hand, are the physical or structural impediments to attaining a goal (like landing a particular job). Examples of such barriers are telephones and audible alarms.

Barriers interact with an *impairment* to cause a *disability*—the inability to perform some function. For example, hearing loss (an impairment) can result in the inability to utilize a standard telephone (a disability). A disability can be overcome by an accommodation, that is, an intervention that results in the removal of barriers. For example, the utilization of new telecommunication technologies (e.g., relay services) removed barriers to telephony for people who are deaf. However, if an accommodation is not made and environmental or attitudinal barriers are not removed, a *disability or difference in ability* becomes a *handicap*.

The removal of barriers does not imply the lowering of expectations with regard to education or work. Rather, it means we make accommodations for individual differences so that persons who are deaf can compete on a level playing field with their peers who hear.

Significant others are well placed to partner with people who are deaf to develop accommodations and eliminate environmental and attitudinal barriers.

Attitudes of Significant Others

I had a moderate hearing loss as a child; however, at around the age of 14 or 15, I experienced a sharp drop to severe deafness. My grades, previously As and Bs, dropped to the B and C levels with no support services. It was assumed by my parents, teachers, and others that I was not "college material" as a result. I went to work in the five-and-dime store after graduation but was fired after a short time because I could not hear the boss yelling from the back of the store. Deciding after all to try college, I was told at the community college that I could not teach and was guided away from my goal of social work. At the age of 21 my hearing dropped from severe to profound. At a nearby university the head of the Deaf education program would not consider me as a candidate because I would not be able to teach young deaf children how to speak. I then spent 6 months interviewing for different types of hospital careers but was told in every instance that a "deaf person" could not do those jobs. Eventually, however, I encountered two individuals who saw my potential and encouraged me to attend university in the communication disorders program, and I was accepted. It was like a lifeline had been thrown to me, and I broke down in tears. I was so overwhelmed and grateful that someone wanted me and believed in me. I decided that I would, from that time on, make my own life decisions.

(Paraphrase of a story related by a successful deaf professional who pursued an exemplary career in counseling)

More than 30 years ago, it was noted that parents dominate the formulation of the concept of deafness constructed by a person who is deaf (Meadows & Nemon, 1976). Meadows and Nemon also indicated that teachers of those who are deaf become important in the formulation of such a definition because they "have early, intensive, and long-term contact with them" (p. 9). Significant others have a profound impact upon the formulation of deaf children's concept of what they can or cannot do and thus significantly affect the construction of aspirations regarding life goals.

Several research studies pertaining to parents' and teachers' expressed attitudes toward advising deaf youth to prepare for various careers have been conducted in various countries over a 20-year period of time (DeCaro, Evans, & Dowaliby, 1982;

DeCaro, Mudgett-DeCaro, & Dowaliby, 2001; Maruggi, 1983; Naidoo, 1989; Parasnis, DeCaro, & Raman, 1996; Hurwitz, Weisel, Parasnis, DeCaro, & Savir, 1997). Each of the countries is culturally quite diverse (respectively, England, Sweden, Italy, South Africa, United States, India, and Israel). Surprisingly, with the exception of India, the results obtained were remarkably consistent in terms of expressed advice for deaf and hearing people to train for various occupations despite differences in time and culture. Generally speaking, the expressed advice, based apparently upon considerations of communication and safety factors, to a *deaf* person was rather consistently more negative than that given to a *hearing* person across a range of occupations.

In cross-cultural analyses of data collected in England and Italy, it was found that parents and teachers did not differ within and between the two countries despite the generally accepted notion that the two cultures are quite different in nature. If a group of parents and teachers from these two countries were to sit together, one would not be able to distinguish between them in their expressed advice regarding training for various occupations. There was no difference between parents' and teachers' expressed advice in spite of the fact that teachers possessed qualifications that the parents did not. For occupations where safety and communication were important issues, deaf people were consistently advised to aim lower than were those who could hear. Deafness tended to diminish the differences between the two countries regarding advice to seek training for various occupations. This occurred even though the school in Italy was an "oral" school and the one in England was a "sign and speech" school.

Even in countries that have been recognized for their progressive disability laws and policies (the United States and Sweden), the expressed advice to hearing people is consistently more positive than for those who are deaf for occupations where communication is a consideration. In the United States, safety also emerged as a consideration; it did not in Sweden because Sweden has very strict safety regulations for worker protection that must be (and by and large are) followed.

Certain attitudes about communication and safety across cultures can mitigate the construction of deafness by a young person who is deaf and limit that construction unnecessarily. The attitudes are a part of the fabric of our society, whose members hold them without even realizing why. In effect, those of us who interact regularly with people who are deaf may be limiting the richness of their lives by imparting attitudes that serve as a barrier to their achievements and life accomplishments.

Approaches to Leadership

As we consider approaches to leadership, we use as a context our responsibility to join in partnership with people who are deaf as they take the lead to remove barriers to access.

In mulling over the stories mentioned earlier, we must address some questions within the context of our responsibility to work with people who are deaf to remove environmental and attitudinal barriers. What went wrong in the case of well-intentioned advice and decisions that took away authorship from deaf individuals? Conversely, what went right that in the end allowed deaf individuals and groups to take authorship of their lives? The following is a discussion of some of the approaches that come to mind in this regard.

First, perhaps we need to remind ourselves that *every person—deaf or hearing—is an individual.* The "typical deaf person" does not exist. Accordingly, there is no such thing as "one size fits all." The diversity among deaf persons includes the entire gamut of differences found in society in general and additionally includes differences in age of deafness onset, degree of deafness, educational history, communication history, and type and effectiveness of medical intervention. A number of principles can guide our thoughts about ethical leadership.

Chief among them is the issue of *high expectations* and a belief in the abilities of persons who are deaf. The absence of such belief underlies advice about careers; two examples are the lack of deaf administrators in earlier times and, more recently, the selection of a hearing president who knew little about deafness over well-qualified deaf candidates at Gallaudet University. This lack of belief in the capabilities of people who are deaf was manifest at the time the chair of the board was reported to have said, "Deaf people are not yet ready."

Pat Mudgett-DeCaro's parents, grandfather, great uncle, aunt, and uncle were all educators of deaf persons. She had ample opportunity to learn through observation that these deaf educators of people who were deaf never accepted or allowed deafness to be used as an excuse for poor performance or "bad" behavior:

> At Pat's mother's passing, there was a memorial service in Jacksonville, Illinois. Many former students came to tell stories about their memories of her. A story that was repeated over and over was how she was so tough and so strict. They didn't like being with her at the time because she always demanded the best of them. However, as adults they thanked her again and again for "saving our lives" by holding high expectations. Pat also remembers with some measure of glee how her mother would challenge every deaf person peddling ABC sign cards on the streets or in airports telling them to stop the self-pity because their "begging" was giving a bad name to deaf persons!

Equally significant is *respect for the knowledge and opinions* of individuals who are deaf. As is often the case, "it is amazing what people can learn if they shut up and listen." Respect involves listening first rather than telling or directing:

> I was called in by my audiologist at my school for the deaf because my house parent and teachers observed that I was not using my hearing aid. I told her I hated the aids. She badgered me for about 45 minutes, telling me that I needed to use my aids. I could not get one sign into the conversation. When she stopped, I told her I hated the aids . . . that I was deaf and that the aids were useless to me. She insisted and went on and on about the benefits of hearing-aid use. I tried to tell her again that the aids were useless. Finally, in frustration, she grabbed the hearing aid and tested it. It was not fitted properly and was of no use to me. Once I was properly fitted, I found them to be helpful!

> (Paraphrase of a story related by a deaf university student)

In short, the preceding example is illustrative of a concrete way in which finally listening to deaf persons led to a better outcome in an area about which people in positions of authority were concerned. Listening is a powerful tool:

> While teaching a masters' degree course in diversity in education, Pat invited in a panel of students who were deaf but were dealing with other challenges. One panelist had retinitis pigmentosa (RP) and therefore had difficulty seeing; another had

cerebral palsy (CP). Each student had a personal story to tell. They described the ways in which they learn best. The student who had RP described the font size and color of overheads that was best, as well as the seating arrangement in a classroom. The student with CP described the ways in which the classroom furniture could be arranged for best movement and interaction. The students ended the discussion by emphasizing, "in order to find out what is the most helpful for a deaf student or what they need, JUST ASK." The masters' degree students related that it was one of the most helpful classes they had ever attended as it proved illuminating.

This story illustrates only a few of the important ways in which *deaf persons are expert.* How many times have those of us in decision-making positions discussed the best way to accomplish some teaching objective without ever asking students how they might best learn it? Through discussion with those who are deaf, we can *learn what barriers* have been encountered and what those persons have found that *empowers them to succeed.* In this aspect of learning, deaf persons are expert, be they youngsters, young adults, or adults. Kavin and Brown-Kurz (2009), in a study of deaf managers in educational and social services settings, offer a wonderful window into the creative interaction and technical solutions that these managers have utilized to address the challenges they encounter in their work.

Another example that illustrates how people who are deaf are expert derives from the study we conducted in Sweden (DeCaro, Mudgett-DeCaro, & Dowaliby, 2001). Deaf respondents in our study were more positive than hearing respondents about advice they would give for several careers, notably salesperson and college professor. When asked to explain why salesperson and university lecturer were not identified as problem careers by the Deaf community leaders, they pointed out that there were multiple ways to set up sales, such as buddy systems and note taking, which made selling feasible. As for university lecturer, the deaf adults explained that interpreters were already available in university classes to facilitate communication between deaf students and hearing lecturers, so what difference did it make, they said, if the students were hearing and the lecturer deaf? Deaf adults (teachers, parents, and deaf community leaders) in Sweden indicated ways that deaf individuals could negotiate occupation barriers in ways that had not come to mind for hearing adults.

In addition to the knowledge that deaf persons have to offer to deaf and hearing persons, there must be *awareness of and emphasis on what successful deaf people can do and have done* rather than upon what they cannot do. That is, *access to a wide variety of positive role models who are deaf* can provide a window into the world faced by people who are deaf that it is hard, if not impossible, for a hearing person to provide:

I am an African American, male social worker who is deaf, and I am employed at a state school for the deaf. On my first day the superintendent introduced me to the students and faculty, asking me to tell them about myself and my job. I proceeded to describe to the students what a social worker does. . . . I was impeccably dressed. The very first question, from a young African American boy was, "So, you are a janitor?" Over a period of several months I needed to continually explain that I was a professional and not a member of the custodial staff. The African American students said they never knew they could become a teacher, social worker, or professional and wanted to understand how I had done so. My answer was that I had studied hard! When I arrived at the school, all the African American students were studying for local high school diplomas. Now, four years later, quite a few are getting ready to go to college.

(Paraphrase of a story related by a young professional who is deaf [June 2009])

Knowledge of the achievement of individuals who are deaf can significantly alter perception of possibilities, both for young individuals who are deaf and for their significant others. Significant interaction with older, mature persons who are deaf in a wide variety of positions can have a positive impact upon the life story created by a deaf youngster. Exposure to these role models can demonstrate that *people who are deaf are capable of a very wide variety of achievements irrespective of their mode of communication.* Students at the National Technical Institute for the Deaf at the Rochester Institute of Technology (RIT) have pointed out that deaf faculty members and administrators are needed so that students can envision the possibilities for themselves. Presently, more than 100 faculty and staff who are deaf work at NTID.

We would also like to suggest some excellent materials that are on the market that can expose deaf youth and their significant others to successful individuals who are deaf. The Postsecondary Education Programs Network (PEPNet) Northeast, housed at the National Technical Institute for the Deaf at RIT, has developed five excellent DVDs (titled "Achieving Goals! Career Stories of Individuals Who Are Deaf and Hard of Hearing") that tell the stories of successful deaf persons in a variety of professional positions (e.g., in business, the arts, social work, IT) and the trades. In these DVDs, successful deaf individuals describe their path to success, the barriers that they have overcome and how they did so, and the tools they use to be successful. They encourage young deaf persons to consider these careers. The reader can find these materials by accessing the following website: http://www.pepnet.org/northeast.

While those who are deaf, like all others, need to be encouraged to achieve their very best, they need to be *allowed to fail* and to be provided guidance regarding learning from failure:

I was sitting in my office at the high school (I am the principal). One of my faculty members called me on the phone in a quandary. He said that a deaf student in his mainstream class was failing but that he really liked the student and was thinking of giving the student a minimally passing grade. I asked one question, "What has the student earned?" When he responded, "An F," I said, "You have answered your question yourself." We then went on to discuss how this F could be utilized to mentor/tutor the student regarding what he had learned from the experience and what he needed to do to improve his performance.

(Paraphrase of a story told by an educational administrator)

It has been our experience in life that we have often learned more from our mistakes and failures than we have from our successes. If utilized as a learning experience, failure is an experience that can add considerably to an individual's set of life skills. As such, we should not protect deaf persons from failure. They should not be deprived of the right to learn from such experience.

Before concluding, there is one final, sensitive area that we feel must be briefly mentioned:

I am preparing to work in the field of deafness. I have worked hard to become a fluent ASL user and have immersed myself in the study of Deaf culture. Unfortunately, some of my teachers and classmates are giving me the impression that I am not welcome in the field. I feel like I am being oppressed by those who are emerging from oppression. Luckily, however, I have found many more Deaf teachers and Deaf students who have not done so and welcomed me with open arms.

(Paraphrase of a story told by a hearing graduate student)

This story is indicative of a condition that has been identified in the literature of liberation pedagogy. Paulo Freire (1972, 1995) has eloquently described the need for an oppressed group to guard against becoming "the oppressors" when they themselves become decision makers or leaders. Those of us who are facilitating, as collaborating authors, the development of a life story of those who are deaf have a responsibility to ensure that the myriad aspects of oppression are considered in life decisions (our own, as well as those of the people we work with on a daily basis). That is, we need to engage in a thorough analysis of what it means to be an oppressor or to be oppressed and what it means to become an oppressor as roles reverse. This understanding will lead us to determine the implications of oppression in the life story we each wish to author for ourselves. The amazing example of Bishop Desmond Tutu in postapartheid South Africa stands as a shining example of a positive and constructive way to address this complex and sensitive issue. To paraphrase the good bishop, "My humanity is bound up in yours [deaf, Deaf, hearing, hard of hearing], for we can only be human *together*. Without *understanding and forgiveness* there is no future."

Conclusion

Those of us (significant others) in positions of authority with regard to people who are deaf are part of the daily decisions that influence their life stories. When we participate in such decision making, we suggest that our responsibilities as leaders require that we *facilitate, as collaborating authors, the development of life stories by those who are deaf so that they become the primary author of their own life story.*

This will require *active participation by people who are deaf, as we serve as partners with them* (Conner, 1988). It is no more acceptable for us to author the life story of people who are deaf than it is to spoon-feed them in the education process. We need to nurture excellence in the life story of persons who are deaf by working in partnership with them. To be better coauthors in the construction of students' life stories, we must understand and then confront the attitudes that we hold about deafness and people who are deaf. We offer the following propositions:

If we have the will to draw forth issues regarding the authorship of students' life stories from the unspoken and subconscious;

if we are courageous enough to confront those issues with an open mind;

if we are willing to persist in developing solutions in partnership with people who are deaf;

if we have the fortitude to execute those solutions in collaboration with people who are deaf;

then we can free ourselves from the strictures that we may impose upon the authorship of a life story of someone who is deaf.

However, there is no reason to believe that we will always get it right no matter how hard we try. But, if we work as collaborators in the authoring of a life story, we can learn together and adjust our behavior to more closely approximate the desired end: that people who are deaf will become the primary authors of their life stories. The lessons we learn from our deaf partners will be enlightening. We will most likely find that we are able to better *envision* a richer life story for ourselves.

References

Conner, K. (1988). Dear colleagues. In *Vision quest: Collected papers* (p. 86). Rochester, NY: National Technical Institute for the Deaf at Rochester Institute of Technology.

DeCaro, J. J. (1988). Concluding remarks. In *Vision quest: Collected papers* (pp. 137–139). Rochester, NY: National Technical Institute for the Deaf at Rochester Institute of Technology.

DeCaro, J. J., Dowaliby, F. J., & Maruggi, E. A. (1983). A cross-cultural examination of parents' and teachers' expectations for deaf youth regarding careers. *British Journal of Educational Psychology, 53*, 358–363.

DeCaro, J. J., & Egleston-Dodd, J. (1982). Towards a dialogue regarding careers for deaf youth. *Journal of the British Association of Teachers of the Deaf, 6*(6), 155–161.

DeCaro, J. J., Evans, L., & Dowaliby, F. J. (1982). Advising deaf youth to train for various occupations: Attitudes of significant others. *British Journal of Educational Psychology, 52*, 220–227.

DeCaro, J. J., Mudgett-DeCaro, P. A., & Dowaliby, F. (2001). Attitudes toward occupations for deaf youth in Sweden. *American Annals of the Deaf, 146*(1), 51–59.

Freire, P. (1972). *Pedagogy of the oppressed.* Harmondsworth: Penguin.

Freire, P. (1995). *Pedagogy of hope: Reliving* Pedagogy of the oppressed. New York: Continuum.

Hurwitz, T. A., Weisel, A., Parasnis, I., DeCaro, J. J., & Savir, H. (1997, March). *Attitudes of teachers, parents, and deaf adults toward career advice to deaf people: A comparative Israel.* Paper presented at the American Educational Research Association Annual Convention, Chicago.

Kavin, D., & Brown-Kurz, K. (2009). The career experiences of deaf supervisors in education and social service professions: Choices, mobility, and networking. *JADARA, 42*(1), 24–47.

Maruggi, E. A. (1983, July). *Occupational role expectations for deaf persons by teachers and parents of deaf children in northern Italy.* Paper presented at the Congress of the World Federation of the Deaf, Palermo, Italy.

Meadows, K. P., & Neamon, A. (1976). Deafness as stigma. *American Rehabilitation, 2*, 7–9.

Naidoo, R. M. (1989). *An examination of parents' and teachers' expressed attitudes towards occupational expectations for deaf persons.* Unpublished doctoral dissertation, University of Kansas.

Parasnis, I., DeCaro, J. J., & Raman, M. L. (1996). Attitudes of teachers and parents in India toward career choice for deaf and hearing people. *American Annals of the Deaf, 141*(4), 303–308.

Part Three

Interpreting Decisions

8

Perceptions of Efficacy of Sign Language Interpreters Working in K–12 Settings

RICO PETERSON AND CHRISTINE MONIKOWSKI

Scenario

Mary, who went on to college right after high school, has just graduated from a well-respected, four-year interpreting education program. She has worked hard, spent time with deaf people in the community so her ASL skills would improve, and took the "Introduction to K–12" course as one of her electives. Mary wants to work in an elementary school setting because she has always enjoyed children. For her practicum, she was placed in a fourth-grade class; her supervisor for that experience was a graduate of the same interpreting program who had been working in that school for three years. Two months before the end of her program, Mary was offered a position as "interpreter" in that school, and she substituted while completing her last few courses. At graduation, she received the "outstanding student" award from her program.

However, as she now completes her first year on the job, Mary is not happy with what she's doing. She feels overwhelmed, unsure, and depressed.

Educational interpreting has been practiced in this country in earnest for at least 35 years. Estimates (Marschark, 2005, p. 57) are that more than 75% of deaf children are mainstreamed, receiving the bulk of their academic experience in circumstances mediated by sign language interpreters. For the first 25 years little was known about this curricular innovation. Educational interpreting was mandated and delivered on a purely theoretical basis, and for a time it sufficed by simply being provided. Its implementation was both pilloried and praised, but for all this the efficacy of interpreters and interpretation in classrooms escaped scientific study. While the cry of "Ready, fire, aim!" is hardly unfamiliar in public education, it is hard to understand how something so vital as the education of generations of deaf children could be treated in such a capricious manner. It is incumbent upon public education to offer evidence that interpreters can

We are grateful to Pamela Brodie, the director of outreach at the Ohio School for the Deaf for coordinating this research project and giving us access to the cadre of educational interpreters working in Ohio. We are also especially grateful to the interpreters who participated in this study, without whose generosity of time, thought, and talent this work would not have been possible.

effectively mediate classroom learning. This is the least we owe deaf children, their parents, and their society. Having invested so much in the credibility of classroom interpreting, is it not logical (not to mention ethical) that we demonstrate its effects?

While K–12 venues are replete with measures of the effective learning and teaching of other populations, the technology of interpreted education for deaf children escaped scrutiny until approximately 10 years ago. The development of the Educational Interpreter Performance Assessment (EIPA) spawned a good deal of investigation. Research (Jones, Clark, and Soltz, 1997; Jones, 2004; Ramsey, 1997; Marschark, Sapere, and colleagues, 2005) has begun to emerge that calls into doubt the ability of interpreters to "level the playing field" for deaf students in mainstream environments. In this chapter we review this history and point out that there is still at least one unexplored aspect of educational interpreting: the perceptions of the interpreters themselves. Knowing how interpreters define success may provide vital information about how effectively students are handling the curriculum.

When PL94-142 (Education for All Handicapped Children Act) was passed in 1975, the "least restrictive environment" was meant to be just that: an academic environment where handicapped children would have the most access and be offered the most opportunities to be equal. At that time, parents of Deaf children had only one choice—the residential school—a choice that was often not an easy one to make. With 94–142, the provision of classroom interpreters enabled parents to place their child in the local school district. This was construed to be the *least restrictive environment* for some children, an opportunity for them to engage in the numerous opportunities afforded other children. The belief was that a "qualified" interpreter in a classroom could and would make things equal for deaf students. It must be noted, however, that then as now, when describing interpreters, the word *qualified* is the devil in the detail.

Federal resources were poured into interpreter training to increase the number of interpreters. At the outset, these programs offered "3-month training courses for individuals without prior interpreting experience" (Cokely, 2005, p. 15). It is crucial to note that, at that time, "there was no meaningful research base upon which to properly understand the linguistic, cognitive, and sociolinguistic demands of interpretation" (p. 15). "[I]n reality only the illusion of access and equality [had] been created" (p. 12). The sad news is that, more than thirty years later:

> the need for research about interpreted education has not gone away. Too many [deaf] students are still being abused in classrooms that fail to provide adequate access to language, to education, and to a "normal" least restricted environment. And too little research has been done to determine whether this practice of mainstreaming has any positive effects. (Winston, 2004, p. 1)

The need for educational interpreting is greater today than ever before, as mainstream academic placement has become the primary means of education for deaf students. More than 75% of deaf children are now mainstreamed (Marschark, Sapere, and colleagues, 2005, p. 57). Seven years earlier, La Bue (1998) reported that "most deaf children [in the United States] are now enrolled in regular public elementary schools and receive instruction in English through a sign language interpreter . . . [and] secondary-level mainstreamed students use educational interpreters in over half of their classes" (pp. 4–5). However, where is the research to assess the efficacy of putting interpreters into the classroom?

The present research looked at interpreters in the state of Ohio, where at the time of this study (2006–2007), some 500 interpreters in K–12 settings were serving 2,546 (2005–2006 enrollment data) students who were deaf and hard of hearing in 88 Ohio counties (2002 Ohio Education Management Information System count). The Interpreting and Sign Language Resources (ISLR) department at the Ohio School for the Deaf, founded in 1998 as a joint venture between the Ohio School for the Deaf and the Office of Exceptional Children at the Ohio Department of Education, serves Ohio pre–K–12 schools, public school interpreters, and interpreting students. This was in response to the passage of the teacher certification and licensure law in Ohio, which requires educational interpreters to have credentials and to engage in ongoing professional development. The ISLR provides professional development, including numerous workshops around the state, for educational interpreters. Additional services include mentoring, internships, American Sign Language assessments, and consultation. However, prior to this limited research project, there was no investigation into whether interpreters themselves viewed their work as successful.

This lack of research into the efficacy of classroom interpretation is a serious national problem inasmuch as too few entities recognize the need for formal investigation into this educational setting for deaf students. The opinions of other members of the academic team—administrators, teachers, parents, and even deaf students themselves—have each been considered to varying degrees. The opinions of the interpreters themselves, on the other hand, are rarely sought and to our knowledge are hardly ever considered at the administrative level, where crucial decisions are made. Interpreters have much to offer this dialogue, and our work here is a vital first step toward making a place at the table for the perspectives of interpreters in educational settings.

Review of Literature

There are, unfortunately, too few researchers whose work has addressed fundamental questions about mainstreaming in the K–12 setting. Ramsey's (1997) observation of both the self-contained class and the mainstream class still brings K–12 interpreters to tears more than ten years after it was published. She found that the three students she followed were "active social beings who observed the world around them at school and engaged in strategic activities" (p. 108) when in the self-contained environment where they could interact with peers and converse with the three adults (two teachers of deaf students and one instructional assistant/interpreter). Although there is no research on this, in speaking with several educators who present workshops for working educational interpreters, it is quite obvious that Ramsey's work challenges their beliefs that the mainstream classroom is a "success" for deaf students. Ramsey continues:

> [T]he mainstreaming classroom afforded deaf students few occasions to interact with others except to the extent that they were on the receiving end of directives and evaluations. In the self-contained classroom, interaction was not only intelligible, it offered [the three deaf students] opportunities to accomplish a variety of social and learning activities. Although there was some social contact for the deaf boys in the mainstreaming classroom, it existed on the surface only. (Ramsey, 1997, p. 92)

Ramsey viewed this imbalance, in part, as a lack of training to prepare regular education teachers to work with deaf students in their classrooms, aside from having an interpreter in the room. "Very limited efforts were devoted to preparing [hearing] teachers and [hearing] students to have deaf children in their midst" (p. 114). She indicated that deaf people seem to understand what hearing people do not. They understand the "illusion of mainstreaming and know that physical integration, even with an interpreter, does not mean that they [deaf students] can fully participate" (p. 113). This seminal work clearly shows that Deaf children thrive when allowed to interact with others (children and adults) with whom they can communicate easily and who can use American Sign Language in conversation in the educational setting. Deaf students in a mainstream setting have an interpreter as their educational accommodation. Typically, this means that their social connections and communication with the majority of the other people in the class are limited.

Given the disturbing lack of insight into the actual work of K–12 interpreters in the classroom, Jones et al. (1997) surveyed 222 educational interpreters in three states (Kansas, Missouri, and Nebraska) and determined demographic characteristics, mode of communication most frequently used, and levels of education and certification for the sample. Two important pieces of information came from this research, information that rocked the emerging field of educational interpreting. First, in addition to the actual task of interpreting, the participants fulfilled numerous "non-interpreting activities such as tutoring, teaching sign language to hearing students, correcting assignments, and other teacher assistance tasks" (p. 260). Second, "perhaps the most distressing finding . . . centers around the qualifications of K–12 educational sign language interpreters in the three states" (p. 264). The results show the following:

> Almost two-thirds of the interpreters working in public schools in Kansas, Missouri, and Nebraska had no certification of any kind to perform the job they were hired to do. This was better than what had been reported ten years earlier in Oregon (87 percent of K–12 interpreters were not certified), but it was still unacceptable. (p. 263)

In recent years, things have not gotten much better. In 2002, M. Mitchell reported that New York State had 15 certified interpreters out of 983 educational interpreters (personal interview, September 5, 2002).

Johnson (1991) conducted research from the *consumer's* perspective, and although she focused on interpreting at the postsecondary level, she provided a much-needed opportunity for deaf students to talk about what they did and did not understand. Johnson, who calls her research "naturalistic" (p. 27) and "ethnographically informed" (p. 4), included herself as one of four subjects in 32 hours of research at 11 different college courses, mostly at the graduate level:

> As a Deaf student, I was aware that I frequently left my classes feeling confused. But I often had little idea of what I was confused about. Only after a few interpreters had discussed with me the various problems in interpreting did I consider that the source of confusion might not lie entirely within me. (p. 3)

Results of her analysis show us that "Deaf people may not know that the information they received in class was inaccurate, or that they did not get all the information that was necessary" (p. 23). It became clear that the misunderstandings "occurred with the greatest frequency when interpreters were unfamiliar with the subject they were interpreting and/or were required to interpret diagrams or verbal descriptions" (p. 1). If this is true of students in graduate school, we can only wonder at the extent to which the younger, less sophisticated student in K–12 experiences the same issues, without the ability to articulate the problem.

Brown Kurz and Caldwell (2004) present another attempt to understand the *consumer's* viewpoint. Twenty deaf and hard of hearing students were interviewed. The individual interviews were conducted in ASL by Brown Kurz and Caldwell, and two interesting findings emerged from those interviews and stories: the students' views of an interpreter's role and responsibilities, as well as a wish list for interpreters. In addition, although the items on this list "should not be seen as representative of what all students want in all situations" (p. 23), they deserve attention from all interpreters. What's the point in asking consumers what they think if we do not take the time to address their opinions? Ethical practice demands that we pay attention to comments such as "interpret everything"; "do not let your personal style interfere with my education"; and "please do not rely on us for information, sign instruction, reassurance, or fun" (pp. 25–26).

Winston (1994, 2004) is arguably the best-known researcher to focus attention on the K–12 setting. Her candid approach in addressing two common "myths" is seminal in our field:

> The myths about interpreting need to be exposed before policies of inclusion through interpreting can be considered rationally. . . . 1) the myth that interpreting is a simple substitute for direct communication and teaching; and 2) the myth that an interpreted education is an "included" education. (1994, p. 55)

Winston describes the constraints that must be addressed before a deaf student is placed in a classroom with an interpreter, most notably that the deaf student "must first have linguistic competence before benefiting from interpreting" (p. 56). Unfortunately, ten years later Monikowski (2004) lamented that this myth had become a reality and that the deaf student's first-language abilities were still questionable at best. Winston (2004) has recognized the even more pressing need for research in the K–12 setting and offered an overview of where we all are today with regard to deaf students, interpreters, and individual education plans (IEPs).

Marschark, Sapere, and colleagues (2005) are emerging as the most prolific researchers in the field of interpretation, but to date their work has focused exclusively on postsecondary and experimental settings (e.g., mock lectures, miniclasses). However, given the dearth of research in the K–12 setting, it is important that we review this work. It is possible that the conclusions of Marschark et al. can be expanded to the K–12 setting. Their primary findings indicate that "deaf students do not comprehend as much as their hearing peers in the [postsecondary] classroom even when provided with highly qualified sign language interpreters in controlled settings" (p. 74). This could be due to "a general language comprehension barrier" or "the possibility that deaf students' conceptual knowledge, world knowledge, or information-processing strategies differ from those of hearing students in ways that create barriers to comprehension of interpreting" (p. 75). It is clear that the question of how students comprehend information needs to be addressed in the K–12 setting as well, so that barriers that arise in postsecondary education can be removed.

Given the limited research on interpreting in the K–12 setting—and none that focuses on the *interpreters'* perspectives of their success—and in light of the growing number of K–12 interpreters in the state of Ohio (500+), we set out to investigate the perceptions of K–12 interpreters with regard to their efficacy. We hold the interpreters' perceptions to be of fundamental interest for two reasons. First, their privileged viewpoint from the "front lines" of classroom interpreting affords them a unique view on the relative effectiveness of their work. In interpreted situations, the interpreters are often the only persons present who are qualified to judge the success of their work. Second, to our knowledge, this crucial point of view has rarely been included in the equation for determining success in interpreter-mediated education. We claim that studying interpreters' opinions about the quality of their work is essential in advancing what is known about interpreting in classrooms.

Methodology

First we developed an online survey, the initial draft of which was reviewed by several interpreters who have experience interpreting in educational settings and are knowledgeable about research procedures. After incorporating their feedback, a pilot survey was distributed to a select group of 12 interpreters in Ohio. Their responses then led us to conduct onsite interviews and focus groups. Based on the resulting data, we then refined the online survey and distributed it to approximately 500 individuals, using the ISLR email list. We indicated that only full-time K–12 interpreters should participate, and we gave them a specific window of time in which to respond. Initially, 87 people completed and returned the surveys. Upon reviewing the data and preparing the final report, we deleted 24 participants because they were not full-time K–12 interpreters. Because not all of the interpreters surveyed responded to each item, the total numbers in the following tables show some variation.

Results

Table 1. Demographics: Gender

Gender	Percentage	Number of Respondents
Female	95.2	60
Male	4.8	3

The field of sign language interpreting is dominated by women. Jones (2004) reported that 99% of K–12 interpreters working in 2001 were females. Our sample was no exception as more than 95% of the respondents were female. Little is known about the female-male ratio of educational interpreters nationally, but this figure is likely to be fairly representative of that number. It is also not known whether this disproportionate number of female interpreters affects the performance and participation of male students in any way. It is conceivable that, in certain situations, a male interpreter would be preferable from the perspective of a male student. The percentage, here, of course, does not suggest that male interpreters are not available in such situations, but it does point to the possible effect of this circumstance as an area of interest for future research.

Table 2. Demographics: Placement and Experience

	Percentage	Number of Respondents
elementary school	31.7%	20
middle school	34.9%	22
high school	47.6%	30

The sample was very evenly distributed between elementary, middle, and secondary school interpreters. Since some interpreters split their time fairly evenly between two or more of these levels, the total here exceeds 100%. Much has been written (Ramsey, 1997; Winston, 1994, 2004; Brown Kurz & Caldwell Langer, 2004) about the necessity for interpreters working at the lower levels to have the most advanced skills. While this study does not address that issue specifically, it does lead to several interesting areas of pursuit. The number of interpreters working in high schools in this sample is 50% higher than the number working in elementary schools. While this is not an issue in smaller schools, where interpreters routinely work with one or two students exclusively, it raises a question about the larger school districts. What circumstances in high schools lead to such a dramatically higher number of interpreters working at that level? Even if the demographics show that high schools have 50% more students than elementary schools, what does it mean for the latter, where, arguably, the resources need to be every bit as rich as they are at the middle- and high-school levels?

Table 3. Grade Level Worked
Specify the grade level in which you work. (*n* = 87)

Grade Level	Percentage	Number of Respondents
K–2	19.0	12
3–5	28.6	18
6–8	36.5	23
9–12	54.0	34

The results in this sample appear to be skewed from the previous item in that a slightly higher number of respondents identified high school as their primary focus. There is some overlap between the divisions in this table and those in the previous chart. For example, elementary school is generally understood to include grades K–5, but, in this item, we were looking for much more specific designations. Still, it is not clear why in the previous item 20 of the respondents identified themselves as interpreters in elementary settings, while in this item the number grew to 30. Again, interpreters are often assigned to more than one primary level, and that dual tasking may account for this anomaly. It is likely that the slightly different phrasing of the items led the respondents to answer differently here.

Table 4. Years of Experience in K–12
How long have you been an interpreter in that specific position? (*n* = 63)

Years of Experience	Percentage	Number of Respondents
1–4	42.9	27
5–9	28.6	18
10–15	20.6	13
other	7.9	5

This finding is significant for training and professional development. With some 42% of the workforce having less than five years' experience, clearly a great deal of attention must go into nurturing these developing interpreters. As the subsequent findings demonstrate, the interpreters in this sample are eager for and appreciative of the state's efforts in this regard.

At the same time it is important to focus on the veteran interpreters, whose needs are often quite different from those of their newer colleagues. Five respondents found that their experience did not match the categories we offered. One had been working less than a year, and the others had experience ranging from 17 to 22 years.

Table 5. Years of Interpreting Experience
How long have you been an interpreter? (*n* = 63)

Years of Experience	Percentage	Number of Respondents
1–4	20.6	13
5–9	19.0	12
10–15	41.3	26
other	19.0	12

It is instructive to compare the length of time interpreters have been working in the classroom with the length of time they have been interpreting in general. In the past, it has not been uncommon for interpreters to work solely in school settings. Although this trend is changing as the number of interpreters working in classrooms increases, the ability to work in both classroom and community settings is a possible indicator of interpreter ability.

The findings here are quite interesting when compared with the previous item. There we saw that some 43% of interpreters had been working in their current position for 1–4 years. Here only 20.6% of the sample had been working as interpreters for that same length of time. From this we can extrapolate that more than half (14 of 27) of the interpreters who have been in their positions came there with significant experience beforehand. This, too, is an indication of the growth and development of the field. It has not always been the case that interpreters had a breadth of experience from which to draw when they entered the venue of classroom interpreting. This finding seems to indicate that this circumstance is changing for the better.

Demographics: Education and Certification

Table 6. Level of Education
What is the highest level of education you have completed? ($n = 64$)

	Percentage	Number of Respondents
high school	4.8	3
some college, no degree	15.9	10
2-year degree	42.9	27
4-year degree	30.2	19
MA/MS	7.9	5

This is a very robust finding in terms of the educational background of interpreters in this state. Nearly three-quarters (73.1%) of interpreters surveyed had postsecondary degrees, and another 15.9% had taken coursework at the postsecondary level. Given the requirements of the Registry of Interpreters for the Deaf (the only organization that certifies interpreters at the national level) that, as of 2009, candidates for certification must possess at minimum an associate's degree, interpreters here seem to be well qualified in this regard.

What is most remarkable is the small percentage (4.8) that had only high school diplomas. This is further evidence of the growth of the profession of sign language interpreter. Prerequisites for employment in many places do not include postsecondary degrees. As of 1998, educational interpreters in Ohio are required to have a degree from an Ohio Department of Education–approved program in interpreting. At this writing there are two 4-year programs in Ohio—one at Kent State University and one at the University of Cincinnati (which offers an online degree); four other face-to-face programs are 2-year programs. The more than 500 interpreters mentioned were counted before licensure and were eligible to be grandfathered without the educational requirement. That such a high percentage of this sample has postsecondary degrees, which surpasses the requirements of the job, is significant in both professional and personal ways. While degrees in interpreting are a relatively new phenomenon (see next item), postsecondary education has been available to interpreters since the profession began in earnest in the late 1960s. Yet, as can be seen by the stipulation that AA degrees be a prerequisite to certification, which the Registry of Interpreters for the Deaf (RID) enacted in 2003, it has not always been the case that interpreters themselves had significant experience in education.

Little work has been done in teasing out these statistics on a nationwide basis, but it seems that Ohio is well ahead of the trend toward requiring that classroom interpreters have proven successful as students themselves. Having successfully negotiated for themselves the environments of higher education, these interpreters are likely much better equipped to interpret in the classroom than were the interpreters of a generation ago.

Table 7. Interpreter Education
Did you graduate from an interpreter education program? ($n = 63$)

	Percentage	Number of Respondents
yes	66.7	42
no	33.3	21

Here, too, there is much reason for optimism. Postsecondary degrees in interpreting have existed since the mid-1970s, but only in the last 15 years or so have they attained any significant numbers and reflected any regard for curriculum standards. Here we see that fully two-thirds of the participants have matriculated through interpreter education programs. Again, there are no national findings for comparison, but anecdotal evidence abounds that this percentage is impressive. The attention to professional development that Ohio affords its interpreters clearly has an effect here. As witnessed in comments from the focus groups (given in a later section), this sample strongly believes that education is vital to success for interpreters in educational settings.

Table 8. Interpreter Performance Evaluations
Have you passed an interpreting performance evaluation? ($n = 67$)

	Percentage	Number of Respondents
no	63.5	40
RID	12.7	8
NAD	19.0	12
other	11.1	7

Until very recently the evaluation of classroom interpreters has been handled on a local, ad hoc level. The advent of the EIPA is ushering in a new era of measurement of performance ability in this venue. However, the EIPA is sufficiently new that only 5 respondents in this study had taken it.

Again, we can only lament that information on performance evaluations for classroom interpreters on the national level is only now emerging (Jones 2004). From these early data, it is evident that the implementation of performance standards is long overdue. The RID standards for certification have not been considered valid for classroom interpreters for a variety of reasons (see later discussion). The overt bias against classroom interpreters that is often seen among community interpreters is rooted in this.

In any event, this finding supports earlier work (Jones, 2004) that suggests that relatively few classroom interpreters have been certified at the national level.

We suspect that the emphasis that Ohio and many other states are placing on the EIPA, as well as RID's recent decision to grant certification to those who pass the EIPA at the level of 4.0 or better (on a 1–5-point scale), will cause this number to change dramatically in the coming years.

Table 9. Years of Signing Experience
How many years have you been signing? (_n_ = 62)

	Percentage	Number of Respondents
1–4 years	8.1	5
5–9 years	21.0	13
10–15 years	33.9	21
other	37.1	23

This finding also shows a healthy trend in the field of educational interpreting. Public Law 94–142 sought to make public school classrooms more accessible to deaf students, but it failed to set any standards for the requisite qualifications of interpreters. This lack of stringent requirements for ability has been the Achilles' heel of educational interpreting ever since. Although many highly qualified interpreters work in this venue, the absence of standards has increasingly come into question. It has also fed the bias we mentioned previously that many community interpreters have against the bona fides of classroom interpreters.

Here, however, a very small (8.1) percentage of interpreters has less than 5 years of experience as signers. Comparing this with the finding that nearly 21% of the respondents have been interpreting for less than 5 years, we can see that these interpreters have more experience as signers than they do as interpreters. While this finding might be unremarkable among spoken language interpreters, it does signal a very healthy development in a field that has only recently begun to look at language and literacy standards as prerequisites to the study of interpreting.

LOGISTICS: NUMBER OF STUDENTS PER INTERPRETER

Table 10. Number of Students per Interpreter
Indicate the largest number of deaf students you interpret for in one class. (_n_ = 59)

	Percentage	Number of Respondents
1–2	65.5	38
3–5	20.7	12
6–8	8.6	5
9 or more	6.9	4

This item is of interest because of the complexities presented by interpreting for multiple parties at the same time. It is quite possible that there are as many language modalities as there are participants in any given interpreted event; thus, the larger the number of students being interpreted for at any given time, the more complicated the task.

The exception here would be assemblies and other large gatherings where students from many classes come together. This is likely to account for the small (6.9) percentage of incidents in which interpreters are interpreting for groups of more than nine students.

These numbers are not out of the ordinary. While issuing the standard caveat about the lack of similar research with which to compare these numbers, we point out that they do comport with the norms.

PERCEPTIONS OF EFFICACY: COMPARATIVE LANGUAGE SKILLS

Table 11. Perceptions of Language Skill
Self-rate your language skills in ASL. ($n = 59$)

	Percentage	Number of Respondents
superior	1.7	1
advanced	44.1	26
intermediate	47.5	28
novice	5.1	3
I don't know	1.7	1

Self-rate your skills in spoken/written English. ($n = 60$)

	Percentage	Number of Respondents
superior	35.0	21
advanced	51.6	31
intermediate	12.1	7
novice	1.7	1
I don't know	0	0

Self-rate your skills in Signed English. ($n = 59$)

	Percentage	Number of Respondents
superior	3.4	2
advanced	41.4	24
intermediate	46.6	27
novice	8.6	5
I don't know	1.7	1

Because these ratings are self-assigned, they are therefore subject to potentially widely varying subjective perspectives. While the categories are those used by many language-measurement instruments, the definition of each is subject to personal interpretation. We are not assessing the interpreters' individual abilities but rather inquiring about their perception of their degree of competence in various modalities. Moreover, we are specific in asking about their perceptions of their *language skills*, not of their ability to interpret.

That said, these self-assessments correlate with much current thought on second-language ability. Indeed, Carroll (1993) asserts the following:

> Some measurements of cognitive ability . . . are not based on psychological or educa-
> tional tests; instead, they can be based on judgments or ratings (either self-ratings or
> ratings by others). . . . Under many conditions, such measurements can have at least
> some validity in assessing given aspects of ability. (p. 5)

A healthy percentage (45.8) stated that their ASL skills are superior or advanced, while the percentage that makes a similar claim about their spoken/written English ability is nearly twice as high, at 89.6 percent. This comports well with standard first- and second-language ability paradigms. Monikowski (1994) found that significantly higher scores in L1 cloze tests resulted in higher levels of proficiency in L1, as compared to cloze test scores in L2. These respondents fit that paradigm.

One of the most interesting findings here involves the respondents' perceptions of their competence in Signed English vis-à-vis that in spoken/written English. Here we see a marked difference. Where nearly 90% rate their abilities in the spoken modality as superior or advanced, less than half of that percentage (44.8) is willing to make the same claim about their proficiency in Signed English.

These numbers call for a deeper analysis. Strong anecdotal evidence suggests that the overwhelming majority of classroom interpreting is carried out in Signed English. That more than half (55.2%) of the respondents rated their abilities in this modality to be intermediate at best is intriguing. Again, these self-ratings may have little or no validity. Still, that a significant number of the respondents have such a relatively low opinion of their skill in Signed English suggests a need for further study.

Another interesting finding is that 8 out of the 60 respondents (13.8%) rated their skills in spoken/written English to be intermediate at best, with one respondent having a self-rating of novice. Again, we cannot know how these subjects define the terms *intermediate* and *novice*, but for people who work as interpreters to rate their *English* language abilities so low is remarkable, especially given that 73% of the respondents indicated they had either a 2- or 4-year college degree.

PERCEPTIONS OF EFFICACY: COMPARATIVE INTERPRETING SKILLS

In this section, we asked interpreters to rate the relative difficulty of typical classroom activities, such as lectures, discussions, reading aloud, and group work. Winston (1994) was the first researcher to focus on the possibility that much of what happens in classrooms is problematic from an interpreting perspective. Much of the meaning conveyed during these activities is taken for granted by people with normal hearing. We are accustomed to circumstances that require us to scan multiple visual sources of information while listening to yet another source (e.g., fast-paced and overlapping conversations, which are essential to collaborative and cooperative learning; sessions where students take turns reading from a source text).

Interpreters, on the other hand, struggle with each of these challenges. The deaf student cannot apprehend multiple visual sources while also watching an interpreter unless the interpretation is carefully choreographed into the flow of information. Given the normal, even nominal lag time that interpreting requires, fast-paced and overlapping conversations can tax even the most expert interpreter. Interpreting for a student who is reading aloud from a text, even when the interpreter has the text open in front of her, requires remarkable discernment and sensitivity. How best to indicate halting speech? How much information is the interpreter getting from the student and how much from the text itself? Issues like these trouble the sleep of even the most competent interpreters. As one of the respondents put it, "Anything other than interpreting for just one person lecturing gets linguistically complex, and my effectiveness declines rapidly."

Before we discuss these findings, we should state that a clear limitation to this study is that terms like *traditional lecture, teacher-led discussion,* and *reading aloud* may well mean different things to different people. The lack of concrete examples for these roughly categorized activities, then, is a clear caution when interpreting the data derived.

Table 12. Perceptions of Relative Difficulty: Lectures
How difficult is this situation to interpret? traditional lecture ($n = 57$)

	Percentage	Number of Respondents
extremely difficult	0	0
fairly difficult	27.6	16
not very difficult	37.9	22
quite easy	22.4	13
very easy	10.3	6

Here 70.6% of respondents found traditional lectures to be relatively easy to interpret. This situation, in which a (presumably) hearing speaker addresses a group of deaf listeners, is one of the most common settings for interpreters. There is little complication here in terms of turn taking or lag time. While rate of speech and the topic of the lecture might add to the difficulty, in general this finding is not at all surprising.

It also points to some related research. As student-centered learning finds a wider audience in schools and classrooms, traditional lectures will certainly be on the wane. The next steps in this research point to reviewing data on the percentage of time that teachers engage in various activities in mainstream classrooms. This information would be very useful to interpreter education programs.

Table 13. Perceptions of Relative Difficulty: Teacher-Led Discussions
How difficult is this situation to interpret? teacher-led discussion
(with no additional visual content) (*n* = 60)

	Percentage	Number of Respondents
extremely difficult	5.2	3
fairly difficult	32.8	19
not very difficult	44.8	26
quite easy	13.8	8
very easy	6.9	4

Respondents here indicated that teacher-led discussions are only slightly more problematic than lectures. The percentage claiming that discussions are not very difficult is
actually larger (44.8% vs. 37.9%) than in the finding on lectures. On the other hand,
the percentage that finds discussions to be difficult is also larger here, by 10 points
(38% vs. 27.6%).

Table 14. Perceptions of Relative Difficulty: Teacher-Led Discussions with Visuals
How difficult is this situation to interpret? teacher-led discussion
(with other visual content) (*n* = 60)

	Percentage	Number of Respondents
extremely difficult	5.2	3
fairly difficult	19.0	11
not very difficult	39.7	23
quite easy	29.3	17
very easy	10.3	6

The most interesting finding here is that this sample indicates that the addition
of other visual content to a teacher-led discussion makes for an easier task than the
one described in the earlier item, where no other visual content was present. This
seems counterintuitive. One would think that the addition of competing visual content
would complicate the interpreter's task. Interpreting is complex enough in and of
itself without the addition of further material. However, the percentage of respondents
who described this situation as easy is nearly twice as high as that in the previous, less-
complicated situation (39.6% vs. 20.7%).

Table 15. Perceptions of Relative Difficulty: Group Work
How difficult is this situation to interpret? group work ($n = 58$)

	Percentage	Number of Respondents
extremely difficult	15.5	9
fairly difficult	31.0	18
not very difficult	41.4	24
quite easy	8.6	5
very easy	3.4	2

This finding was one of the more surprising in the survey, as it conflicts with conventional wisdom, the experience of the researchers, and many of the comments made both in focus groups and in the respondents' extended comments on survey items. Still, that 46.5 % described interpreting for students working in groups to be difficult is significant. Follow-up work would certainly clarify this, especially with regard to the effect of interpreter experience on the perception of difficulty. For example, do interpreters with fewer than 5 years of experience find group work more (or less) difficult than interpreters with 10 years of experience? Is this putative difference in perception correlated more strongly to perspectives of the task or the assessment of one's ability to successfully interpret an event? How does experience influence an interpreter's ability to discern and deal with relative difficulty?

In general, the issue of perception of difficulty needs to be studied much more carefully. Issues of length of interpreter experience, familiarity with topic, and comfort with student and group are all confounding factors here, and each needs to be explored more fully.

Table 16. Perceptions of Relative Difficulty: Reading Aloud
How difficult is this situation to interpret? reading aloud ($n = 58$)

	Percentage	Number of Respondents
extremely difficult	29.8	17
fairly difficult	33.3	19
not very difficult	24.6	14
quite easy	14.0	8
very easy	0	0

Although slightly more than one-third of respondents disagreed, reading aloud is widely thought to be among the most difficult situations for classroom interpreters. Of all the situations posed to interpreters on this survey, this one elicited the strongest finding. More than 6 in 10 respondents described this work as difficult. As the respondents' comments reveal, many interpreters find interpreting for students who are reading aloud from texts to be problematic.

ELABORATIONS ON PERCEPTIONS OF RELATIVE DIFFICULTY

Here again we issue the standard disclaimer about the limited value of subjective reckonings of ease and difficulty. Given that this is an exploratory study designed to lead to areas of productive research in the future, the terms are well suited to our purpose. They should not, however, be taken to mean anything beyond general observations about how this particular sample felt about these very particular situations. We have, earlier in this chapter and elsewhere, argued for aggregating findings from subsequent research into categories based on years of experience, certification, and EIPA level. Clearly that is a promising direction for future research of this type.

Please Identify And Describe Any Situations or Assignments You Think Are Easy.

a) *Educational interpreting is a difficult task every day. Getting the meaning to the student is daunting and taxing on your brain and body. If this is a class that I have interpreted previously and the student has a great command of the language and is working on grade level . . . maybe then it is easy.*

b) *Since I have been doing (first through third) grade for 9 years, it is easy for me. But I have tried other grades (fourth and fifth) for a day, and it seemed a little harder since I didn't know that material beforehand.*

c) *I am not sure I find any situation "easy" to interpret. I feel if there is the possibility of having time to prepare yourself for what will be happening, this may make things easier. I guess I would have to say the assignments I find easier are those I have been able to prepare for or have a first-hand knowledge of, or have interpreted in the past.*

d) *I don't feel that "easy" is a good term to use. However, "easier" may be the more appropriate term relating to various factors such as background knowledge and preparation for the assignment.*

These comments, as all of the comments in this chapter, are taken from focus group follow-ups and elaborations made by the interpreters on the survey instrument. The common theme in all such remarks is that experience is the great equalizer in the interpreters' eyes. Having multiple, regular opportunities to interpret a text or situation allows interpreters to feel more comfortable; thus, they are likely to give a more accurate interpretation. Much of what an interpreter deals with is transitory; it comes in a rush and is gone in a flash. Moment by moment, class by class, day by day, this juggernaut of information demanding to be woven into meaning by the interpreter can seem like an impossible challenge. Here, however, we see that interpreters recognize the value of becoming familiar with the texts they interpret by preparation and by multiple exposures to the text or, ideally, both.

Please Identify and Describe any Situations Oor Assignments You Think Are Difficult.

A desire to see interpreting through the eyes of interpreters is at the heart of this study. The responses to this item were a rich and wonderful resource. The strengths and weaknesses of interpreters are as many and varied as the interpreters themselves. Although the education of deaf students has itself been studied now for hundreds of years, the inclusion of interpreters into that educational equation is a relatively new phenomenon. The further inclusion of the perspectives of those interpreters is largely terra incognita in educational research.

The following comments represent only a fraction of the responses this item yielded. The question predominated in the focus groups and elicited the most detailed information of any of the elaborated items on the survey. Here is a brief sample of the interpreters' perspectives on problematic issues in educational interpreting:

a)   *rapid-fire [presentations], changing subjects, trivia kinds of lessons (like a 5-minute discussion of all the morning news); working with special ed students in mainstream classrooms because their language level isn't at the level the lecture and discussion are occurring in, and they don't have enough background info on the subject to understand without explanation.*

b)   *I think earth physical science is very difficult. Sometimes there aren't signs for the vocabulary, or I'm not familiar with the vocabulary, and it's just very hard.*

c)   *small-group work because students don't speak in complete ideas or don't speak clearly; assemblies for "teasers" for school plays/musicals (because we never get info ahead of time).*

d)   *foreign language, reading aloud, student presentations. These are situations when students talk fast, mumble, and try to finish in record time.*

e)   *Situations in which there is a lot of interaction between students and teacher or if students don't take turns talking but talk over each other are difficult situations. Music class is difficult.*

Although reading aloud was mentioned frequently in terms of degree of difficulty in the elaborations and focus groups, it was not the activity that elicited the most responses. Table 17 lists circumstances that interpreters identified as difficult and the number of times these circumstances were mentioned.

Table 17. Interpreter-Identified Challenges

Circumstance	Number of Mentions
technical vocabulary	8
assemblies	7
group work	7
working without preparation	6
reading aloud	4
presentations	4
subbing	3
foreign language	3
literature classes	3
music	2

Clearly, knowing what interpreters find difficult and why they find it so is vital to both the training and professional advancement of educational interpreters. This preliminary study shows many promising areas of future pursuit. One wonders about the extent to which interpreting students are adequately prepared by their educational programs for the types of situations listed in table 17. On a similar note, how much training is afforded working interpreters in professional development? Giving interpreters a stronger voice and then listening to that voice has been a hallmark of the professional development afforded them in Ohio. It is our sincere hope that this research gives support for opinions previously expressed and new attention to areas that have yet to be treated adequately.

PREPARATION

Table 18. Preparation Time
Are you regularly given time to prepare for your classes? ($n = 53$)

	Percentage	Number of Respondents
yes	46.4	26
no	48.2	27

Slightly more than half of the respondents indicated that they did not receive regular (or adequate) prep time for their classes. In general, the interpreters indicated that they did not get sufficient time to prepare for their work in the classroom:

a) *This [prep time] is something that should be given just as a teacher has . . . [prep] time. I do, however, make sure I am as prepared as possible. I have been known to take all of the books, lectures, lesson plans, stories, assembly information, etc., home with me to prepare— for the benefit of my students and myself!*

b) *[I get] some time but never enough. I often have to give it up to fill in for interpreters who are out and there is no sub for the day.*

c) *At home. Not during the workday.*

d) *[I] gave up prep time to teach much-needed sign classes to 7th-grade students.*

Some interpreters, on the other hand, felt that they did receive adequate prep time:

a) *Well, actually, it is not called prep time; however, we almost always have a free period in which to use the time to prepare.*

b) *More now than in years past.*

c) *I have enough "down time" to prepare.*

d) *I insist on prep time the same as a teacher would have. It is inadequate, as there are several teachers, subjects, and much new material, but it is fair.*

The issue of prep time is certainly much on the interpreters' minds. Recall the previous finding that working without preparation was among the most difficult things that they had to do. As previously mentioned, when interpreters were first brought into classrooms in the 1970s, school administrators had remarkably little understanding of what interpreters did and how they did it. In the last 10 years we have seen important advances in the study of educational interpreting. As our understanding improves, so should the conditions in which interpreters work.

ERGONOMICS

We are most certainly not the first to state that interpreting is difficult work. It taxes one physically, cognitively, and emotionally. Ergonomics, the study of human efficiency in the workplace, is today being applied to interpreting in many venues. So little is known about the human capacity for sustained work as an interpreter that we must begin to reckon with its limitations and how they affect the quality of interpreters' work.

With that in mind, we asked several questions, both on the survey and in follow-up focus groups, about working conditions.

How Much Time Do You Have Between Classes?

With the exception of block schedule days, most of the respondents reported that they had an average of 3–5 minutes between classes, which seems like a reasonable amount of time. In light of the following question about breaks, however, this finding suggests that perhaps interpreters need more "down time" than is presently afforded them.

How Many Hours Are in a Typical Workday For You?

Most of the respondents reported that they work between 6 and 8 hours every day (mean = 6.7 hours). This number in isolation does not appear to be overtaxing; however, it should be looked at in light of several other factors, including pay rate and break time.

Table 19. Breaks
How long are you required to work before you are given a break? ($n = 60$)

	Percentage	Number of Respondents
0–30 minutes	16.1	9
30–50 minutes	32.1	18
1 hour	5.4	3
other	53.6	30

These findings show that breaks seem to be decided entirely on a local basis. As evidenced by these comments, many schools schedule no breaks whatsoever:

a) *Lunch is break* ☺
b) *Break!? What break?*

c) *What break? I am the only interpreter in my school, and my break comes at lunch or when I excuse myself to take one.*

d) *We are not given a break. They consider our "break" the time between classes, or if there is independent work, that is a "break," but we can't leave the room.*

e) *Haha, break, what's that??*

f) *Break? Only if there is seat work or a test assigned.*

These findings are somewhat problematic. There can be no question that interpreters work long, hard hours. That they do so largely without regulated break times is reminiscent of a time gone by in labor history. This finding cries out for further examination and clarification.

PERCEPTIONS OF ROLES AND RESPONSIBILITIES

Table 20. Perceptions of Roles
I am seen as a member of the academic team. ($n = 57$)

	Percentage	Number of Respondents
strongly agree	26.8	15
agree	33.9	19
neutral	19.6	11
disagree	16.1	9
strongly disagree	5.4	3

Classroom teachers respect and value my role in their classrooms. ($n = 58$)

	Percentage	Number of Respondents
strongly agree	25.0	14
agree	55.4	31
neutral	5.4	3
disagree	12.5	7
strongly disagree	5.4	3

Taken together, the findings of these two items are very positive. More than 60% of respondents agreed that they are seen as members of the academic team. More than 80% believe that teachers respect and value their roles in the classroom. These numbers are very significant given the sometimes rocky path educational interpreting has negotiated over the last 30 years. It has not always been the case that interpreters (or deaf students, for that matter) were welcome in mainstream classrooms. Take, for example, the comment made by one interpreter in this study: "In previous years the staff was very good to work with and treated me like an equal, etc., etc., etc. This year I worked in a school with a team of interpreters, and we were treated like a necessary evil, and the ones in authority had no interest in whether we had what we needed to do a good job or not, just that they could prove we were in place according to IEPs."

To be sure, over the years much has been done to improve the situation. The fact that today 80.4% of interpreters in this study can say that teachers value and respect them and 70.7% say that they are considered to be members of the academic team is a huge step forward and a very welcome finding. That comments like the preceding one are few and far between also speaks well of the educational environment within which these interpreters are working.

Table 21. Teacher Awareness of the Interpreter's Role
Teachers understand the role of interpreters in the education of deaf
children, ($n = 57$)

	Percentage	Number of Respondents
all teachers	7.1	4
most teachers	26.8	15
many teachers	35.7	20
some teachers	25.0	14
few teachers	7.1	4

These findings come remarkably close to a standard normal distribution, a bell curve. It indicates that it is the opinion of interpreters that "many" teachers understand their role in the education of deaf children. This would be an excellent finding if it were true. To be sure, we have seen enormous advances over the last 30 years in the attitudes and understanding of teachers, staff, and administrators toward interpreters. This finding, must, however, be put in different relief when taken together with the findings from the next topic.

Are You Asked To Perform Roles Other Than Interpreting?

Here things are a bit more complicated. Put simply, the rules of conduct for interpreters in the educational setting are different from those in almost every other venue. We are talking here about the K–12 setting. With the notable exception of video relay interpreting, the role of the interpreter in most other venues is strictly to interpret. Interpreters outside of the educational sphere do not typically assume any other responsibilities. This is not so in educational interpreting, however, where most interpreters have a host of other responsibilities in addition to their interpreting work (Jones et al., 1997.) This is seen in the job titles in many places, where interpreters are labeled "interpreter/aide" or a similar designation. This, in part, explains the stigma we have mentioned that educational interpreters sometimes experience from interpreters outside of education.

One could argue quite effectively that the norms for K–12 are different for teachers, too, and that many people in these schools work beyond strict job definitions. Certainly "other duties as defined" applies to many people in schools. The issue here is that while a teacher may also be doing lunch duty, no one confuses the role of the teacher in that situation. The teacher is seen and paid as a highly skilled professional. Educational interpreters, in many venues, have a long way to go before they are accorded similar respect and compensation.

It is unsurprising then to see the list of "other" duties handled by interpreters in this sample. These include all of the duties one might expect in a K–12 setting such as copying, lunch duty, bus duty, tutoring, monitoring the classroom, and assisting the teacher. As one interpreter puts it:

> [Other duties include] bus duty, lunch duty, recess duty, and [I] have offered to help with [the] minor classroom preps thing: copying, laminating, preparing art or science projects with the understanding—and I've stated this numerous times to the classroom teacher where I am assigned, as well as the building principal—that my interpreting responsibilities supersede anything else. They always respect that, although I am told that a principal in another building does not.

This last comment is especially significant as it comes up repeatedly in these data. The role of interpreters as seen by school administrators is inconsistent from one school to the next. This suggests that there is not a common understanding among them about what interpreters do and how they do it.

Conclusion

This preliminary study suggests several areas that are ripe for further study. We have mentioned that interpreters' perceptions of difficulty are likely to be influenced by factors such as their years of experience and familiarity with material. It would be very useful to be able to gauge more precisely what is meant by exposure and experience. For example, certain problem areas, like vocabulary and unfamiliar details in subjects like history, math, and science, could likely be remedied relatively quickly. Other problem areas, such as overlapping dialogue and interpreting challenges in music and foreign language classes, are likely to require much more strenuous treatment. Interpreters have proven to be successful in all of these venues, so it is clearly possible to find ways to negotiate these situations. It remains for us to plot a path to successful practice that can be used by interpreters of varying skill levels. We hold this to be a crucial area for future pursuit.

One clear possibility is seen in the findings on preparation time. No correlation is evident at present, but we suggest that interpreters who get adequate prep time are more successful in interpreting and in turn provide their students with a greater chance at success. This is an area where bringing interpreters into the administrative dialogue could be very effective. Certainly time and money constraints have meant that little or no prep time is afforded interpreters. Even if we were able to show a clear connection between prep time for interpreters and academic success for students, it is not clear that this finding would trump the fiscal and policy constraints under which schools operate. Still, a finding like this could well shed light on other areas of success-ful practice, perhaps ones that are more easily implemented.

The topic of "down time" needs additional exploration. It is not clear whether inter-preters distinguish between what we call "break time" and "prep time." Given some of the respondents' comments, it is clear that they have precious little time off task (i.e., time to themselves during the day). Knowing how interpreters make these distinctions would be quite valuable. Little is known about interpreter fatigue and how it affects performance (Brasel, 1976; Vidal, 1997). However, standard practice outside of academic settings has interpreters working in teams for any assignment that lasts longer than two hours. Given the length of time interpreters report working, fatigue is a concern. The effect this has on the quality of their performance is also a significant subject for future research.

We would be remiss in not including a further exploration of the many things that seem to be working well. Interpreters report that they feel valued and respected. They acknowledge the benefits of a strong professional development program when one is made available to them. They are a talented and committed group of professionals. It is often easier to look at areas where things are not working so well. Here we find it imperative to call attention to the quality of the environment in which interpreters work, a circumstance that shows Ohio to be well ahead of the curve when it comes to attending to the various needs of its educational interpreters.

Like any preliminary study, this one is fraught with limitations. We have mentioned sampling a relatively small number of participants. In using a wide-mesh net, we have limited the nature of our screening to the most obvious details. Our objective was to begin isolating those details and to use them as pointers toward the next step in this area of investigation. These early findings call for finer detail of the sort that can come only from further efforts, such as classroom observation and individual interviews. At some point it will also be necessary to bring other stakeholders into this research. Teachers' perspectives on interpreter success are a key part of the puzzle, as are those of administrators, parents, and the deaf students themselves. To get a clear picture of the efficacy of interpreters in educational settings it will be necessary to investigate each of the following valuable points of view:

DISCUSSION POINTS

1. Are interpreters provided to students from other linguistic and cultural groups? Why are the educational circumstances for deaf children so different from those of other English language learners?

2. Typically, K–12 interpreting is widely considered to be entry-level work for new graduates of interpreting education programs. How likely is it that as little as two years of signing experience (and far less of interpreting) is adequate preparation for this task?

3. How can the field of K–12 interpreting benefit from current research?

The answers to these and other questions will inform the field of educational inter-preting and indeed the field of education of deaf students in significant ways in the future. Providing the very best interpreting situation for all deaf learners is a shared responsibility.

References

Brasel, B. (1976). The effects of fatigue on the competence of interpreters for the deaf. In H. Murphy (Ed.), *Selected Readings in the integration of deaf students at CSUN* (pp. 19–22). Northridge: California State University Press.

Brown Kurz, K., & Caldwell Langer, E. (2004). Student perspectives on educational interpreting: Twenty deaf and hard-of-hearing students offer insights and suggestions. In E. Winston (Ed.), *Educational interpreting: How it can succeed* (pp. 9–47). Washington, DC: Gallaudet University Press.

Carroll, J. (1993). *Human cognitive abilities: A survey of factor analytic studies.* New York: Cambridge University Press.

Cokely, D. (2005). Shifting positionality: A critical examination of the turning point in the relations of interpreters and the Deaf community. In M. Marschark, R. Peterson, and E. Winston (Eds.), *Sign language interpreting and interpreter education: Directions for research and practice* (pp. 3–28). New York: Oxford University Press.

Johnson, K. (1991, Spring). Miscommunication in interpreted classroom interaction. *Sign Language Studies, 70*(1), 1–34.

Jones, B. (2004). Competencies of K–12 educational interpreters. In E. Winston (Ed.), *Educational interpreting: How it can succeed* (pp. 113–131). Washington, DC: Gallaudet University Press.

Jones, B., Clark, G., & Soltz, D. (1997). Characteristics and practices of sign language interpreters in inclusive educational programs. *Exceptional Children, 63*(2), 257–268.

La Bue, M. A. (1998). Interpreted education: A study of Deaf students' access to the content and form of literacy instruction in a mainstreamed high school English class. (Doctoral dissertation, Harvard University, 1998). *Dissertation Abstracts International, 59*(4), 1057A.

Marschark, M., Peterson, R., & Winston, E. (Eds.). (2005). *Sign language interpreting and interpreter education: Directions for research and practice.* New York: Oxford University Press.

Marschark, M., Sapere, P., Convertino, C., and Seewagen, R. (2005). Educational interpreting: Access and outcomes. In M. Marschark, R. Peterson, & E. Winston (Eds.), *Sign language interpreting and interpreter education: Directions for research and practice* (pp. 57–83). New York: Oxford University Press.

Monikowski, C. (1994). *ASL proficiency in interpreters: Assessing L2 with a videotaped cloze test.* Unpublished doctoral dissertation, University of New Mexico, Albuquerque.

Monikowski, C. (2004). Language myths in interpreted education: First language, second language, what language? In E. Winston (Ed.), *Educational interpreting: How it can succeed* (pp. 48–60). Washington, DC: Gallaudet University Press.

Ramsey, C. (1997). *Deaf children in public schools: Placement, context, and consequences.* Washington, DC: Gallaudet University Press.

Vidal, M. (1997, Winter). New study on fatigue confirms need for working in teams. *Proteus, 6*(1). Retrieved July 26, 2010 from http://najit.org/members_only/proteus/back_issues/vidal.htm.

Winston, E. (1994). An interpreted education: Inclusion or exclusion? In R. Johnson & O. Cohen (Eds.), *Implications and complications for deaf students of the full inclusion movement* (pp. 55–62). Occasional Paper 94-2. Washington, DC: Gallaudet Research Institute. ED380917.

Winston, E. (Ed.). (2004). *Educational interpreting: How it can succeed.* Washington, DC: Gallaudet University Press.

9

Opening Our Eyes

The Complexity of Competing Visual Demands in Interpreted Classrooms

MELISSA B. SMITH

Signed languages are visual languages. The importance of this quality was emphasized almost one hundred years ago by George Veditz, a prominent leader in the Deaf community and former president of the National Association of the Deaf. Veditz (1912) delivered a passionate argument in support of American Sign Language even in the face of intense political pressures, punctuated by the 1880 decision in Milan, Italy, to ban the use of sign language in public schools. In this address he characterized Deaf people as "first, last, and of all time the people of the eye." The fundamentally visual nature of American Sign Language and the people who use it validated his case for the preservation of this language at a time when it seemed on the verge of eradication. Nearly a century later, some Deaf leaders are celebrating the process of discovering what it truly means to be Deaf (Ladd, 2003) and champion the essential aspect of vision at its core (Bahan, 2008; Lentz, 2007).

American Sign Language has, in fact, not only survived but also attained wide recognition and support. The California Department of Education's vision for California's deaf and hard of hearing students states that each of these students will be provided with the means to "develop age-appropriate communication skills, in his/her preferred mode of communication . . . which will allow him/her to acquire the academic, social, emotional, and vocational skills needed for the establishment of social relationships, economic self-sufficiency, and the assumption of civic responsibility" (2000, p. 1). In a report of the California Deaf and Hard-of-Hearing Education Advisory Task Force, American Sign Language is listed as one of the communication options that should be made available (1999).

I am eternally grateful to all of the people who made this research and this chapter possible. Sincerest appreciation goes to Pam Long for teaching me to honor my writing process and for being an amazing writing coach. Thank you to Pam, Cheryl Forbes, and my life partner, Annette Miner, for invaluable input on numerous drafts and issues related to the education of Deaf students; to the UCSD faculty who advised me; and to the interpreters, teachers, school administrators, students and parents who allowed me to come into the classroom with video cameras. I am so lucky to have such a wonderfully supportive family. Thank you for the encouragement, time, and space I needed to work.

Although ASL is largely recognized today, for Deaf and hard of hearing learners in K–12 classrooms, the struggle has now become focused on their true inclusion in and access to a quality education. The typical classroom environment makes meeting their needs inherently and intensely complex. To date, schools have largely failed Deaf and hard of hearing students (Commission on Education of the Deaf [COED], 1988; California Deaf and Hard-of-Hearing Education Advisory Task Force, 1999; O'Connell, 2007). In mainstream education, students are expected to adapt to the regular classroom, whereby inclusion implies that the classroom and the teachers are supposed to adapt to meet the needs of the students (Stinson & Antia, 1999). "Philosophically, inclusion implies more than mainstreaming. Inclusion refers to full membership in a regular classroom" (Seal, 2004, p. 1). Many Deaf and hard of hearing students attend regular classrooms with interpreters, yet concerns about the efficacy of an interpreter-mediated education remain.

There is no doubt about the moral imperative to create change in the dismal statistics on the educational outcomes of Deaf and hard of hearing students. In his 2007 address on the state of education in California, Jack O'Connell reported that only 8% of Deaf students and 15% of hard of hearing students attain a score of at least "proficient" on English language arts standards. Because school success is largely predictive of employment options, the stakes are incredibly high when making decisions about how to most effectively meet the needs of Deaf and hard of hearing students in inclusive classrooms. If the general assumption and legislative reality are that the provision of a qualified interpreter is a sufficient means for Deaf and hard of hearing students to be fully included in mainstream school contexts, then we have an obligation to determine the factors that need to be in place so that they are truly afforded the opportunity to achieve socially and academically to their greatest potential.

Dean and Pollard (2006) have brought Niebuhr's moral philosophy of responsibility to the attention of professional interpreters. In 1963 Niebuhr described the moral person as one who responds appropriately to a given situation, a respon se that is characterized by a process of first asking oneself, "not about what is good or right, but about what is fitting to do in the light of what is actually going on" (West, 1965, p. 3). Professional ethics obligate practitioners to rely on their specialized knowledge and training to make decisions that take into account the likely outcomes of a chosen action (or intentional nonaction). Dean and Pollard (2006) suggest that interpreters must first consider the context in which the interpreted interaction takes place and the identification of the circumstances that require a response: "An ethical response cannot be determined absent of knowledge regarding what it is that one is attempting to respond to, that is, what the situation or question is that has predicated the opportunity for a response" (p. 121). They further elaborate that "careful consideration and judgment regarding situational and human interaction factors are central to doing effective [interpreting] work" (p. 259).

Based on interviews with Deaf and hard of hearing students, Brown Kurz and Caldwell Langer (2004) have determined that "a constellation of factors has to be properly aligned to achieve adequate access to education through an interpreter. Even if that alignment were achieved, these participants are quite aware that they still would not have equal access to education because of inherent alterations associated with the interpreting process" (p. 11). This alarming tacit acceptance of a lack of equal access confirms the need for extensive investigation into the possibilities and pitfalls of an interpreted education. In inclusive teaching environments, effective and responsible educational interpreters must carefully consider a constellation of academic, contextual, and situational factors along with a myriad of student- and teacher-related factors in order to make decisions appropriate for each interpreted interaction. In fact, it is only upon consideration of multiple factors that real interpreting can occur (Turner, 2005). The question that remains is what factors interpreters should consider when making decisions that affect Deaf and hard of hearing students' school experiences.

Concerns about barriers to access and inclusion (Antia & Kreimeyer, 2001; Brown Kurz & Caldwell Langer, 2004; Komesaroff & McLean, 2006; Lane, 1995; Mertens, 1990; Power & Hyde, 2002; Ramsey, 1997; Schildroth & Hotto, 1994; Winston, 1994, 2004), equivalence of interpretations, and amount of instruction comprehended by Deaf and hard of hearing students in comparison to their hearing peers (Harrington, 2000; Jacobs, 1977; Johnson, 1991; La Bue, 1998; Marschark, Sapere, Convertino, Seewagen, & Maltzen, 2004; Marschark, Sapere, Convertino, & Seewagen, 2005; Russell, 2006, 2008), as well as the roles, practices, and qualifications of educational interpreters (Hayes, 1992; Jones, 1993, 2004; Metzger & Fleetwood, 2004; Monikowski & Winston, 2003; Schick & Williams, 2004; Schick, Williams, & Bolster, 1999; Stewart & Kluwin, 1996; Stuckless, Avery, & Hurwitz, 1989; Taylor & Elliott, 1994) have been amply documented. Several researchers have expressed a specific concern about meeting the visual needs of Deaf and hard of hearing students in educational settings.

Although it is impossible for Deaf and hard of hearing students to watch the interpreter and attend simultaneously to other visual stimuli, Winston (1994, 2004) has noted that educational settings are riddled with practices that result in just such conflicting agendas. Seal (2004) cautions that interpreting during art demonstrations or computer work "poses another challenge for interpreters who must negotiate competing visual referents" (p. 94) and mentions that multiple factors will likely complicate interpreters' decisions when teachers show captioned video. Competing demands for visual attention exist when a Deaf or hard of hearing student needs to attend visually to a signed interpretation while also locating and/or viewing another source of visual input.

Classroom teachers depend on a multitude of visual aids (such as whiteboards, overhead transparencies, charts, and textbooks) and are accustomed to working with hearing students, who can look at visual input while simultaneously listening to instruction. Therefore, teachers typically keep talking while referring to other sources of important visual information, inadvertently creating difficulties for Deaf and hard of hearing students, who need to look at an interpreter to access classroom discourse. These students must have an opportunity to alternate between looking at other visual stimuli and attending visually to the interpreted communication.

The primacy (first in sequence rather than importance) of the visual nature of people who depend on sign language for communication is vital before even beginning to consider the semantic equivalence necessary for effective interpretation. Interpreters must undoubtedly be proficient in both sign language and English in order to produce an equivalent interpretation. However, if an interpretation is not accessible (visible for signed communication), it is without value. For this reason, it is critical to explore visual access first—even before getting into the complexities involved in language and interpretation. Deaf and hard of hearing students must look at the interpreter in order to have access to classroom discourse, yet their need to take in interpreted information through their eyes is in addition to the abundance of visual information that is already integral to public school contexts. Deaf and hard of hearing students must be provided with visual access to the multiple sources of input that are a critical component of the pathway to academic success for all students.

Interpreters working in educational contexts, perhaps more than those in any other context, have a professional obligation to remain cognizant of and respond appropriately to Deaf and hard of hearing students' need to access information visually. In mainstream classrooms, competing demands for visual attention inhibit Deaf and hard of hearing students' opportunity to access the same information as their hearing peers. Educational interpreters, as the primary gatekeepers of access, must recognize these competing visual demands and respond to the fundamental visual nature of Deaf and hard of hearing students.

It was not until about a decade ago that the first thorough discussion of best practices in educational interpreting was published (Seal, 1998). Winston (1994, 2004), Seal (2004), and Marschark et al. (2005) discuss the challenges that are associated with competing demands for Deaf and hard of hearing students' attention in interpreted classrooms. However, there is no research documenting specific strategies used by educational interpreters in response to this reality or discussing the factors that influence their decisions. It is important to deepen our understanding of what interpreters need to know in order to make the best decisions so that Deaf and hard of hearing students might have a better chance of participating in inclusive classsrooms.

Description of the Study

The remainder of this chapter presents a portion of a study Smith (2010) designed to expand existing knowledge about what interpreters do in K–12 settings and to explore the factors that inform their decisions on a moment-to-moment basis. For this study, three interpreters each working at a different school in California were videotaped on the job. One interpreter who participated in the study is a native signer with a graduate degree in education holding certificates of interpretation and transliteration (CI and CT, respectively) from the Registry of Interpreters for the Deaf (RID) and with more than 25 years of interpreting experience at the time of the study. Another interpreter holds an associate's degree in interpreting from a program that focused on interpreting in educational settings. She achieved a 4.2 on the Educational Interpreter Performance Assessment (EIPA), taken 3 months after data collection, and had 7 years of experience. The third interpreter holds a bachelor's degree in interpreting and had only 8 months of interpreting experience. She obtained a 3.0 on the Educational Sign Skills Evaluation (ESSE), taken 2 months after the data were collected. She subsequently obtained a 4.2 on the EIPA, taken 1 year after data collection. Within 2 months of data collection, all three met the then existing minimum standards of qualification for interpreting in K–12 settings in California.[1] Table 1 outlines the qualifications of all three interpreters. For the scope of this project, this chapter focuses on reporting the findings from a single science lesson that took place over the course of 2 days in a class interpreted by Camie (pseudonyms have been used for all participants and school sites).

Table 1. Participating Interpreter Qualifications

Interpreter	AJ	Camie	Marina
type of certification held	RID CI & CT	EIPA 3.7 in 6/03; 4.2 in 6/06	ESSE 3.0 in 6/06; EIPA 4.2 in 4/07
met CA standards of qualification	yes	yes	no (met 2 months after data collection)
educational degree	MA/Ed.S.	AA	BA
field of study	psych/education	general studies	interpreting
# of years signing	40	8	4
# of years interpreting	26	7	8 months
formal interpreter education	workshops and conferences	certificate from a 2-year online educational interpreting program with summer intensive onsite sessions	4-year BA program in interpreting

Live observation of these interpreters ranged from 1½ to 3 working days, and 39 total hours of video were recorded for analysis. In addition, video elicitation interviews were conducted with each of the interpreters. All of the interviews were transcribed for analysis. As these three interpreters watched video of themselves at work, they explained what was going on—shining a spotlight on the factors they took into account when making moment-to-moment decisions. Table 2 documents the quantity and type of data collection.

As an interpreter educator and a certified interpreter[2] with more than 25 years of experience, I closely and repeatedly examined the video of interpreters at work. I relied on interview data to draw my attention to frequently occurring patterns or to those phenomena that seemed unsettling to interpreters or about which they appeared particularly passionate. Two of the major themes that appeared in the data were related to Deaf and hard of hearing students' visual needs, as well as their readiness for the material (especially as compared to their peers) in terms of their language (sign language and English) and prior knowledge.

Findings of Smith's (2010) study confirm the prevalence of competing demands for Deaf and hard of hearing students' visual attention. For the purposes of the study, competing visual demands were coded as such whenever spoken discourse to be interpreted and some other competing visual stimulus occurred at the same time. For example, as long as a particular visual aid was either the focus of attention or remained in view as a relevant feature of continued discussion, it was characterized as present. Based on discussions with teacher educators, the assumption made is that whether or not a teacher is actively pointing to a visual referent, hearing students can and do look back and forth between the teacher and other visual input as long as it is available. In contrast, Deaf and hard of hearing students risk missing relevant aspects of the discus-

Table 2. Documentation of Data Collection: Video/Observation and Interviews

School Name, Site Description, and Grade Levels Served	Total Number of Interpreters Observed and Videotaped	Total Hours of Data Collection	
		Days and hours of classroom video/ observation	Hours of interpreter interviews
Via Portal urban K–6	1	1½ school days 8 hours	3½ hours
Meadowbrook rural K–8	1	3 school days 18 hours	6 hours
Azalea suburban K–6	1	2 school days 13 hours	2½ hours
Total	3	39 hours	12 hours

sion whenever they look away from the interpreter. Competing visual demands were both a visible and quantifiable feature of the data that were collected. For example, in an analysis of 9 hours and 54 minutes of recorded video, during which there was substantive classroom discourse to interpret (e.g., teacher and/or students talking as a class), there were at least 8 hours and 20 minutes (84%) of overlapping visual input. This percentage represents the measure reported by the rater with the lowest identified occurrence of competing visual demands. One reason for the discrepancy was that the raters watched a video of the interpreter in which the teacher was not always visible. The Deaf rater could not always tell that the teacher was speaking unless the interpreter was signing; therefore, the Deaf rater identified a slightly lower prevalence of competing sources of visual input (but the overall interrater reliability was high). Figure 1 lists the types of activities during which Deaf or hard of hearing students were expected to watch the interpreter for the signed interpretation of spoken discourse while other visual information was being presented.

The following description of the findings is extremely detailed in order to begin the arduous task of documenting what K–12 interpreters are doing and considering in the course of their work. The difficulty of the writing task—describing each response separately when, in fact, responses shift frequently because of the overlapping nature of the factors affecting interpreters' decisions and because each decision results in a new set of factors to be considered—reflects the complexity of interpreters' moment-to-moment decision-making processes.

The interpreters in the study employed multiple strategies in their efforts to optimize Deaf and hard of hearing students' access to various sources of visual input. In spite of their best efforts, they recognized that equivalent access was not being provided and struggled to make the most of a less than ideal situation.[3]

Sources of Competing Visual Input

A. locating materials such as a particular page of text, paper, pencil, or hand-outs

B. looking at visual aids such as maps, charts, number lines, bulletin boards, props, computer-based graphics or presentations, video (without captioning), overhead transparencies, facial expressions, and/or gestures

C. reading printed information such as in handouts, textbooks, captioned video, computer-based text, or PowerPoint presentations

D. generating written information such as completing a worksheet, correcting written responses, and/or taking notes

E. participating in a hands-on activity either individually or in groups

---

Figure 1. Sources of competing visual input.

Four of these strategies and the implications of the findings are the focus of this chapter. They were both the most obvious and the most prevalent techniques that the interpreters employed in this study, and they provide a means for examining in more detail the complexity of dealing with competing visual demands in K–12 classrooms. While these four strategies are not new discoveries, previous research has not included observation and description of these techniques as they were employed in actual K–12 classrooms by educational interpreters at work. Moreover, in other studies, educational interpreters have not been interviewed to determine what factors influence their decisions. Data from both classroom video and interpreter interviews are presented as evidence of the multitude of variables and the interweaving of contextual and participant-related factors that make educational interpreting such an inherently complex task.

Techniques for Responding to the Presence of Competing Visual Demands

The four primary techniques used by K–12 interpreters when responding to the presence of competing visual demands identified in the Smith (2010) study are the following: (1) adjusting physical position in the classroom, (2) directing students' attention, (3) adjusting the timing of the interpretation, and (4) modifying the interpretation itself. While these four particular courses of action were both prevalent and obvious, it is important to note that they were not the only strategies used during this study and that interpreters likely utilize additional ones when encountering competing demands for Deaf and hard of hearing students' visual attention. Therefore, the techniques discussed here are not meant to be an exhaustive list. Although this study just begins to scratch the surface of examining what educational interpreters do when confronted with the reality of multiple sources of visual input, the findings provide new insights into the complexities and challenges involved in optimizing Deaf and hard of hearing students' access to visual information.

Visual access is fundamental to the ability of these students to reach their greatest academic potential in educational contexts and is therefore critical for educational interpreters to choreograph effectively and wisely. It is also important to note that although the findings of this study are organized by technique and described separately as distinct responses to the presence of competing visual demands, in fact, the responses are inherently intertwined. While each action is in itself important, chosen responses are highly interdependent and overlapping. Inevitably, the success of one course of action is either facilitated or impeded by the implementation (or lack thereof) of another, and additional responses are often necessary because of the strategies chosen. It is because of the variability of conditions and interrelatedness of factors that the roles, responsibilities, and tasks of interpreting have heretofore been difficult to pin down.

Although the four strategies highlighted in this chapter are not unique to educational interpreting, they are complicated by the educational context. Before examining these strategies, an overview of each of these four techniques and the norms associated with each is warranted. First, in order to be most clearly seen, interpreters often adjust their physical position. They typically position themselves close to the primary speaker, adjusting as needed to create optimal sight lines. In educational settings, the interpreter usually sits between the teacher and the Deaf or hard of hearing student. Ideally, interpreters will be in the same line of sight as both the teacher and other visual input (such as a whiteboard). Deaf and hard of hearing students can then see what they need to see by either looking over the interpreter's head or just to the side of the interpreter. The assumption, although arguable and not yet proven, is that while students are looking at the interpreter when the teacher is talking, they can also see the teacher's facial expressions, gestures, and body language either with their peripheral vision or an occasional glance.

Directing visual attention is a second strategy commonly used by interpreters to ensure that Deaf and hard of hearing participants know to look at salient visual information. Interpreters frequently point to things and people that a Deaf or hard of hearing participant needs to see. Similarly, educational interpreters typically point to a student or teacher so that Deaf and hard of hearing students can identify who is speaking.

A third strategy used by interpreters in all settings is adjusting the timing of the interpretation. When interpreters choose to point out salient visual input, they must then wait for Deaf and hard of hearing participants to reestablish eye contact before resuming their interpretation. Because of the time it takes for interpreters to direct students' attention to visual input, as well as the time it takes for both the student and the interpreter to visually process the information, educational interpreters must frequently wait to interpret classroom discourse. If the reference is relatively brief and simple, such as signifying that a different person is now speaking, the corresponding timing delay will be brief, and interpreters will simply pause momentarily so that students can see who is talking. If, however, the visual input is more complex or prolonged, the timing delay will increase. The findings of this study show that there is a preponderance of references to salient visual input that requires sustained attention in K–12 classrooms.

A fourth strategy interpreters use to provide access to visual input is modifying the interpretation in some way, such as adding information to clarify (Metzger, 1999;

Metzger & Fleetwood, 2004). For example, if a teacher calls on a student by pointing at him rather than calling on him by name and the interpreter *knows* the name of the student, a statement may be added to the interpretation of the student response, such as "Patrick says . . ." When interpreters do *not* know the name of the speaker, they may add a physical description to their interpretation, such as "the boy in the pink T-shirt," so that the Deaf student can more easily locate and identify who is speaking. Interpreters may also reduce or compress the information in some way, such as by delivering a summarized version or even deliberately omitting information as a conscious strategy (Napier, 2003, 2004, 2005).

Strategies such as adjusting physical position, directing student attention, adjusting the timing of the interpretation, and/or modifying the interpretation itself are certainly familiar to interpreters. However, the following findings deepen our knowledge about what interpreters must do to optimize Deaf and hard of hearing students' visual access. Through this discussion, we can begin to illuminate the intricate choreography of responses based on the infinite number of contextual and human factors that potentially influence interpreters' moment-to-moment decisions.

Again, although discussing these strategies as separate processes is an artificial distinction, it serves to focus our attention on what interpreters do and why. Educational interpreters employ multiple strategies simultaneously, wherein the use of particular techniques in combination is intricately interwoven, context specific, and highly individualized. The findings presented in this chapter show that educational interpreters apply multiple, simultaneous, and interdependent strategies, providing evidence of the striking complexities involved in responding to the presence of competing demands for Deaf and hard of hearing students' visual attention.

SCIENCE LESSON: VOLCANOES

The following scenario describes what happened during a science lesson in Mr. Harrison's sixth-grade classroom over the course of 2 days (approximately 30 minutes each day, totaling 1 hour of video data). During a science lesson about volcanoes, the students took turns reading aloud from the textbook (one textbook for every two students) while each student completed a directed reading worksheet (DRW) to answer questions based on what they had read. An engaging use of visual aids created competing visual demands for Emily, a Deaf student mainstreamed in Mr. Harrison's classroom. The scenario highlights what Camie, the interpreter, did in response to Emily's need to access multiple sources of visual input (e.g., see and look at visual stimuli).

Science Lesson: Volcanoes, Day One

When Mr. Harrison called on Olivia to read at "when tectonic plates collide," Camie signed to Emily to begin reading at the top of page 203, turning her own book toward Emily to show her exactly where to begin. While Olivia read, Camie did not interpret. However, when Mr. Harrison sat down at the desk between Emily and Camie and began talking as he conducted an experiment described in the book (i.e., pushing two pieces of paper together to see what would happen), Camie got up from her seat and walked a few feet to her left, standing while interpreting Mr. Harrison's commentary during the demonstration. As students subsequently stood to read aloud, Camie made sure Emily knew where to read, giving descriptive instructions like "second paragraph under 'predicting eruptions'"; however, she did not interpret the text as it was read aloud. Whenever Mr. Harrison elaborated on a section of text, Camie waved to get Emily's attention and interpreted his explanation.

As the lesson progressed, Mr. Harrison used a laser pointer to indicate geological formations at specific locations on a world map displayed on the back wall of the classroom, describing how the movement of oceanic plates will eventually result in the creation of new volcanoes. The students, including Emily, had to turn around to see where he was pointing. Although the hearing students could hear Mr. Harrison's explanation while looking at the locations as they were pointed out on the map behind them, Emily could not see the interpreter while looking at the map. Camie pointed to the map at the back of the room and waited to interpret until Emily looked back at her again. By the time Emily turned back around to see the interpreter, Mr. Harrison was pointing out another location on the map behind her. At one point, Camie pointed to the back of the room for Emily to look, but by the time Emily did so, Mr. Harrison had turned off the laser pointer. Sometimes, instead of pointing and waiting, Camie incorporated the name of the specific location and signed it in a space consistent with an imaginary map in front of her. For example, as Mr. Harrison pointed out the "ring of fire," North America, South America, the northern and southern parts of Africa, Camie signed them in a space corresponding to their actual relative positions.

Further into the lesson, Mr. Harrison said, "Hawaii just looks like a little island like this," and asked the students to look at his hands. Camie pointed to him, but as he kept his hands in one position while talking about what was happening under the surface of the water, she then incorporated his gesture into her own interpretation. Immediately after using his hands to describe a shield volcano in Hawaii, Mr. Harrison said, "Now, here's the weird thing. And I think I'd rather you look there instead of the book." As he spoke, he again shone his laser pointer at the map. At that point, Camie walked to the back of the room. She did not sign while she walked but continued to listen to Mr. Harrison. Once Camie was standing next to the map in a position where she was not blocking any of the students' view, she began interpreting and delivered a condensed version of most of Mr. Harrison's comments about the map thus far, occasionally looking behind her at the map to see what he was pointing out. Because she could not easily see where Mr. Harrison was pointing or point to the map without turning around herself, she tried to find a better position and moved to her right, closer to the center of the map. In this position, Camie was blocking some of the students' view of the map, and she was in the path of Mr. Harrison's laser beam. Camie quickly moved to her left (back to her previous position) to get out of the way. After interpreting a sentence or two, Camie walked all the way over to the left side of the map, hugging the bookcase next to the map so she would not block anyone's view.

When Mr. Harrison wrapped up his discussion in reference to the map, Camie returned to her seat in time to cue Emily where to resume reading. In a few minutes, Mr. Harrison again used his hands to indicate how tilt meters measure the steepness of slopes to predict volcanic eruptions. Camie waved to get Emily's attention before she began interpreting his comments, then alternated between pointing and waiting to interpret, looking at Mr. Harrison's gestures and incorporating them into the interpretation, or using a combination of both strategies.

Science Lesson: Volcanoes, Day Two

On the following day, Mr. Harrison decided to go through the DRWs with the class. Camie spent 44 seconds getting a copy of the DRW packet for her own reference as Mr. Harrison tried to solicit and clarify a student's answer to number one. Camie returned to her seat just in time to interpret his comments about the first DRW question and response (not the clarification discussion). Except for the laser pointer, all of the sources of visual input from the previous day were observed, but there were two additional ones for Camie to address. Again, all of the students had their textbooks and their DRW packets, and Mr. Harrison continued to engage the students with a multitude of visual aids. On this particular day, he used a busy whiteboard to draw pictures, used his hands (even in interaction with his drawing) to demonstrate geological formations and characteristics, and used a paper and pen as a three-dimensional model of specific geological phenomena. In addition, Emily (as always) needed to watch the interpreter almost constantly to access the stream of spoken discourse generated by her teacher and peers.

When Mr. Harrison was asked why lava wouldn't clog up the volcano in Hawaii since lava hardens when it reaches water, he decided to draw a picture to illustrate. Camie followed him to the whiteboard but walked past him so that Mr. Harrison stood to the left of the picture being drawn, and Camie stood to the right. Camie could then see what Mr. Harrison was drawing and which part of the drawing he was pointing to. When it was most relevant to the interpretation, Camie now and then pointed directly at the drawing. Camie also asked Emily whether she could see. When Emily nodded, Camie continued interpreting. As Mr. Harrison drew a second picture close to the left side of the whiteboard, Camie looked to her left (away from the drawing) and determined that moving closer to Mr. Harrison would put her in a position that would block several students' view of the drawing, so she stayed where she was, incorporating features of the drawing and Mr. Harrison's gestures (when she saw them) into her interpretation.

Once Mr. Harrison and Camie had returned to their seats, Mr. Harrison picked up a piece of paper and a pen to create a three-dimensional representation of the geological phenomenon he was discussing. Camie responded by standing up and moving closer to Mr. Harrison so that Emily could see both the interpretation and the demonstration. As he manipulated the paper and pen to demonstrate how oceanic plates move over a magma plume, he rotated his shoulders slightly away from Camie. In order to see his demonstration herself, she stepped and leaned forward, using what she saw to aid in her own comprehension and corresponding interpretation.

On one section of their DRWs, the students were to match definitions with vocabulary words. Mr. Harrison went fairly quickly, reading each definition aloud, asking students for the corresponding letter, then reading or repeating the word. Throughout this section, any additional comments were always interpreted, as were the numbers and their correct answers. The definitions and the words themselves were sometimes interpreted. For example, when Mr. Harrison said, "Sixteen. What's the main product of a nonexplosive eruption?" Camie signed only, "Sixteen. What's sixteen?"

Camie prompted Emily to raise her hand if she knew the answer to the question. When Emily raised her hand, Mr. Harrison had already called on Hunter, who gave the correct answer. Camie looked at Emily and Mr. Harrison, snapping her fingers as if to say, "Shoot!" Camie then looked back at Emily, signed that Hunter had already given the answer and prompted Emily to look at the next question. In this instance and in several subsequent examples, Camie was actually prompting Emily to jump the gun and look ahead at her answer to the next question. Then Mr. Harrison read the next definition and called on a student, who gave an incorrect answer. Camie did not interpret what either Mr. Harrison or the student said. Instead, she signed, "Do you know? Do you know? Raise your hand." Emily did, just as the other student gave the wrong answer. Camie told Emily to wait, then at the right time, to raise her hand. He repeated the question, "What's magma after it's been exploded out?" He then called on Emily, who gave the correct answer, "pyroclastic material."

Sometimes Emily signed her answers as she raised her hand, and Camie included in her interpretation whether Emily's answers were correct or not and even praised her for correct answers. For example, when Mr. Harrison said that an answer was "false," as Emily simultaneously signed FALSE, Mr. Harrison said that answer was "false." Camie interpreted that the correct answer was "false" and then gave a thumbs up to Emily.

The four primary strategies Camie used in response to the presence of competing demands for Emily's visual attention that are highlighted in the following discussion are adjusting physical position, directing visual attention, adjusting the timing of the interpretation, and modifying the interpretation.

ADJUSTING PHYSICAL POSITION

In this scenario, when Mr. Harrison sat at a vacant student desk at the front of the classroom to demonstrate what happens when tectonic plates collide, he obstructed the sight line between Camie and Emily. Camie immediately stood up and moved to Mr. Harrison's left so that Emily could see what her teacher was demonstrating and also see Camie (over Mr. Harrison's shoulder) as she interpreted. A few minutes later, it was Mr. Harrison's use of a laser pointer that created a need for Camie to make a more complicated decision about how to optimize Emily's visual access. Without the laser pointer, Mr. Harrison would have had to walk across the room in order to point out specific locations on the map. Rather than having to make the decision herself about whether to stay where she was or move closer to the map, Camie would have simply followed him. However, Mr. Harrison's use of the pointer meant that Camie needed to predict how sustained or repeated the reference to the map would be. If it were a fleeting or even gratuitous use of the laser pointer, then choosing to stay where she was made sense. Another factor that came into play was the fact that the back of the room provided limited space. In this case, she initially chose to stay. She stayed in this position for several minutes, pointing to the map and incorporating Mr. Harrison's geographical references into the interpretation.

In contrast, when he specified that he wanted students to look at the map on the back wall rather than their books, Camie waited for a moment and listened, then chose to move closer to the map and leave Mr. Harrison behind. In so doing, the potentially important extralinguistic information in Mr. Harrison's facial expressions and gestures would no longer be visually accessible to Emily. However, Camie decided that the map was more important for Emily to see, perhaps at least in part because of Mr. Harrison's explicit statement of preference for the students to look at the map on the back wall.

When Camie walked to the back of the room (which took 7 seconds), she stopped in front of the right side of the map and turned back toward Emily to interpret. In this position, Emily could see both the interpretation and where Mr. Harrison was pointing (around the Hawaiian Islands) with his laser beam without having to turn around. Now, however, Camie had to turn around to see what Mr. Harrison was pointing out behind her, and Emily still had to look back and forth between the left side of the map and Camie (on the right side of the map). To find a better location from which to interpret, Camie moved farther to her right (closer to the center of the map), but in so doing she blocked some of the students' view of the map. Moreover, she obstructed Mr. Harrison's laser beam. She danced a little bit to the right and left, trying to quickly get out of the way and find a place where she was not blocking any of the students' view or Mr. Harrison's laser and where Emily could see the interpretation and the map at the same time without having to look back and forth. After interpreting a sentence or two in this position (still unable to easily see the map herself), Camie walked to the far left side of the map. Because there were built-in bookcases on the left side of the map and shelves in front of and below the map, finding a place to stand that would not block anyone's view required Camie to stand very close to the bookcase to the left of the map. However, standing in this position on the far left side afforded Camie, Mr. Harrison, Emily, and all of the other students an unobstructed view of the map. Less than a minute later, Mr. Harrison wrapped up his discussion of the map, and Camie returned to her seat in time to interpret as Mr. Harrison called on another student to read aloud and reminded students to read along, starting at "Predicting Volcanic Eruptions."

As Mr. Harrison began going through the DRWs with his students during science class the second day, Camie did not have to adjust her physical position for almost 15 minutes. She moved for the first time during this lesson when Mr. Harrison decided to respond to a student's question by drawing a picture on the whiteboard. After following him to the board, Camie stood on the opposite side of the drawing as Mr. Harrison, where she could see and point directly to specific parts of the drawing or the drawing as a whole. Camie even asked Emily directly whether she could see, making sure Emily's visual needs were met. Camie's physical position allowed Emily to see the drawing, the interpretation, and Mr. Harrison all at once. It also allowed Camie to see and point to specific features of the drawing.

However, when Mr. Harrison decided to draw a second picture, additional factors came into play. Because there was already a chart on the board just to the left of where he had drawn the first picture (near the center of the board), Mr. Harrison drew the second picture to the left of the chart (on the far left side of the board). Rather than immediately moving to a more optimal position closer to the second drawing, Camie looked to her left and determined that if she moved, she would obstruct some of the students' view, so she chose to remain in place.

After Mr. Harrison returned to his seat at the podium and Camie to her seat, a student asked another question, which prompted Mr. Harrison to return to the board. Seeing him approach, Camie leaned back to let him pass, then followed him to the board, passing him as he stopped to reflect on his first drawing. She returned to a standing position on the right side of the picture and interpreted from there until he returned to the podium.

Of necessity, Camie had to move again when Mr. Harrison began using a piece of paper and a pen to create a three-dimensional model to demonstrate how oceanic plates move slowly over magma plumes. Emily needed to see his demonstration, so Camie stood up and moved closer to Mr. Harrison. As he manipulated the paper and pen to demonstrate the movement of the plates, he rotated his shoulders slightly away from Camie. As a result, Camie needed to step and lean forward to see the model herself, aiding in her own comprehension and corresponding interpretation.

In this study, part of what governed the interpreters' decisions about where to stand or sit was the degree to which they saw themselves imposing upon the speaker's personal space and/or disrupting the rest of the students in the class. All of the interpreters in this study expressed a concern about unnecessarily interrupting the typical flow of classroom discourse. They held a comparably high regard for allowing Deaf and hard of hearing students to maintain momentum rather than interrupting them and getting their attention to interpret every single sound or spoken word. Moreover, as is apparent in this study, physical space may also present numerous variables that affect interpreters' decisions about whether, when, and where to move. The physical construction of the classroom, location of shelving, and number and arrangement of desks necessary to accommodate the class size made it more difficult for Camie to secure an optimal position from which to interpret. Securing a position that maintained clear sight lines for everyone—Emily, Camie, Mr. Harrison, and all of the hearing students—proved to be problematic. Furthermore, one thing that often complicates the issue of the interpreters' physical position in classrooms is that they are sharing what has traditionally been regarded as the teachers' space. Therefore, a comfortable rapport and solid professional relationship between teachers and interpreters is critical.

The importance of this professional relationship and shared space was evident in comments made by AJ, another interpreter in this study, when she explained what conditions would have to be in place in order for her to approach the teacher and point directly to the board. She said that she would have to be a regular classroom interpreter (when, in fact, in this study she was working as a substitute interpreter) and indicated that she would need to have a history and a good working relationship with the teacher. She elaborated: "I would have to feel like this teacher *really is* invested in the Deaf student's education. Because if they are not, [having someone up there pointing at their stuff] could really be annoying." She went on to emphasize the point that some teachers are less than comfortable with the thought of having an interpreter, another adult, on their turf.

During the interviews, Mr. Harrison and Camie both stated that they had a good professional relationship. Each felt that the other was supportive and helpful and that they worked as a team to figure out how to best meet Emily's needs. Camie said she felt comfortable sharing the space with Mr. Harrison. By asking Camie questions about what she needed in order to do her job well and by responding to those needs, Mr. Harrison created an environment in which Camie felt free to make decisions that she deemed appropriate. He also provided a desk for Camie to store her own copy of class resources and materials, as well as a few personal items. He reported being comfortable working with Camie and stressed that he valued her professionalism and her input about how to work more effectively with Emily. As a result of the excellent working relationship and mutual respect between Camie and Mr. Harrison, Camie was able to do as she saw fit in order to meet Emily's needs, even standing right next to Mr. Harrison at his podium and sharing the paper he was using to dictate sentences during language arts. Camie felt at ease moving wherever she needed to be in order to optimize Emily's visual access because Mr. Harrison respected Camie's knowledge and expertise regarding how to best meet Emily's learning needs. Rather than being concerned about bothering Mr. Harrison or interfering with the class, Camie was able to move to the right place at the right time, maximizing her physical position in order to afford Emily the greatest opportunity for academic success.

In summary, during this science lesson about volcanoes and other geological phenomena, Camie had to change her physical position several times in order to optimize Emily's visual access. Each change in physical position involved a complex set of judgments on Camie's part. She had to predict where she would most need to be and to prioritize one source of visual input over another. Moreover, she had to identify the available options and make sure that her chosen position did not block anyone else's view of salient visual information. Particular courses of action had to be selected as quickly as possible. Camie not only had to balance all of these concerns but also attend to the ongoing stream of spoken instruction, which she might subsequently need to interpret. Because a good working relationship with Mr. Harrison had been developed, Camie could choose the physical location that would provide the most benefit to Emily. It is important to emphasize that however complicated this situation was, it was simplified somewhat by Camie's ability to work collaboratively with Mr. Harrison. If she had not had such a good working relationship with the teacher, there would have been an additional layer of concerns to consider. Discerning an appropriate physical position is not as simple as choosing whether and where to stand or sit. Educational interpreters must consider and be prepared to handle a complex array of factors in order to optimize Deaf and hard of hearing students' access and alleviate the competing demands for their visual attention.

DIRECTING STUDENT ATTENTION

Camie's decisions about optimizing Emily's visual access and alleviating the competing visual demands for her attention depended on, but required more than, moving closer. Instead of operating under the assumption that Emily could see what she needed to see on the map (or at the board) as long as Camie was close enough to the primary source of visual input, she also showed Emily exactly where to look. The two techniques she used to direct Emily's attention were pointing at the visual stimulus and taking a moment to look at it herself, the latter while keeping her hands down and in a neutral position.

As the lesson began, Mr. Harrison asked Olivia to read at "When tectonic plates collide . . ." Camie signed to begin reading at the top of page 203, then turned her own book around and pointed to the exact spot on the page, holding the book facing Emily until Emily nodded. Having directed Emily's attention to the right place in the book, Camie kept her hands down and read along in her own book. By choosing not to interpret, Camie eliminated one potential source of visual input—the interpretation—allowing and prompting Emily to read from the book as her classmates were reading.

Similarly, once Camie had decided to walk to the back of the room rather than perpetuating the competing demand for Emily's visual attention by continuing to interpret, the fact that Camie did not sign essentially directed Emily's focus to the remaining source of visual input, the map. Although Camie positioned herself next to the map, she could not easily see where Mr. Harrison was pointing, nor could she herself point to specific locations on the map when it was relevant to the part of instruction she was interpreting at the time. Although a bit awkward, her final position at the left side of the map proved to be the most effective not only because everyone could see the map but also because Emily could then see both the map and the interpretation. Her height also provided an advantage over a shorter interpreter in that Camie was tall enough so that Emily could see her over the other students' heads as long as her classmates remained seated. In addition, having moved closer to the map, Camie could then point directly at it—even touching it to direct Emily's attention to very specific locations.

Examples of how directing student attention is affected by the physical position of the interpreter—in relation to not only the students but also the location of other sources of visual input—are apparent in this study. When Camie was close enough to both the teacher and another source of visual input for Emily to see both clearly and easily, and when sight lines between Camie and Emily were also clear, Camie used another technique besides pointing. For example, when Mr. Harrison used his hands to represent Hawaii and when he picked up a pen and paper to create a three-dimensional model to illustrate the movement of oceanic plates, Camie stopped signing and watched Mr. Harrison's demonstration, thereby alleviating the competing visual demand and directing Emily's attention to the right place. At the whiteboard, Camie's physical proximity and position were instrumental in enabling her to direct Emily's visual attention to Mr. Harrison's drawing. By standing on the opposite side of the drawing as Mr. Harrison, she had an unobstructed view of the board, and she was again able to look at and/or point directly to the relevant part of the picture in order to direct Emily's attention to the right place. Had she been standing behind him, her position would have been problematic. He would have become a barrier between Camie and the drawing, preventing her from seeing it clearly herself and using it as a resource (both to aid in comprehension and as a physical prop) for her interpretation. Whether or not she deliberately made the decision to stand to the right of the drawing, Camie was optimally positioned for directing Emily's attention to whatever Camie felt Emily needed to see.

In summary, educational interpreters direct Deaf and hard of hearing students' attention so that these students do not have to divide their focus between the almost perpetual sources of competing visual input in classrooms. Courses of action selected by K–12 interpreters to optimize Deaf and hard of hearing students' visual access are not chosen in isolation, and numerous contextual and student-related realities significantly inform their decisions. So, in addition to making sure she was in a good physical position since it could either enhance or inhibit her ability to direct Emily's visual attention, Camie further alleviated numerous competing demands for Emily's visual attention by explicitly showing her where to look. Furthermore, she had to predict what visual input was important enough for Emily to see, decide whether to point and/or look at it, and/or lower her hands in order to direct Emily's attention to the right place. What K–12 interpreters do depends on a variety of intertwined environmental, academic, and interrelational factors relevant to meeting Deaf and hard of hearing students' needs, each one in turn affecting subsequent decisions by interpreters, who are endeavoring to assess and respond to the needs of students and teachers. Looking at what interpreters do through the lens of competing visual demands for Deaf and hard of hearing students' attention sheds light on one critical aspect of why educational interpreters do what they do in the classroom. It is, in fact, *because* of their efforts to alleviate competing visual demands that interpreters decide when, where, and how to move around the classroom, stand or sit, and explicitly direct Deaf and hard of hearing students' attention to essential visual input. To complicate matters further, K–12 interpreters consider the needs and goals not only of Deaf and hard of hearing students but also of the other students in the classroom, as well as the needs of teachers and other support staff.

ADJUSTING TIMING OF INTERPRETATION

Further evidence of the complexity of interpreters' decision-making processes and the intertwined nature of the factors they consider is evident in the frequent timing delays during an interpreted lesson. Delays are inherent to all interpretations simply because of the time it takes an interpreter to take in the information, decide how to convey the meaning in the target language, and then deliver the interpretation. In addition, school settings are riddled with situations that result in numerous brief interruptions in Deaf and hard of hearing students' ability to concentrate on interpretations because they cannot look at two different places at the same time. For example, they may look away to find and pick up a dropped pencil, to turn to a specified page of text, or to glance (or stare) at a classmate. Given the active and crowded nature of a typical classroom context, these kinds of interruptions are quite common. At times, interpreters can simply wait to interpret until the Deaf and hard of hearing students have time to pick up a dropped pencil, find a particular page in a book, or look to see which of their classmates is speaking. However, they must weigh several factors when making decisions about timing. For example, they must decide how much time is available for students to look at something in comparison to its relative importance to the task at hand and to get the knowledge they will need to successfully participate in visually rich and highly interactive school classrooms. In considering how to ensure that Deaf and hard of hearing students can see salient visual information, interpreters must first determine how long a particular source of visual input will be available. For visual references that are temporary rather than permanent, educational interpreters rely on an additional constellation of factors to decide how to optimize students' visual access.

During the scope of 1 hour of a two-part science lesson on volcanoes, Mr. Harrison capitalized on the use of various visual aids, some of which were permanent (such as the map, printed worksheets, and textbooks) and others that were used only briefly. When he told the students to begin reading at "When tectonic plates collide," there was no doubt that the printed words on the specified page would still be there a few seconds later. Camie was therefore able to point out the particular page of text, holding her own book up until Emily indicated that she had found the right place in the text and was ready to read.

By contrast, Mr. Harrison's swift use of his hands as a physical representation of Hawaii (above and below the surface of the water) and to describe how tilt meters work were short-term sources of visual input. Similarly, his paper-and-pen demonstration of how oceanic plates move over magma plumes was temporary rather than permanent. In other words, Mr. Harrison could have put the paper and pen down or moved on to something else at any time. Since Camie could not predict how long the model would be visible (unlike a specified page of text), she immediately directed Emily's attention to the demonstration as it was taking place. In this instance, Camie adjusted the timing of the interpretation by changing the sequence of presentation. Therefore, Emily could first take in the visual demonstration and then focus on the corresponding interpretation. By doing so, Camie optimized Emily's access to the visual input over which Camie had less control—Mr. Harrison's demonstration—while it was visible.

Having decided the information was important enough for Emily to see and having directed her attention to the demonstration, Camie then had to delay the interpretation long enough for Emily to watch the demonstration. While it may seem like a simple enough judgment, a number of different considerations are at play in this situation. Camie had to predict how long Emily would need to look at the model and decide when to interpret the explanation that was meant to accompany that part of the demonstration; she also had to take in the visual information herself and be prepared to quickly redirect Emily's visual attention if necessary.

Once Camie decided to resume the interpretation pertinent to the demonstration, she raised her hands to a clasped position and looked back toward Emily; however, she then had to wait for Emily to reestablish eye contact before again beginning to interpret. Camie's lifting her hands signaled that she herself had looked at the visual demonstration long enough and was again ready to interpret. Lifting her hands to a different position seemed to serve as enough of a cue for Emily to reestablish eye contact with Camie and indicate readiness for more information. However, sometimes Emily continued watching a demonstration or looking at something other than the interpreter. When she did so, Camie chose either to wait until Emily reestablished eye contact or to wave to get Emily's attention, thereby directing Emily's visual attention back to the interpretation itself. If Mr. Harrison had made a clarification of an earlier point or elaborated on some piece of pertinent information (e.g., "an understanding of this will help you on the test tomorrow"), Camie would most likely interrupt Emily's visual observation by waving to get her attention, interpret the pertinent information, then allow Emily an opportunity to look again with this newly acquired piece of information. If Mr. Harrison was moving on, once Camie felt she had enough relevant information and would not be able to retain it unless she began interpreting, she would also wave to redirect Emily's visual attention back to the interpretation.

Interpreters in this study all reported a reluctance to interfere with Deaf and hard of hearing students' right to look at something or to work on something that required their visual attention (e.g., looking at a graphic or completing a worksheet). They frequently made decisions about when precedence should be given to other sources of visual input over the interpretation of spoken discourse and vice versa.

The timing of the interpretation was less of an issue when Mr. Harrison decided to draw on the whiteboard. Since his explanations were not as rapid or detailed as some of his other instruction (perhaps because he was also focused on drawing and/or thinking), Camie had ample time to interpret. Also, in her position to the right of the drawing and opposite Mr. Harrison, as when standing to the left of the map, she could point to the picture when it was most relevant to the interpretation. Both of these strategies used in conjunction afforded Emily an opportunity to look at the drawing and take in the accompanying interpretation.

The map, although a permanent fixture, became problematic in terms of timing because of the temporal nature of laser pointers (or any other technique instructors use to point out particular objects, words, locations, etc.). Several factors complicated Camie's decision of whether to adjust her physical position, direct Emily's visual attention by pointing, or adjust the timing of the interpretation. One factor was the difficulty of predicting how long Mr. Harrison would leave the pointer in place. A second factor was the difficulty of directing Emily's visual attention (showing Emily where to look and when) because of Camie's physical position in relation to Emily and the map. A third complicating factor was the lack of available space. The relative physical positions of Camie, Emily and her classmates, Mr. Harrison, and the map further complicated the decision-making process.

Whereas Camie could easily point to a student and wait long enough for Emily to see who was speaking before interpreting, she could not rely on the point-and-wait technique for Mr. Harrison's discussion with regard to the map. Camie could not predict how long Mr. Harrison would point at a particular geographic location, and in all probability he would not keep the laser beam in place long enough for Camie to interpret before directing Emily's attention to the map. Therefore, instead of interpreting what Mr. Harrison said and then pointing, Camie initially tried to point so Emily could first look to see where he was pointing, and then she interpreted what he was saying about that location, adjusting the timing of the interpretation by changing the sequence of presentation. Although this technique worked to some degree, it soon proved to be inadequate. In one instance, Camie pointed to the back of the room, but by the time Emily turned around to look, Mr. Harrison had turned off the laser. When Emily looked back at the interpreter, Camie signed a brief explanation with an apologetic expression that he had turned it off before she again began to interpret. In this situation, the technique of pointing (directing student attention) and waiting (adjusting the timing of the interpretation) did not work at least in part, because Camie could not predict how long Mr. Harrison would leave the laser in place.

Moreover, because of where Emily and Camie were in relation to the map, it was difficult for Camie to direct Emily's attention to the right place at the right time. Emily could not see the map and Camie without looking back and forth (in front of and behind her). As a result, Emily often did not look in the direction that would have been the most helpful. Camie could not effectively direct Emily's visual attention until she walked to the back of the room and took up a position next to the map, where both she and Emily could easily see where Mr. Harrison was pointing. Each of these factors and Camie's chosen actions resulted in concomitant timing delays. Although some timing delays were deliberate, such as changing the sequence of presentation and waiting for Emily to look at something, others were a result of the particular combination of variables affecting that interaction. Several delays were a result of the time it took for Camie to decide on a particular strategy. Even more delays resulted because of where Emily herself chose to look at any given moment.

In addition to making decisions about physical placement and directing students' attention, the need for timing adjustments adds yet a third layer of complexity to interpreters' nearly constant challenge of alleviating the competing visual demands for Deaf and hard of hearing students' attention. Since teachers are accustomed to a style of classroom discourse in which it is acceptable and even desirable for them to speak while referring to visual input, these findings show that K–12 interpreters often intentionally delay the interpretation. Because simply being close to a source of visual input and showing Deaf and hard of hearing students exactly where to look would not sufficiently alleviate competing visual demands, interpreters must also afford students the time to look by deliberately adjusting the timing of their interpretations. These adjustments then require another series of decisions and actions—predicting how long a student will need to look at sources of visual input, waiting for the student to look back, identifying and remembering significant instructional points, and constructing and delivering a modified interpretation. Accurate predictions about how to optimize visual access for Deaf and hard of hearing students likely further complicate interpreters' decisions. Additionally, interpreters must determine what information is most important and the order in which it must be accessed. Furthermore, they must decide when respecting Deaf and hard of hearing students' need to look at salient visual input is trumped by a greater and more immediate need for some even more important information that also requires their visual attention. Moreover, it is important to understand that the length of time needed for Deaf and hard of hearing students to take in information visually varies according to the individual. Interpreters must be prepared either to meet students' individual needs by waiting as long as necessary for students to attend visually or to select a different course of action. Moreover, interpreters may need some time to assess the situation and make a decision. All of these delays are in addition to the delay already inherent to the process of message analysis, which is essential for effective and accurate interpretation. Furthermore, as both references to visual information and corresponding timing delays accumulate, educational interpreters' decisions become more complex and require additional skills in order to alleviate competing visual demands for Deaf and hard of hearing students' attention.

MODIFYING THE INTERPRETATION

Although it is critical for educational interpreters to adjust their physical position, direct students' attention, and adjust the timing of their interpretation, none of these strategies provides adequate means of ensuring that Deaf and hard of hearing students have sufficient opportunity to attend to all of the salient visual input. In fact, even when used in conjunction, all of these strategies still fail to provide a fully accessible environment when considering a single reality—the competing demands for Deaf and hard of hearing students' visual attention. Although these three techniques were valuable and necessary, Camie recognized (whether consciously or not) that further action was imperative. The fourth strategy that she used to optimize Emily's visual access was to modify the content of the interpretation.

Modifying the interpretation refers to either augmenting or reducing the content of the interpretation. Relatively simple, yet crucial, modifications of the interpretation occurred in this study when a teacher used referents such as "this," "that," "here," "there," "these," and "those" and expected the students to look at a visual aid. Modifying the interpretation can mean clarifying the information. It can also include strategies such as being either more specific or more general than the source information or reducing the original message by paraphrasing, summarizing, or even consciously omitting information.

As I have mentioned, because of the time delay inherent in interpretation, by the time a teacher's instruction to "take a look at this" is interpreted, the teacher has often stopped pointing at whatever "this" is, and the visual information is no longer available. Conversely, the discussion of the visual aid the teacher is referring to may be extended, and the teacher expects the students to look at the visual while simultaneously listening to the instructions or description. In order to include the visual aid and the information accompanying it, interpreters often modify the interpretation by including it explicitly.

In the volcanoes lesson, as Mr. Harrison mentioned and pointed out North America, South America, the "ring of fire," and Africa, Camie chose to include the names of the specific geographic locations in her interpretation. When she did so, she made a deliberate decision *not* to prompt Emily to look at the locations that Mr. Harrison was pointing to (even though he was pointing to them and using referents such as "right here" as he named them). Camie did not direct Emily's attention to the other visual input. In so doing, she eliminated the competing demand for Emily's visual attention by giving precedence to the interpretation. In order for this decision to be a viable choice, Camie had to be cognizant of what Emily already knew. Camie had to know that Emily could identify North and South America, as well as the "ring of fire," on the map. Camie did use the signing space in front of her and various features of ASL to reference the locations Mr. Harrison was pointing out. She simply interpreted these familiar geographic locations without prompting Emily to turn around. When Mr. Harrison talked about how two different plates under Africa were moving in different directions, however, Camie pointed so that Emily could look to see, waited for Emily to look back at the map, and then reestablish eye contact. She then included the specific information in her interpretation, describing how the plate under the northern part of Africa was moving in one direction while the plate under the southern region was moving in another direction.

Camie modified her interpretation again when Mr. Harrison used his hands to talk about the island of Hawaii. As he held his hands in one position, he began to elaborate on the fact that although we can see only a tiny part of Hawaii, the volcano continues under the surface of the water all the way to the ocean floor. Although Camie did direct Emily's visual attention to Mr. Harrison's representation of Hawaii by pointing at it, she then incorporated his hand formations into her interpretation as he continued to speak. Later Mr. Harrison used his hands to demonstrate how tilt meters predict volcanic eruptions by measuring changes in the steepness of a volcano's slopes. He did so again when discussing the limitations of tilt meters, saying, "So, instead of this, you might get that." In these instances, Camie often looked at his gestures but did not point, drop her hands, or prompt Emily to look. Instead, she incorporated his gestures into her own interpretation so that Emily would see them at the right time—along with the interpretation of the corresponding description. For example, Camie signed that the slopes change, then incorporated Mr. Harrison's gestures into her own interpretation to show that slopes get steeper as the pressure of magma increases inside the volcano (see figure 2).

Modifying an interpretation by re-creating visual resources (e.g., gestures) within it presents several advantages. First, the interpreter often looked at and pointed to the visual aid before incorporating it into the interpretation. This allowed both the student and the interpreter to benefit from looking at the visual resource. Second, for the Deaf student, the competing demands of watching the interpretation and simultaneously trying to access the visual aid were eliminated. The interpreter assumed the cognitive burden of looking at and comprehending the visual aid while holding the information still forthcoming in the teacher's discourse rather than passing the burden of two visual demands on to the student. A third benefit was that once the visual stimulus was re-created within the interpretation, Camie could then choose to refer to the actual visual aid itself or return to the gesture or other visual information she had incorporated within the interpretation or both. In other words, this strategy opened the door to an additional resource for Camie's later use. Once an interpreter has created a representation of the visual information in her own signing space, she creates the option of referring to that visual stimulus even when it is no longer present (e.g., the drawing has been erased from the board, the teacher's hands are no longer in that position).

The cumulative nature of timing delays further complicates decisions about how and when to modify the content of interpretations. The time delay inherent in interpretation (the fact that an interpreter has to listen to and understand a spoken message before beginning to interpret it), the visual nature of sign language and Deaf and

Figure 2. Camie incorporates Mr. Harrison's gestures.

hard of hearing students, and the visually laden overlapping information input of the K–12 classroom all lead to a need to compensate for lost time. Even more timing delays arise from the time interpreters spend getting to a desired location, the time it takes for them to direct students' attention to the right place, and the time students need in order to take in information visually once they are looking at the salient visual input. In this scenario, because of the time Camie spent waiting for Emily to look back and forth between Camie and the map and because of the time it took for Camie to walk closer to the map, the delay in the interpretation was particularly prolonged. While Mr. Harrison continued talking, Camie had to listen to him, look at the map, and analyze the incoming message as she walked—just as if she were still interpreting. Moreover, by virtue of the fact that there was such a long delay before Camie resumed interpreting, she had to rely on her memory of what had been said—analyzing that message and then giving priority to the most important points while intentionally letting go of less academically relevant discourse. Of the range of possible options available to her at that point, Camie chose to omit much of what Mr. Harrison had said. Awareness of what Emily already knew likely influenced Camie's decisions about what she could omit. If the information was new and she believed Emily would be held accountable, Camie would have had to seek other options. With introductory material, for example, she might have chosen to interrupt Mr. Harrison and ask him to wait, repeat, rephrase, and/or clarify (actions that were observed on numerous other occasions).

Camie also modified her interpretation when Mr. Harrison prompted the students to begin reading at "When tectonic plates collide," by signing to begin reading at the top of page 203. This description got Emily to the same place, but rather than giving her an entire fingerspelled English phrase to look for, Camie chose a description that would likely be faster, thereby allowing Emily more time to locate the specified excerpt. As Olivia began to read aloud, Camie did not interpret. In this case, Camie deliberately chose to modify the interpretation by completely omitting information.

In this study, when visual input was dense, sustained, and/or complex, as is the case with printed text (or captioned movies), it was not possible to adjust the pacing and timing of the interpretation enough so that students could attend sequentially rather than simultaneously to the signed interpretation and the other visual input. Because Deaf and hard of hearing students cannot read written text and simultaneously watch an interpretation when a teacher or hearing student reads aloud, interpreters have to decide whether and to what extent to interpret the text being read aloud. Sans a change in teaching style, interpreters can approach the situation in two ways. An interpreter can choose to respond by not signing, thereby eliminating the competing demand by deliberately omitting information from the interpretation. The other possible response is to interpret, knowing that the students will not be able to see the printed text. In other words, in order to alleviate the competing demand, the interpreter must decide whether to give priority to the interpretation or the text. Since both approaches are far less than ideal, educational interpreters experience a great deal of conflict (expressed uncertainty) about such decisions. If they are making these decisions without teacher input, they may not be aligned with the most appropriate learning objectives. Camie, like many educational interpreters, also reported that concerns about physical injury (e.g., repetitive motion injuries) contributed to her decision not to interpret extended and designated read-aloud sessions. She did, however, interpret printed instructions and handouts that were read aloud.

In spite of the dilemma presented by read-aloud sessions, the practice was prevalent during the course of my observations. Examples of printed information read out loud included printed instructions and questions (e.g., handouts and worksheets), passages from textbooks, information written or posted on the board, audiotaped recordings of scripted information, and captioned videos. On a weekly basis, Mr. Harrison's students were asked to recite a poem they had memorized. Emily was excused from this activity. Minimal Deaf and hard of hearing student participation was observed during the read-aloud sessions. As a matter of fact, during my observations (39 hours), there was only one instance of a Deaf or hard of hearing student actively participating in a read-aloud activity. According to the interpreter (Marina), this was likely a result of the researcher's presence in the room rather than standard practice. Alleviating demands for Deaf and hard of hearing students' visual attention is highly problematic during read-alouds.

SUMMARY OF GEOLOGICAL FORMATIONS

Interpreting is a complex task. Given the frequency, duration, and potential significance of multiple sources of visual input in K–12 schools, educational interpreters have the additional challenge of reducing the competing visual demands for Deaf and hard of hearing students' attention. To accomplish this they use strategies like adjusting their physical position, directing students' visual attention, adjusting the timing of the interpretation, and modifying the scope and/or content of the interpretation. Multiple layers of complexity were a striking feature of this study. In order to optimize Emily's visual access to educationally relevant input and because Camie encountered several situational changes during Mr. Harrison's geology lesson, Camie was required to make a complex set of overlapping and simultaneous judgments. She had to assess each situation quickly, determine when a response was necessary, consider the range of possible options, predict which strategies would alleviate the competing demands for Emily's visual attention, and finally, select and pursue a particular course of action. Furthermore, she needed to prioritize the content of Mr. Harrison's instruction by deciding what information would take precedence at any given moment and what information could be sacrificed from the interpretation. In determining priorities, compromises were inevitable. Either Emily did not have as much time to look at the visual input as her classmates, or, given that Camie needed to deliver a condensed version of the interpretation, Emily did not have access to everything her classmates and Mr. Harrison said. At the very least, Emily had less time to take in each of these important and primary sources of information. Since it would have been difficult for Emily to guess what was important to see at any given time, Camie's moment-to-moment actions were critical in choreographing Emily's visual attention. Moreover, as a result of the frequent and sometimes prolonged timing delays, Camie needed to be able to identify which points were academically most relevant in order to make principled choices about what information could be eliminated from the interpretation.

Decisions for optimizing visual access make the already complex and cognitively challenging task of interpreting even more difficult. The choices involved are not necessarily intuitive, and most of them need to be made while interpreters also continue to process teacher-delivered instruction for meaning, determine an equivalent interpretation, and deliver it clearly. Furthermore, the process of condensing and summarizing instructional content involves academic expertise that interpreters may or may not have. Generating a consolidated version of salient academic points is a process that, in and of itself, depends on fairly advanced linguistic skills in *any* language, especially in a second language. It becomes even more challenging because interpreters are processing two different languages at the same time. Add to that the fact that these decisions are taking place in an environment known for being inundated with visual and communicative activity. So, while interpretation in K–12 classrooms may, to the untrained eye, seem no more complex than interpreting in any other context, the data from this scenario in Mr. Harrison's classroom make it clear that even something as simple as walking across the classroom is neither simple nor merely about walking.

Study Summary: The Complexities of Responding to Competing Visual Demands

Upon thorough examination of the actions of K–12 interpreters working in elementary school classrooms, the complexities of the task became immediately and conspicuously evident. Analysis of a single lesson led to the identification of four strategies used by interpreters in response to the presence of competing demands for Deaf and hard-of-hearing students' visual attention. The four strategies include adjusting physical position, directing Deaf and hard of hearing students' visual attention, adjusting the timing of the interpretation, and modifying the interpretation.

As a reminder, the first strategy interpreters used in this study was adjusting physical position. A decision as seemingly simple as whether to move must be based on frequent and ongoing analysis of the situation as a whole. Educational interpreters must determine which source of visual information should take precedence over another at any given moment and determine where they should sit or stand in order to optimize Deaf and hard of hearing students' visual access. If they choose to adjust their physical position, interpreters must first ascertain what positions and locations are available to them. Additionally, they must consider which (if any) of those are least likely to create an unnecessary distraction. They must determine how and where to move without getting in the teacher's way or obstructing the view of the other students. These decisions and the act of physically moving take various lengths of time, which in turn presents another set of variables for interpreters to consider. Moreover, the act of adjusting one's physical position to be in the most ideal location/position for optimizing Deaf and hard of hearing students' visual access is not in itself an adequate means of ensuring visual access. Therefore, further action is often required.

In addition to determining and securing the best position for Deaf and hard of hearing students to see, interpreters in K–12 settings used a second strategy—directing students' attention to salient visual input. To recap, some of the techniques for guiding students' visual attention to the right place include waving or tapping on something within the students' line of sight, touching the student according to Deaf cultural norms (e.g., a gentle tap on the arm), pointing and/or looking at a visual referent, putting their hands up to indicate readiness to interpret, and/or putting their hands down to eliminate one of the competing sources of visual input. However, once interpreters have directed a student's attention to a particular visual referent, they must either afford the student an opportunity to look or they must redirect or reclaim the student's visual attention, perhaps by waving and resuming the interpretation.

Decisions about where to direct students' visual attention and when to redirect or reclaim it rely on the interpreters' ability to accurately predict and prioritize. Not only must they predict how long a visual referent will be available (e.g., when a slide will be switched or a gesture will be dropped), they must also predict or determine the degree to which a particular referent can subsequently be accessed or re-created (e.g., the interpreter can copy a gesture used by the teacher). Perhaps most important, interpreters must determine which sources of visual information are most relevant to a particular student and which are most important to access first. Once they make those determinations, they can direct Deaf and hard of hearing students' visual attention to the most appropriate and beneficial source of input.

The third strategy used by educational interpreters to optimize visual access was adjusting the timing of the interpretation. These decisions result from their assessment of which sources of visual input should be given precedence at any given time. Upon determining that a visual referent must be seen in order for the corresponding interpretation to make sense, interpreters stop interpreting. Similarly, if interpreters predict that a particular visual referent may not be available in a few moments, they may immediately stop interpreting, direct the student's visual attention to the right place, and wait as long as they deem necessary for the student to look. If the visual referent is relatively simple and/or if the teacher's accompanying explanation is relatively short and straightforward, an appropriate approach might be to change the sequence of presentation (e.g., let students look first and then deliver the interpretation). If, however, either the visual stimulus is more involved and/or the accompanying instructions more elaborate, interpreters must make decisions at yet a deeper level of analysis. Moreover, because of the cumulative nature of timing delays resulting from adjusting their physical positions, directing students' visual attention, and affording students not only the opportunity but also the time to look as long as is warranted (another process of prediction and ongoing assessment) at each source of salient visual input, new demands then arise for educational interpreters. The findings of this study clearly indicate that even the use of all three of these strategies in conjunction with each other were insufficient to provide the visual access that Deaf and hard of hearing students need.

The fourth strategy involved modifying the interpretation. The decision to change the scope and/or content of the interpretation was often a direct result of the cumulative nature of timing delays, which were in response to the Deaf and hard of hearing students' need to access information visually (and sequentially) and the existence of multiple sources of visual input. In order to alleviate or eliminate these competing visual demands, interpreters frequently make decisions about what can be eliminated or omitted. Studies conducted with interpreters working in universities indicate that even highly skilled interpreters make conscious strategic decisions to omit information that they determine to be less relevant in order to render a more effective interpretation (Napier, 2003; Napier & Barker, 2004). Similarly, the interpreters in this study chose to omit information based on the needs of Deaf and hard of hearing students in the classroom.

Interpreters in K–12 classrooms deliberately chose not to interpret certain information in order to promote visual access, especially when they determined that the spoken discourse was less pertinent to the task at hand than whatever activity was holding the Deaf or hard of hearing students' visual attention at the time. Rather than omit information entirely, sometimes the interpreters chose to condense or summarize the information—modifying the interpretation by reducing it in some fashion. Conversely, when they determined that the spoken discourse was more important than another source of visual input, rather than direct the students' visual attention to that source, they sometimes continued interpreting without any reference to the other visual input. However, a decision not to direct the students' attention to another visual referent was often addressed by making the information explicit in the interpretation, that is, modifying the interpretation by adding to it in some fashion. For example, when the teacher said, "What about this one?" while pointing to number two on the board, the interpreter would explicitly sign NUMBER TWO in the interpretation. When cumulative timing delays caused Deaf and hard of hearing students to miss out on an opportunity to respond publicly and the interpreters were aware of their answers, the interpreters often praised Deaf and hard of hearing students directly, signing GOOD JOB! This frequent occurrence is an example of modifying the interpretation by adding to it. The interpreters in this study described this practice as being parallel to classroom teachers' use of positive reinforcement. They expressed a belief that doing so was at least an attempt to compensate for the indirect nature of an interpreter-mediated education.

The interpreters in this study highly valued the active participation of Deaf and hard of hearing students in class activities, so they created opportunities for them to respond by using a combination of the strategies discussed in this scenario. When teachers asked students to respond to printed questions, interpreters often directed Deaf and hard of hearing students' visual attention to the subsequent question. In doing so, the interpreters deliberately omitted information from the previous response (the one that the student had already answered correctly), as long as no new information was being provided. Moreover, they adjusted the timing of the interpretation by moving ahead of the class to the next question. They then modified the interpretation by adding to it in a way that was consistent with the teacher's approach to previous questions—prompting students to be prepared to answer (students even checked their answers with the interpreter in advance) and cuing them to raise their hands at the right time. The interpreters were cognizant of the students' readiness to risk participation. During interviews, they expressed sensitivity to the need to find a balance between promoting student independence and creating an environment in which students who traditionally remain bystanders feel safe and comfortable enough to participate actively.

It should be mentioned that when the interpreters had enough time, they would often use multiple strategies. The less time afforded to the interpreter because of the teacher's pacing, density and complexity of the material, and the accumulation of timing delays because of chosen responses to competing visual demands, the fewer strategies interpreters used in conjunction with one another. Sadly, the implication of this reality is that just when Deaf and hard of hearing students have a greater need for a slower and clearer presentation of material (as is arguably true for their hearing peers) to allow for visual access, fewer support structures may be provided.

As simple as each of these four strategies appears to be on the surface, it is the necessity of considering the affects of implementing each strategy and the resulting need for subsequent action that truly complicate interpreters' decisions. In addition, the question of what interpreters do in light of the existence of competing demands for Deaf and hard of hearing students' visual attention is not entirely answered by the identification of these four strategies. In fact, the findings discussed in this study have primarily focused on only those that can be employed while interpreting. If interpreters determine that accommodations or adjustments regarding teaching style, information, or activities are warranted, reliance on these four strategies would be inadequate. Interpreters might choose to collaborate with classroom teachers to optimize Deaf and hard of hearing students' visual access, either during the presentation of a lesson or after it has been completed. An interpreter might even go so far as to interfere completely with an activity in order to ensure visual access. For example, Camie might have chosen to interrupt Mr. Harrison and ask him to wait for her to get to the other side of the room. If there were more space available near the map, she may even have chosen to ask him to move with her. After the lesson had been completed, she might follow up with Mr. Harrison by informing him of the fact that the laser pointer presented a problem in terms of Emily's ability to see both the interpretation and the map. By doing so, they could then work collaboratively to identify strategies for optimizing Emily's visual access.

In order to shed some light on practices that appear most likely to enhance the school experiences of Deaf and hard of hearing students, much of this study focused on descriptions of strategies that worked to some degree. It is important to remember that all of the interpreters who participated in the study reported not always being certain about what to do or well-equipped to effectively interpret in every situation they encountered. Camie had worked as an interpreter in public schools for seven years and had received a score of 3.7 on the Educational Interpreter Performance Assessment (EIPA) three years before data collection. At the time of the study, she held an AA degree and had almost completed a two year interpreting program which focused on K-12 interpreting. Three months after data collection, she earned a 4.2 on the EIPA. In spite of the fact that she met or exceeded minimum qualifications for K-12 interpreters in most states, Camie struggled to meet Emily's visual needs.

As Mr. Harrison used a laser pointer to refer to locations on the world map on the back wall of the room, Camie eventually found an appropriate place to stand. It was not until her sixth position that Camie found a place where Emily could see and Camie's position did not block other students' view or interfere with Mr. Harrison's ability to use the laser pointer. However, Camie did not make a decision to move until more than six and a half minutes after Mr. Harrison first used the laser pointer. During that time, she struggled to direct Emily's attention to the right place at the right time. Complicating the issue was the fact that even if Camie chose to interpret a particular concept, she had to stop when Emily looked away. Naturally, whenever the students around her looked back toward the map, Emily looked too. In so doing, whatever Camie was signing at the moment was lost. Moreover, Mr. Harrison's visual referents were missed several times. For example, he explained, "Magma has risen up through the continental crust, through the lithosphere and is extruding pyroclastic material." After Camie interpreted that magma came through the continental crust, she pointed to the back of the room, directing Emily's visual attention to the map. By the time Emily turned to look, Mr. Harrison had turned off the laser. Emily looked back to Camie, who explained apologetically that he had turned the laser off. Camie tried a variety of strategies, each to no avail. She tried pointing and waiting, summarizing information whenever possible. She tried changing the sequence, but when she was interpreting, Emily looked away to follow the gaze of her classmates. She used specific names of geographic locations and geological features, which worked to some degree, but left Emily without the opportunity to see and be reminded of where each was located.

In spite of Camie's willingness to move in other situations in order to create clear sightlines, several factors converged to contribute to Camie's reluctance to move in this particular instance. First of all, because of the physical layout of the room, the shelving, and the seating arrangement, there simply was not a good place for Camie to stand. Another constraining factor was Camie's lack of ability to predict how long Mr. Harrison would be referring to the map. In the meantime, he also told students to look at his hands to demonstrate another phenomenon. Because he was at the front of the room and the map was at the back of the room, this added yet another visual referent to further complicate the situation. In addition, students were looking at their Directed Reading Worksheets as well as their textbooks (all while Emily was also supposed to be watching the interpreter), so Camie had to prioritize between several sources of visual input (the interpretation, the map, the book and DRW that Emily had at her desk, and Mr. Harrison). Emily made her own contribution to the visual choreography when she looked away from the interpretation (often in the middle of a sentence) because her classmates looked to the back of the room en masse.

Camie finally chose to stand six minutes and twenty seconds later when Mr. Harrison said, "I think I'd rather you look there [at the map] instead of the book" and pointed with his laser to the map at the back of the room. Although she stood and could visibly be seen considering her options, she did not move yet. After another round of visual ping pong, Camie finally chose to move to the back of the room. However, Camie's conundrum became immediately apparent upon her arrival, as she chose positions that blocked Mr. Harrison's laser pointer, Emily's view, and other students' views. In her haste to get out of everyone's way, Camie even retreated to a previous location that did not allow Camie herself to easily see the map and the laser pointer. Finally, Camie crossed to the opposite side of the room and stood to the left side of the map. She pressed herself close to a bookshelf and reached to point at the locations on the map when they were most relevant to the interpretation (several seconds after Mr. Harrison had pointed them out with the laser) (see figure 3).

The position that she finally settled on may not have worked as well if Camie were not tall. A shorter interpreter might have had to stand closer to the map and very likely blocked the view of at least a few students. It took nearly eight and a half minutes for Camie to find a location from which she could effectively direct Emily's visual attention. By the time she did so, Mr. Harrison was ready to put away the laser pointer for good (less than a minute later). The fact that Deaf and hard of hearing students need to look at a signed interpretation and other visual sources of information sequentially rather than simultaneously has serious implications in terms of the amount of time available for each of these important activities. It is not feasible to expect interpreters to be able to interpret all of the spoken discourse in less time than it took for the

Camie looking back over her shoulder at the map

Laser beam on back of Camie's hand

Final position next to tall bookshelf (left) with laser beam on map (near Camie's elbow)

Figure 3.

teacher to deliver the original discourse. As long as teachers continue to speak and teach while expecting students to look at multiple sources of visual input, Deaf and hard of hearing students will not have access to the same information as their hearing peers. The effects of this mismatch will certainly differ depending on several variables, including the frequency and significance of the visual input, teacher pacing and presentation style, complexity of content, student readiness, and the ability of individual interpreters to accurately assess and prioritize students' needs in order to determine and implement appropriate and effective courses of action. Interpreters working in K–12 classrooms must do far more than we might have realized thus far. Not only must they think critically as they simultaneously continue to listen to and analyze the source message for meaning and function, consider a host of additional factors regarding context, language and culture, and engage in the cognitively demanding task of interpreting, but they must also monitor and assess Deaf and hard of hearing students' visual needs along with additional language and learning needs, identify and evaluate the available options, predict potential outcomes and consequences of a chosen approach, and select and implement what they believe to be an effective response to the current set of circumstances. They must then follow through until an appropriate resolution has been reached. It is imperative to create a visually accessible environment for Deaf and hard of hearing students, however, an interpreter cannot do that in isolation. Collaboration with classroom teachers is crucial.

A Critical Need for Research

The importance of the visual needs of Deaf and hard of hearing students becomes extremely apparent when interpreters work in mainstream classrooms. When teachers teach in their accustomed manner, which involves delivering a steady stream of spoken discourse while presenting an infinite number of visual referents, the cumulative timing delays imposed on interpreters become progressively more problematic. Moreover, interpreters who do not have adequate knowledge, skills, and resources at their disposal may not make effective decisions quickly—resulting in more delays at the very least. The likelihood that these students will miss salient information increases exponentially. Research must be conducted to determine how interpreters' decisions and responses to a range of predictable conditions will affect Deaf and hard of hearing students' school experiences and learning outcomes.

Schick (2004) states, "Put simply, educating children with the use of an interpreter is an educational experiment. Although published demographic data documents [*sic*] the number of children who are being educated in classrooms with educational interpreters (Kluwin, Moores, & Gaustad 1992), no studies have been done to document how well these students are doing" (p. 73). It is glaringly evident that extensive research and ongoing dialogue must take place in order to ensure that Deaf and hard of hearing students do not continue to fall through the cracks. Some students are able to succeed in educational settings, but it seems to be more a matter of happenstance than of any strategic design based on what works.

This chapter has brought to light some of the many factors involved in K–12 interpreters' attempts to respond to the visual needs of Deaf and hard of hearing students. By now it is clear that each decision or change in circumstance may lead to a completely different approach. Because the process of responding to competing visual demands is socomplex, the information presented here only hints at how complicated and challenging the task of interpreting effectively really is. It would be negligent not to mention that the needs of each individual student must be taken into account when constructing interpretations that facilitate language development in both English and sign language—based on each student's language realities and prior knowledge. We cannot continue to expect that simply placing an interpreter in a classroom with one or more Deaf or hard of hearing students (who likely have different language needs and prior knowledge) is adequate.

Taylor (2004) suggests that when hiring educational interpreters, administrators should assess the candidate's "skills, expertise, knowledge of the subject matter, and ability to suit the needs of the situation and the individual child. Interpreters must be competent to provide interpretation for the specific teachers and students for whom they are being hired" (p. 179). Competence depends on numerous factors, including the interpreter's ability to adjust the interpretation according to the context, teaching and learning goals, and the needs of the participants. Since Deaf and hard of hearing students may not have had exposure to the same linguistic and cultural capital and funds of knowledge as their hearing classmates, Schick (2004) proposes that "appropriate scaffolding and guided participation for a hearing child at any point in development may not scaffold the Deaf or hard of hearing child's learning. The Deaf or hard of hearing child may need interaction and teaching that is more fine-tuned to his or her level of skills and understanding" (p. 81). She suggests that training interpreters to become a working part of the educational team might be more reasonable than the "model of interpreting that was developed by interpreters who work in the adult community where the gold standard is to represent everything the teacher and classmates say" (p. 81).

According to interpreters' professional ethics, their specialized knowledge requires them to respond to the various sets of circumstances that either promote or hinder inclusion. Yet, ironically, professional codes of conduct for interpreters and routine protocol in academic settings have often prevented educational interpreters from taking whatever action is necessary to promote true inclusion—full membership—for Deaf and hard of hearing students in K–12 schools. Often interpreters do not know who to turn to for help, advice, and support, and when they do, they may be denied the assistance they request. For example, interpreters may not be made aware of a student's IEP goals. Sans this information, they are making decisions in isolation and with an incomplete picture of what the educational team members (including the parents) have agreed upon. It seems logical that interpreters and teachers must work together toward a common goal, but how to create opportunities for effective collaboration remains to be seen. Although the teachers in this study were especially receptive to the idea of having interpreters in their classes and open to their advice, they still inadvertently created situations that were problematic. Furthermore, not all teachers are enthusiastic about sharing their classrooms and changing their teaching style to accommodate a single student. With increased class sizes and pressures of accountability, teachers are often overburdened. Incentives such as extra prep time might provide not only the time but also the structure for teachers and interpreters to engage in ongoing dialogue about strategies for meeting the unique needs of Deaf and hard of hearing students.

Call to Action

Not until recently has legislation mandated the specific qualifications for educational interpreters working in K–12 settings in the United States. Although this is clearly a step in the right direction, assessing interpreting proficiencies and cognitive knowledge does nothing to ensure that educational interpreters will respond effectively to other crucial factors such as competing demands for Deaf and hard of hearing students' visual attention and their readiness for interpreted material in light of each student's language ability (in both English and sign language) and prior knowledge.

To date, we have largely neglected the field of educational interpreting—oftentimes marginalizing those who work in K–12 settings while failing to provide them with the support, research, education, and training necessary to do their jobs effectively.

In addition, there is much controversy and confusion about the expected roles and responsibilities of educational interpreters (affecting their perceived status as professionals). The complexity and variability of situational/contextual and human/interactional factors make it difficult to predict the range and depth of required knowledge and skills. Furthermore, educational interpreters have traditionally been poorly compensated and offered few (if any) opportunities for in-service training.

Particularly troublesome is the fact that K–12 interpreters have most often been left to their own sense of what works—without a thorough understanding of the implications of their decisions. In fact, they must independently figure out what to do once on the job, although the field has not reached agreement about what should be happening in K–12 classrooms. Hopefully educational interpreters have a good sense of the needs of Deaf and hard of hearing students. However, it is negligent to rely on individual interpreters' decision-making skills without providing a means for them to acquire these skills and learn how to make the decisions necessary for interpreting effectively within school environments.

There has been a conspicuous lack of research on the extent to which learning through interpreters might work. That research can and should be conducted only after we know that the interpreters participating in the research are well prepared for the task. It makes no sense to examine how well a process works until we clarify what it is that educational interpreters should be doing. Moreover, it is absolutely absurd to do research on how well interpreting works without considering the diversity of individual students' needs. Investigation that focuses only on linguistic competence and equivalence in interpretation will not give us a complete picture. Educational interpreters must critically analyze each situation in light of multiple factors and take into account the context, goals, participants, interactional dynamics, and individual needs of each Deaf and hard of hearing student.

In order to clarify the skills and knowledge that interpreters must have in order to interpret effectively in mainstream educational contexts, it is crucial to invest substantially in the development of a considerable body of research. Moreover, teams of experts—including researchers, first- and second-language-acquisition experts, interpreters, interpreter educators, Deaf education teachers, Deaf and hard of hearing students, parents, general education teachers, and teacher educators—must work collaboratively and extensively to determine what critical components must be in place in order for Deaf and hard of hearing students to be fully included. We need to determine what interpreters and teachers must do, what physical resources and support structures should be provided, how to meet Deaf and hard of hearing students' language and learning needs while ensuring visual access, and how to promote full participation and true inclusion (not only academically but socially as well). It is time to define the set of factors that must be properly aligned and the knowledge and skills that are fundamental to the task of interpreting in K–12 settings so that we can begin to determine whether and under what conditions educational interpreting is most likely to be effective. We are obligated to provide Deaf and hard of hearing students with outstanding and enjoyable school experiences that allow them "to acquire the academic, social, emotional, and vocational skills needed for the establishment of social relationships, economic self-sufficiency, and the assumption of civic responsibility" (California Department of Education, 2000, p. 1). Until that happens, we cannot rest.

Notes

1. As of July 1, 2009, K–12 interpreters in California joined Alaska and Nevada in requiring at least a 4.0 on the EIPA, ESSE, or other equivalent assessment.

2. RID CI and CT, NAD V, and EIPA 4.9.

3. All of the interpreters in the Smith (2010) study discussed the challenge of responding effectively to competing demands for Deaf and hard of hearing students' visual attention. For example, during his sixth-grade language arts lesson, Mr. Harrison told the students to write down a series of dictated sentences that included their spelling words. The students were to spell the words correctly and define each one based on the context of the sentence. While hearing students can listen and sound out the words as they are spoken aloud in English, Deaf and hard of hearing students are engaged in a much different task. Although the language and translation aspect of the activity is in itself worthy of further discussion, the issue here is that Deaf and hard of hearing students need to look at their papers to write the words, then back up to the interpreter to get the rest of the sentence. While interpreting the lesson, Camie, the interpreter, was concerned about Emily, the Deaf student, in Mr. Harrison's class: "I hate when he does that because Emily can't do that! That's like telling her brain to go in three different places—look at me, focus on the spelling, focus on trying to figure out what this word is [while writing the sentences]. That's *impossible* to do!" Expressing similar frustrations, interpreters in this study reported having asked teachers to refrain from talking while presenting visual stimuli, and although the classroom teachers were very receptive to the idea of adapting their teaching style to better meet the Deaf and hard of hearing students' visual needs, they still unintentionally, albeit habitually, created problematic situations.

   Consequently, competing demands for visual attention result in an intense responsibility for interpreters. They must respond to the students' need to access visual information and concentrate on the accompanying interpretation of spoken discourse, knowing that the students cannot look at both sources of information at the same time. Considering the fact that young Deaf and hard of hearing students may be at an extreme disadvantage when unable to simultaneously access visual information and explanations, the prevalence of competing visual demands (more than 84%) found in the fifth- and sixth-grade classrooms in this study was disquieting.

References

Antia, S. D., & Kreimeyer, K. H. (2001). The role of interpreters in inclusive classrooms. *American Annals of the Deaf, 146*(4), 355–365.

Bahan, B. (2008). Upon the formation of a visual variety of the human race. In H-D. L. Bauman (Ed.), *Open your eyes: Deaf studies talking* (pp. 83–99). Minneapolis: University of Minnesota Press.

Brown Kurz, K., & Caldwell Langer, E. (2004). Student perspectives on educational interpreting: Twenty deaf and hard of hearing students offer insights and suggestions. In E. A. Winston (Ed.), *Educational interpreting: How it can succeed* (pp. 9–47). Washington, DC: Gallaudet University Press.

California Deaf and Hard-of-Hearing Education Advisory Task Force. (1999). *Communication access and quality education for deaf and hard-of-hearing children: The report of the California deaf and hard-of-hearing education advisory task force.* Sacramento: California Department of Education.

California Department of Education. (2000). *Programs for deaf and hard-of-hearing students: Guidelines for quality standards.* Sacramento: California Department of Education.

Commission on Education of the Deaf. (1988). Toward equality: Education of the deaf. Washington, DC: U.S. Government Printing Office.

Dean, R. K., & Pollard, R. Q. (2005). Consumers and service effectiveness in interpreting work: A practice profession perspective. In M. Marschark, R. Peterson, & E. Winston (Eds.), *Interpreting and interpreter education: Directions for research and practice* (pp. 259–282). New York: Oxford University Press.

Dean, R. K., & Pollard, R. Q. (2006). From best practice to best practice process: Shifting ethical thinking and teaching. In E. M. Maroney (Ed.), *A new chapter in interpreter education: Accreditation, research, and technology* (pp. 119–131). Proceedings of the sixteenth national convention of the Conference of Interpreter Trainers (CIT). Monmouth, OR: CIT.

Harrington, F. J. (2000). Sign language interpreters and access for deaf students to university curricula: The ideal and the reality. In R. Roberts, S. A. Carr, D. Abraham, and A. Dufour (Eds.), *The Critical Link 2: Interpreters in the community* (pp. 219–273). Benjamins Translation Library, vol. 31. Philadelphia: Benjamins.

Hayes, P. L. (1992). Educational interpreters for deaf students: Their responsibilities, problems, and concerns. *Journal of Interpretation, 5*(1), 5–24.

Hurwitz, T. A. (1995). Current issues: Interpreters in the educational setting. Paper presented at the Eighteenth International Congress on Education of the Deaf, Tel Aviv, Israel, July 16–20, 1995. ED390240.

Jacobs, L. R. (1977). The efficacy of interpreting input for processing lecture information by Deaf college students. *Journal of Rehabilitation of the Deaf, 11,* 10–14.

Johnson, K. (1991). Miscommunication in interpreted classroom interaction. *Sign Language Studies, 70*(1), 1–34.

Johnson, R. C., & Cohen, O. P. (Eds.). (1994). *Implications and complications for deaf students of the full inclusion movement.* Occasional Paper 94-2. Washington, DC: Gallaudet Research Institute. ED380917.

Jones, B. E. (1993). *Responsibilities of educational sign language interpreters in K–12 public school in Kansas, Missouri, and Nebraska.* Unpublished doctoral dissertation, University of Kansas, Lawrence.

Jones, B. E. (2004). Competencies of K–12 educational interpreters: What we need versus what we have. In E. A. Winston (Ed.), *Educational interpreting: How it can succeed* (pp. 132–167). Washington, DC: Gallaudet University Press.

Komesaroff, L. R., & McLean, M. A. (2006). Being there is not enough: Inclusion is both deaf and hearing. In *Deafness and Education International, 8*(2), 88–100. Burwood, Australia: Wiley. Retrieved June 9, 2009, from http://dx.doi.org/10.1002/dei.192.

La Bue, M. (1998). *Interpreted education: A study of deaf students' access to the content and form of literacy instruction in a mainstreamed high school English class.* Unpublished doctoral dissertation, Harvard University, Cambridge, MA.

Ladd, P. (2003). Understanding Deaf Culture: In Search of Deafhood, Multilingual Matters Ltd.

Lane, Harlan. (1995). The education of deaf children: Drowning in the mainstream and the sidestream. In J. M. Kauffman and D. P. Hallahan (Eds.), *The illusion of full inclusion: A comprehensive critique of a current special education bandwagon.* Austin: PRO-ED. ED376639.

Lentz, E. M. (2007, February). *People of the eye . . . Community of vision.* Paper presented at the meeting of the San Diego chapter of the American Sign Language Teachers Association, San Diego.

Marschark, M., Lang, H. G., & Albertini, J. A. (2002). *Educating deaf students: From research to practice.* New York: Oxford University Press.

Marschark, M., Sapere, P., Convertino, C. M., & Pelz, J. (2008). Learning via direct and mediated instruction by deaf students. In *Journal of Deaf Studies and Deaf Education, 13*(4), 546–561. New York: Oxford University Press.

Marschark, M., Sapere, P., Convertino, C. M., & Seewagen, R. (2005). Educational interpreting: Access and outcomes. In M. Marschark, R. Peterson, & E. A. Winston (Eds.), *Sign language interpreting and interpreter education: Directions for research and practice* (pp. 57–83). New York: Oxford University Press.

Marschark, M., Sapere, P., Convertino, C. M., Seewagen, R., & Maltzen, H. (2004). Comprehension of sign language interpreting: Deciphering a complex task situation. *Sign Language Studies, 4*(4), 345–368. The Hague: Mouton.

Mertens, D. M. (1990). Teachers working with interpreters: The deaf student's educational experience. *American Annals of the Deaf, 136*(1), 48–52.

Metzger, M. M. (1999). *Sign language interpreting: Deconstructing the myth of neutrality.* Washington, DC: Gallaudet University Press.

Metzger, M. M., & Fleetwood, E. (2004). Educational interpreting: Developing standards of practice. In E. A. Winston (Ed.), *Educational interpreting: How it can succeed* (pp. 171–177). Washington, DC: Gallaudet University Press.

Monikowski, C., & Winston, E. A. (2003). Interpreters and interpreter education. In M. Marschark, & Spencer, P. E. (Eds.), *Oxford handbook of deaf studies, language, and education* (pp. 347–360). New York: Oxford University Press.

Napier, J. (2003). A sociolinguistic analysis of the occurrence and types of omissions produced by Australian Sign Language/English interpreters. In M. Metzger, S. Collins, V. Dively, & R. Shaw (Eds.), *From topic boundaries to omission: Research on interpretation* (pp. 99–153). Washington, DC: Gallaudet University Press.

Napier, J. (2004). Interpreting omissions: A new perspective. *Interpreting, 6*(2), 117–142.

Napier, J. (2005). Linguistic features and strategies of interpreting: From research to education to practice. In M. Marschark, R. Peterson, & E. A. Winston (Eds.), *Sign language interpreting and interpreter education: Directions for research and practice* (pp. 84–111). New York: Oxford University Press.

Napier, J., & Barker, R. (2004). Accessing university education: Perceptions, preferences, and expectations for interpreting by deaf students. *Journal of Deaf Studies and Deaf Education, 9*(2), 228–238.

O'Connell, J. (2007). Achievement gap for the deaf. State of education address 2007 by Superintendent O'Connell on the status of education in California. Retrieved June 4, 2009, from http://www.cde.ca.gov/eo/in/se/agdeaf.asp.

Power, D., & Hyde, M. (2002). The characteristics and extent of participation of deaf and hard-of-hearing students in regular classes in Australian schools. *Journal of Deaf Studies and Deaf Education, 7*(4), 302–311.

Ramsey, C. L. (1997). Deaf children in public schools: Placement, context, and consequences. Washington, DC: Gallaudet University Press.

Ramsey, C. L. (2004). Theoretical tools for educational interpreters, or "the true confessions of an ex-educational interpreter." In E. A. Winston (Ed.), *Educational interpreting: How it can succeed* (pp. 132–167). Washington, DC: Gallaudet University Press.

Russell, D. (2006). Inclusion or the illusion of inclusion: A study of interpreters working with deaf students in inclusive education settings. *Critical Link 5*. Sydney, Australia.

Russell, D. (2008, November). Getting to Skopos in a mediated educational environment: Bridging research and practice. Paper presented at the National Convention of the Conference of Interpreter Trainers (CIT), San Juan, Puerto Rico.

Schick, B. 2004. How might learning through an interpreter influence cognitive development? In E. A. Winston (Ed.), *Educational interpreting: How it can succeed* (pp. 73–87). Washington, DC: Gallaudet University Press.

Schick, B., & Williams, K. T. (2004). The educational interpreter performance assessment: Current structure and practices. In E. A. Winston (Ed.), *Educational interpreting: How it can succeed* (pp. 186–205). Washington, DC: Gallaudet University Press.

Schick, B., Williams, K. T., & Bolster, L. (1999). Skill levels of educational interpreters working in public schools. *Journal of Deaf Studies and Deaf Education, 4*(2), 144–155.

Schick, B., Williams, K. T., & Kupermintz, H. (2006). Look who's being left behind: Educational interpreters and access to education for deaf and hard-of-hearing students. *Journal of Deaf Studies and Deaf Education, 11*(1), 3–20.

Schildroth, A. N., & Hotto, S. (1994). Deaf students and full inclusion: Who wants to be excluded? In R. C. Johnson & O. P. Cohen (Eds.), *Implications and complications for deaf students of the full inclusion movement* (pp. 7–30). Occasional Paper 94-2. Washington, DC: Gallaudet Research Institute. ED380917.

Seal, B. C. (1998). *Best practices in educational interpreting*. Boston: Allyn & Bacon.

Seal, B. C. (2004). *Best practices in educational interpreting* (2nd ed.). Boston: Allyn & Bacon.

Smith, Melissa B. (2010). *More than meets the eye: Revealing the complexities of K–12 interpreting*. Unpublished doctoral dissertation, University of California–San Diego.

Stewart, D., & Kluwin, T. (1996). The gap between guidelines, practice, and knowledge in interpreting services for deaf students. *Journal of Deaf Studies and Deaf Education, 1*(1), 29–39.

Stinson, M., & Antia, S. (1999). Considerations in educating deaf and hard-of-hearing students in inclusive settings. In *Journal of Deaf Studies and Deaf Education, 4*, 163–175.

Stinson, M., & Lang, H. (1994). The potential impact on deaf students of the full inclusion movement. In R. C. Johnson & O. P. Cohen (Eds.), *Implications and complications for deaf students of the full inclusion movement*. Occasional Paper 94-2. Washington, DC: Gallaudet Research Institute. ED380917.

Stuckless, R. E., Avery, J., & Hurwitz, A. (1989). *Educational interpreting for deaf students: Report of the National Task Force on Educational Interpreting*. Rochester, NY: National Technical Institute of the Deaf.

Taylor, C., & Elliott, R. N. (1994). Identifying areas of competence needed by educational interpreters. *Sign Language Studies, 83*, 179–190.

Taylor, M. M. (1993). *Interpretation skills: English to American Sign Language*. Edmonton: Interpreting Consolidated.

Taylor, M. M. (2004). Assessment and supervision of educational interpreters: What job? Who's job? Is this process necessary? In E. A. Winston (Ed.), *Educational interpreting: How it can succeed* (pp. 178–185). Washington, DC: Gallaudet University Press.

Turner, G. H. (2005). Toward real interpreting. In M. Marschark, R. Peterson, & E. A. Winston (Eds.), *Sign language interpreting and interpreter education: Directions for research and practice* (pp. 29–56). New York: Oxford University Press.

Veditz, G. (1912). President's message in *Proceedings of the ninth convention of the National Association of the Deaf*, 1910. Philadelphia: Philocophus.

West, C. C. (1965). Book review of *The Responsible Self* by H. Richard Niebuhr (published 1963). *Theology Today, 21*(4). Retrieved March 26, 2009, from http://theologytoday. ptsem.edu/jan1965/v21-4-bookreview6.htm.

Winston, E. A. (1994). An interpreted education: Inclusion or exclusion? In R. C. Johnson & O. P. Cohen (Eds.), *Implications and complications for deaf students of the full inclusion movement* (pp. 55–62). Occasional Paper 94-2. Washington, DC: Gallaudet Research Institute. ED380917.

Winston, E. A. (2004). Interpretability and accessibility of mainstream classrooms. In E. A.Winston (Ed.), *Educational interpreting: How it can succeed* (pp. 132–167). Washington, DC: Gallaudet University Press.

Conclusion: Confounded by Language

KATHEE MANGAN CHRISTENSEN

Attitude is a little thing that makes a big difference.

—Winston Churchill

Education is much more than a matter of imparting the knowledge and skills by which narrow goals are achieved. It is also about opening the child's eyes to the needs and rights of others.

—His Holiness the Dalai Lama

Anyone who has attempted to learn a new language, especially during school age or later, would agree that it is not an easy task. Our abilities to learn syntax, vocabulary, and cultural nuances vary from individual to individual, and the skill level of our instructors is yet another variable. Looking back on my two years of college French, I recall wondering how a few students were comfortably exchanging pleasantries with our instructor after just a week or two while the rest of us looked on in baffled amazement. Languages are not learned according to "seat time" and rote memorization. Much more is required, not the least of which is individual motivation. As difficult as language learning may be, once a student is able to understand and be understood in a new language, the rewards are great. Perhaps the most daunting challenge of educators of deaf children is to provide stimulating, comprehensible, and meaningful language experiences for their students consistently and over the course of many years. Decisions must be made for children as soon as their deafness is diagnosed. Many of these decisions center on communication. What communication mode or modes will be best for the child? Which is the best communication environment? Who will be responsible for providing comprehensible, consistent input? How will the child, the family, and the extended family interact? These and other questions are raised and addressed often before the child is 1 year old.

Sadly, emotions, expectations, and conventions may interfere with or bias the decision-making process. Since the majority of deaf children are born into hearing families, who may have little or no knowledge of deafness and the Deaf community, parents often rely heavily on medical professionals for advice. While the medical community can certainly offer a perspective based on current medical practice, parents may benefit from "thinking beyond the ear." A general discussion of communication options, including the benefits and limitations of each, would help parents make informed decisions about the future of their deaf baby. If, as mentioned in previous chapters of this book, it is beneficial to provide "both/and" rather than "either/or" educational options, it makes sense to consider an early, comprehensible bilingual approach for profoundly, congenitally deaf children whose hearing parents speak English. Is this possible?

At least two examples merit consideration. Chapter 4 of this book describes the situation of PJ, who, empowered by his parents and teachers, began his educational trek exposed to three languages: English, Spanish, and American Sign Language (ASL). Sensitivity to his needs prevailed, and PJ, over time, acquired fluency in English and ASL. He also knows rudimentary Spanish and is continuing to study this language, his heritage language, for personal reasons. A second example is that of hearing children of deaf adults (codas). These hearing children often acquire signed language as infants and spoken language as they grow older; thus, they are able to communicate fluently in both languages by the time they enter kindergarten. In both instances, the outcome is positive: Language is viewed as a resource, and the children's world is expanded to include natural bilingual interaction.

All too often, parents are given information that leads them to believe that only one language is "best" for their deaf child. Therefore, attention is given to just one communicative option, be it oral/aural or visual/spatial, and other options are placed in abeyance. They are suppressed. In the case of PJ in chapter 4, all of the language options were present, and the child was able to demonstrate which choice worked best at a given time. Teachers and others had their eyes on PJ as they considered his goals. The child's strengths were allowed to guide the decision making and eventually led to bilingual ability. Noted Harvard child psychiatrist Robert Coles has encouraged adults to observe, record, and interpret children's communication, "especially through the children's own words, uttered in their homes . . . in a manner that might do justice to them" (1986, 10). Chapter 7 of this book describes how educational leaders can model and facilitate independent decision making for deaf children. The intent is that these children become authors of their own lives with the ability to make educated choices, including choices about language. In all fairness, the question we as educators, parents, and others involved with young deaf children must ask is this: Given what we know about the positive impact of bilingual ability on cognitive development and educational achievement, is it in the deaf child's best interest to focus solely on only one communication option early in the child's life?

When motivated, children eventually acquire languages to which they are exposed consistently and comprehensibly over time. *Eventual Bilingualism* is a term coined to describe this process which happens to each child at a time unique to that child. For example, fluent in ASL, PJ chose to add spoken English to his repertoire at age 8. Other deaf children, fluent in written and/or spoken English for academic purposes, may acquire ASL fluency in middle school for social reasons. There are so many varied ways in which bilingual access and ability can serve as a resource for deaf children. The situation of Ann and her daughter, Ellen, is a case in point. Ann and her husband adopted Ellen as an infant. Ellen, at age 2, was diagnosed with profound, bilateral deafness, Ann was instructed by the audiologist at their local clinic to enroll Ellen in a private oral school for infants, toddlers, and young children. The school did not allow signed language of any kind. Ellen spent 6 years in the oral school and was able to communicate quite well through speech with her parents and others familiar with her speech patterns. When Ellen was 8, her father was transferred to another city and the family moved. There was no private oral school in the area, so Ellen was enrolled in an oral classroom within a comprehensive public school program serving all deaf children in the city. Her oral classroom was adjacent to the classroom where other 8 year old deaf children used what was called Total Communication (TC) including Signed English and ASL. Ellen was intrigued and it wasn't long before she was engaged in sign language on the playground with children from the TC class. She acquired signs readily. By the time she entered high school, she was fluent in ASL, immersed in the Deaf social scene, and still able to communicate in spoken and written English at home and elsewhere when the need arose.

As Ellen was on her journey into Deaf culture, her mother enrolled in a graduate program at a local university that prepared teachers of the deaf. Although Ann's goal was to teach in an oral program for deaf children, she was required to take basic ASL courses as part of her teacher preparation. Ellen was thrilled and encouraged her mother to sign with her and with Ellen's deaf friends. Ann soon realized that Ellen's social life was primarily with Deaf peers. Since she wanted to maintain a close relationship with her daughter, Ann began to use sign language more often as a social option with Ellen and her friends. Eventually, Ann became quite fluent in ASL. This was fortunate for the family, since Ellen married a deaf man. Their hearing children, whom Ann adored, were, of course, codas and used ASL as their first language.

In this family, Ellen eventually, and at her own pace, acquired the ability to use both English and ASL. Her eventual career, in fact, was teaching ASL at a community college. Her mother, in an effort to support Ellen's goals, used English with her in academic situations and learned basic ASL for social interactions. In later life, Ann was comfortable communicating in English and ASL, according to the situation. Her bilingual abilities flourished after the age of 50. Eventually, both Ellen and Ann became bilingual according to the dictates of their situations.

There are numerous examples of a "both/and" communication philosophy at work in families with bilingual and even trilingual situations. Given support, motivation, and a positive, open-minded outlook, Eventual Bilingualism can give deaf individuals and their families a variety of options for successful communication that grow and change throughout life. If two languages are available, and the child is able to choose the one that fits in a specific situation at a given time, Eventual Bilingualism can be a positive outcome. Ellen's situation demonstrates how and Eventual Bilingual model can be effective with deaf students and their families when all of the aspects are in place and respected. Figure 1 delineates this process.

Clearly, a bilingual acquisition model requires an individualized plan for ongoing and interrelated use of both options as determined by the child's strengths and preferences. Visual/spatial support and aural/oral support systems must be in place, along with a variety of both communication opportunities and fluent adult communication partners. As the model suggests, all children are born into an environment where communication is expected. Initially, caregivers communicate with the child in various ways, including gestures, facial expression, sounding, and language. Babies and toddlers react and respond to those stimuli that are the most meaningful. A deaf

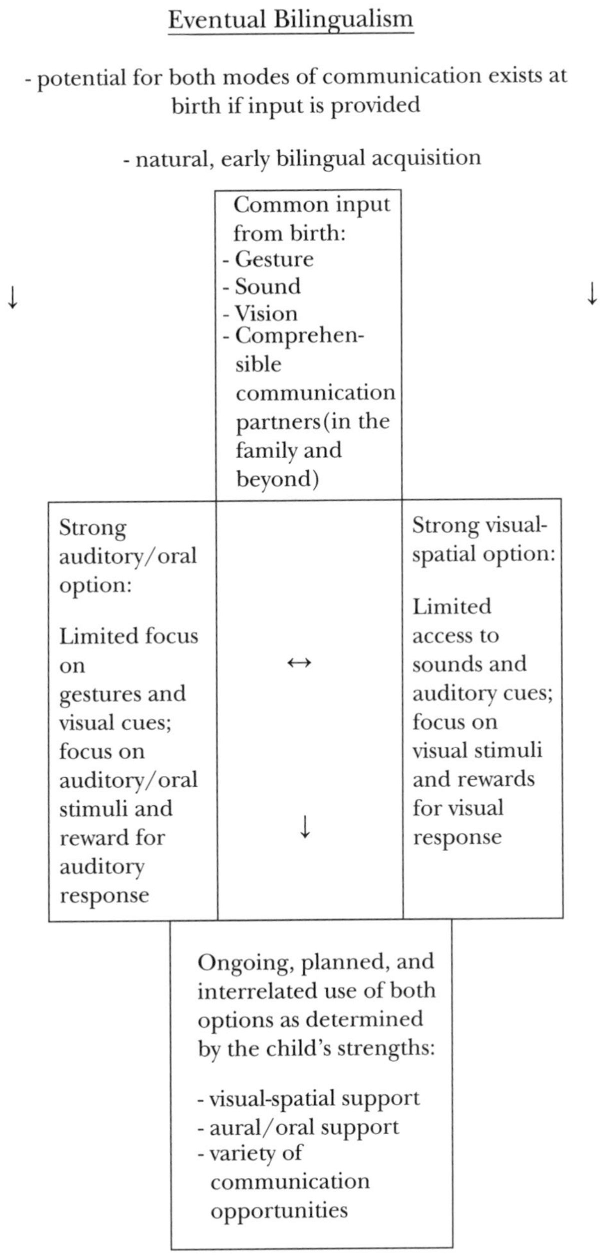

Eventual Bilingualism

- potential for both modes of communication exists at
birth if input is provided

- natural, early bilingual acquisition

	Common input from birth: - Gesture - Sound - Vision - Comprehensible communication partners (in the family and beyond)	
Strong auditory/oral option: Limited focus on gestures and visual cues; focus on auditory/oral stimuli and reward for auditory response	↔ ↓	Strong visual-spatial option: Limited access to sounds and auditory cues; focus on visual stimuli and rewards for visual response
	Ongoing, planned, and interrelated use of both options as determined by the child's strengths: - visual-spatial support - aural/oral support - variety of communication opportunities	

↓ ↓

Figure 1. Eventual Bilingualism.

baby who babbles, attempts to vocalize in response to a parent's spoken words, and/or reacts appropriately to environmental sounds may be demonstrating an early oral/aural preference. As the child matures, more visually salient input may be required to understand fully what is happening around the child. Gestures and signs can be used to expand and strengthen basic aural/oral interpersonal communication skills and vice versa. A child who shows early preference for visual/spatial communication may eventually benefit from aural/auditory stimuli enhanced by hearing aids or other technology. Rather than predetermining that one modality is "best" for a child and failing to observe the child's communication strengths and preferences, decision makers should look to the child for guidance. As in the case of PJ and others like him, communication needs ebb and flow. For example, ASL may help a child to better understand geometric principles, while English certainly supports the child's ability to enjoy a captioned film. In other words, a "both/and" approach to language can serve a child well in both academic and social settings as the child matures into adulthood.

One of my former graduate students sent me a story that illustrates the benefits of having bilingual input with deaf children in an educational setting. Her personal experience as a coda, a credentialed teacher of deaf students, and a certified interpreter allowed her to provide optimum communication for the deaf child. She writes:

> I'm on my way to another interpreting job. This time it is with a psychologist and a young boy who is deaf. I don't have much information about the job other than the boy "doesn't sign very well." I arrive and meet the psychologist. It is clear from her comments to me that she knows very little about deafness.
>
> The family arrives, and we go in to start the session. They are there to determine if the boy, I'll call him John, has ADHD. John was very talkative. My first thought was his language skills in ASL are ok. He is pretty easy to understand. I notice John has a cochlear implant and can speak clearly—a few words here and there. His mother knows very little ASL. She has shared with me her desire to learn sign language through a DVD. I can already sense that it will be difficult for me to keep to my code of ethics. I'm a coda, and I have a master's degree in Deaf education. Oh boy—here we go.
>
> We start off with John talking about an incident that happened at school. John was in trouble for pushing a boy on the playground. As the conversation continues, I start to see the gaps in John's language. I have seen this before. John's use of referencing and pronouns in ASL is very weak. At times it makes it difficult to know whom he is talking about and the time line of the events that got him in trouble. It is obvious he wants to explain himself. He starts repeating his story over and over. The psychologist is trying to redirect him. She is not doing a very good job of pacing herself or rephrasing her questions to be more direct. I'm trying to make adjustments to get things flowing. The mother is asking questions to try to understand his story. Tension and frustration are starting to build. At times John uses his voice when he hears the psychologist talking. I notice his English is similar to his ASL—gaps in his grammar. He is not connecting his thoughts clearly. At the same time, I also can see he is very smart. He is working hard to put all the pieces together. He is trying to understand what is going on and why he is here.
>
> It is the same old thing. Hearing people think that just because they say something, the deaf child understands them. I wonder why hearing people really don't comprehend what the word *deaf* means. John is a child who has so many gaps of information and misunderstandings occurring each and every day of his life. He works hard to understand. The adults see the problem as the child's deafness—not that the adults aren't communicating clearly. Why is the burden of communication always put on the deaf child? Deaf children of Deaf parents don't usually have this problem.
>
> The psychologist decides to try a new approach. She wants John to ask her a question. I interpret this and can see that John doesn't quite get it. I can understand

why this doesn't make sense to him. He is not sure why he is here. He doesn't seem to fully understand the role of the interpreter. He is asked to create an unnatural communication function, and he is not proficient in high-level skills of discourse and communication. This may seem to be an easy task when you are an adult with an intact language. This is where the coda and the educator in me will have a hard time staying inside the limits of my role as an interpreter as described in the ethics document. The question is asked again. John still doesn't understand. I adjust my signing. No luck. His mother tells us that John doesn't know how to ask a question and that that has been an ongoing problem. At this point, I can see so many factors coming into play to make this situation a lost cause. If I were to stay in my role as an interpreter, nothing will get done. John will most likely be labeled as incompetent at some level.

I interject and ask the psychologist if I could try a different approach. I explain my background and education. The psychologist and mother happily agree. I also explain how I am stepping out of my role but assure them this will work. I move over to the couch and sit next to John. At this point I am signing and using my voice when communicating so all parties can understand. The goal is to get John to ask a question. I look at John and begin to tell him what I am thinking. I tell him, with one hand up, blocking the psychologist as if we are having a private conversation, that I don't know her name. I say it again. Next I tell John that I will ask her a question, and I ask him to watch me. I sign and voice to the psychologist, "What is your name?" She says, "Norma." I look back toward John and with a big nod of satisfaction sign to him, "Her name is Norma." I then continue with my next curiosity. I tell John that I don't know where she lives and that I will ask her where she lives. John watches me ask Norma the question. Norma tells me, and I share that information with John. Now we start talking about how we all arrived here either by bus, bike, or car. Now John is fully participating in the conversation. John naturally starts asking questions about what kind of cars we have. He asks in ASL with proper grammatical markers "Toyota? (head leaning forward and eye brows raised). "Honda?" (same grammatical markers).

I point out to the psychologist and mother that John can ask questions. He does seem to have a hard time answering "why" or "how" questions correctly, but he is not far from achieving that skill. The session is now over. We didn't get very far, but we did make progress. If I hadn't stepped out of my role [as interpreter], I think everyone would have left that meeting unsatisfied. The mother was very impressed with how I was able to get John to participate so naturally. I am not sharing this to pat myself on the back. I am sharing this story to remind people that a deaf child is working hard to figure out our world, and we are not doing enough to help. I think the key that helped John understand was to show him that I have thoughts and questions in my head. We need to show the deaf child how we think.

John's mother brought up her need to learn ASL but wanted to learn through a DVD. I strongly advised her to go to the Deaf community, take a class, and interact with people. Learning alone is not going to work. Unfortunately, she still just wanted to learn from a DVD and wasn't aware there was a Deaf community service organization. The psychologist didn't have any information or knowledge about the Deaf community. It's such a shame to see that very little has changed in providing education for deaf children. How is it possible in this age of technology and information at our fingertips that families and psychologists still don't know basic information regarding what to do for a deaf child?

This story is another example of how "both/and" thinking can benefit our decision-making process. If the interpreter had not requested a role change, the outcome of the meeting with the psychologist would have been much different. The interpreter's sensitivity to the situation and her ability to switch roles as needed made a positive impact on the conclusion of the meeting. Joan Chittister (2004) writes about "cross-over times" or moments of intense possibility. In our profession, these moments must not be overlooked. When the needs of children are acknowledged and respected, those children will learn a valuable lesson about their own human rights and those of others.

The overall theme of this book is ethical decision making; that is, each decision is based upon a unique situation. There is not a single "right way" that can be applied to each challenge. . However, in reading and rereading the chapters, several overarching, mutually supportive themes emerge. Although each author wrote independently, it is worth noting that they considered many of the same critical issues as they thought about and composed their chapters. The authors have been true to interpretive thinking anchored by fact in the form of direct personal experience, empirical research, or a combination of both. In my observation, the following issues emerge as threads that weave the chapters into a coherent whole:

1. the need for communication-rich, barrier-free educational environments
2. the depression or frustration felt by both teachers and interpreters, which may lead to a high drop-out rate
3. the fact that good intentions may run amok
4. the understanding that life stories help us to consider professional issues more clearly
5. the knowledge that Deafhood is an important, yet little-understood, concept
6. the need to address issues of accountability among teachers, interpreters, and other professionals
7. the need to move from educational experimentation to informed practice
8. the importance of respect for the desires of children and parents at all stages; the understanding that every human being has a personal ethic and personal goals.

Along with these common threads is the need for everyone involved in the educational world of deaf children to consider a "both/and" approach to decision making. In a recent PBS discussion on cochlear implants (November 3, 2009), the moderator brought up the following question: "Will cochlear implants destroy deaf culture?" She called on the audiologist on the panel to answer the question. I held my breath . . . will there be a "both/and" response? The audiologist answered, "No, ASL will continue to exist because it is a beautiful language with its own literature and poetry." He evidently missed the point of the question and simply equated deaf culture with ASL. Although language is a critical component of culture, there is so much more to culture than language alone. It occurred to me that a more appropriate question would have been: "What impact will the use of cochlear implants have on Deafhood?" I thought about the Baby Signs classes for hearing children: Do those babies learn about the broader issues—about deafness, Deaf culture and communication across cultures? This brought to mind a Langston Hughes poem, "Note on Commercial Theatre" (1940), which gives a perspective on "taking" just part of a culture. As you read the poem, suppose that the word "blues" is replaced by the word "signs." Imagine that the word "Black" is the word "Deaf":

>You've taken my blues and gone—
>You sing 'em on Broadway
>And you sing 'em in Hollywood Bowl,
>And you mixed 'em up with symphonies
>And you fixed 'em
>So they don't sound like me.
>Yep, you done taken my blues and gone.
>
>[and later he states]
>
>[. . .] someday somebody'll
>Stand up and talk about me,
>And write about me—
>Black and beautiful—
>And sing about me,
>And put on plays about me!
>I reckon it'll be
>Me myself!

It is difficult, to be sure, to understand all of the sensitive issues involved in a different culture. There is much to learn, but we cannot ignore the challenge. To paraphrase John F. Kennedy's classic quote concerning the space program, we choose to do important things not because they are easy but because they are hard. In a "both/and" approach to the education of deaf children, there is much to know. Regardless of the presence or absence of a cochlear implant, whether deafness is congenital or acquired, whether one chooses to capitalize "Deaf" or not, when children are born deaf, their experience is fundamentally different from that of persons born with hearing ability intact. Visual experience impacts all aspects of development and overlaps all educational options. Educators, parents, and others can begin to understand the visual world of deaf children by observing, by listening, and by making discoveries each and every day. We can attempt to see clearly what is in front of us and make honest decisions regardless of our own personal biases and allegiances. To quote the *New York Times Magazine* Ethicist, "Making a good ethical decision can depend on making an accurate assessment of what's going on in a situation, a matter of anthropology as much as morality" (Cohen, 2010, p. 17). We can find common ground in education of deaf and hard of hearing students. We can consider more, not less. It is our ethical responsibility to do so.

References

Bloom, P. (2000). *Buddhist acts of compassion.* Berkeley: Conari.

Cavanaugh, M. (Nov. 3, 2009). How the deaf community is dealing with cochlear implants. *These Days.* San Diego, CA: KPBS radio.

Chittister, J. (2004). *Called to question: A spiritual memoir.* Chicago: Sheed and Ward.

Cohen, R, (2010). Breaking and entering and doubting. *New York Times Magazine,* p. 17.

Coles, R. (1986). *The moral life of children.* New York: Atlantic Monthly Press.

Rampersad, A., & Roessel, D. (Eds.) (2001). *The collected poems of Langston Hughes.* Columbia: University of Missouri Press.

Contributors

Mathew Call is a consultant, author, interpreter, and translator. He performs consulting for schools and businesses regarding how to effectively serve multicultural deaf populations. He is the author of a series of articles regarding ethics in interpreting, trilingual interpreting, and cross-cultural discourse involving immigrant families with deaf/hard of hearing children. He is a certified ASL and Spanish interpreter and translator and has worked in a wide variety of venues using all language combinations (ASL/Spanish/English). Mathew Call holds related degrees in sociology from Brigham Young University and interpreting from American River College. He is also a member of the Lifeprint.com Sign Language and Deaf Studies Presenters Network. He resides in Sacramento, California.

Kathee Mangan Christensen is Professor Emerita, San Diego State University, School of Speech, Language and Hearing Sciences. She has over 40 years of experience teaching deaf children, directing a clinic for deaf, hard of hearing, and deafblind children and preparing teachers of children who are deaf or deaf with special needs. She earned her Ph.D. from the Claremont Graduate University and her areas of research include multicultural issues in deafness, nonverbal cognitive development, and language acquisition in children who are deaf or deafblind. Dr. Christensen is active nationally and internationally through ChristensenConsults.com.

James J. DeCaro is Professor and Dean Emeritus at the National Technical Institute for the Deaf at Rochester Institute of Technology. He has been at NTID since 1971, serving as a faculty member, instructional developer, chairperson, center director, dean of the college, and interim president. He has been a Fulbright Senior Scholar at Orebro University in Sweden and a Rotary Foundation Scholar at the University of Newcastle-upon-Tyne in England. For the past 10 years he has been directing a multinational collaborative (PEN-International) which strives to improve postsecondary deaf education in the developing world. His areas of research interests are employment of people who are deaf and attitudes towards employment of people who are deaf.

Patricia A. Mudgett-DeCaro holds degrees and certifications in biology, counseling, and sociology of deaf education and has worked in various capacities, as teacher, counselor, researcher, and consultant in the field of deafness since 1970. She was a long-time faculty member in the National Technical Institute for the Deaf (NTID) Masters of Science in Secondary Education for Deaf Students (MSSE) at Rochester Institute of Technology (RIT). She taught Foundations of Educational Research, as well as on-campus and distance-learning courses regarding curriculum design for inclusion of a wide diversity of students who are deaf or hard of hearing. She is retired and is a member of the organizing committee of the Rochester School for the Deaf Archives.

Wendy S. Harbour is the Lawrence B. Taishoff Professor of Inclusive Education at Syracuse University in New York state, in the departments of Cultural Foundations of Education, Disability Studies, and Teaching and Leadership. She is also executive director of the Lawrence B. Taishoff Center for Inclusive Higher Education, which conducts research and training related to college students with disabilities. Dr. Harbour has served on the editorial boards for the Harvard Educational Review and the Journal on Postsecondary Education and Disability, has written about universal design, inclusion, and postsecondary interpreting, and has conducted research or federal grant projects with the Postsecondary Education Programs Network (PEPNet), the Association on Higher Education and Disability (AHEAD), CAST, Inc., and Gallaudet University. She completed her doctorate in education from Harvard University, where she is currently an adjunct instructor in the Graduate School of Education. Her master's degrees are from Harvard University and the University of Minnesota.

Melissa Herzig obtained her bachelor of arts degree at Gallaudet University and earned both degrees, master of arts and doctorate in education, at University of California, San Diego. For eight years, she was a teacher at Chula Vista High School. At the time of publication, she divides her time as a student teacher supervisor at Educational Studies and a postdoctoral researcher in Center for Research in Language at University of California, San Diego. She spends her free time with her family and two dogs.

Kary Krumdick earned his bachelor of arts at Gallaudet University and his master of arts degree in deaf education at San Diego State University. He currently resides in San Diego and is an elementary school teacher at Davila Day School. He has eight years of prior teaching experiences in middle school and high school. He's the proud father of two boys.

Marybeth Lauderdale has an Ed.S. Degree from Gallaudet University, as well as a master's in educational administration from University of Illinois at Springfield and a BS in Deaf and Elementary Education from MacMurray College. She is currently the superintendent of the Illinois School for the Deaf, and recently assumed the duties of superintendent of the Illinois School for the Visually Impaired. Both schools are in Jacksonville, Illinois.

A teacher of the Deaf/hard of hearing for twenty years, Ms. Lauderdale has been an administrator for the past ten years. Next to her children and grandchildren, the schools are her favorite subject!

Christine Monikowski is a professor in the Department of ASL and Interpreting Education at National Technical Institute for the Deaf/Rochester Institute of Technology where she has taught courses in American Sign Language and ASL/English interpretation for the past 18 years. She has over 30 years experience working as a certified interpreter (CSC) and 25 years as a teacher of interpreting in higher education.

She holds a doctorate in educational linguistics from the University of New Mexico. Dr. Monikowski presents local and national workshops for interpreters and interpreter educators. Her areas of interest include second language acquisition, educational interpreting, distance learning for interpreter educators, and teaching/learning in higher education and she has authored and co-authored numerous chapters and articles related to those topics. She lives in Rochester, N.Y. with her husband and enjoys bicycling when the western N.Y. weather cooperates!

Katrin Neumann is director of the Department of Phoniatrics and Pediatric Audiology at the University of Frankfurt am Main, Germany. She chairs the Audiology Committee of the International Association of Logopedics and Phoniatrics, is second vice president of the German Society of Phoniatrics & Pediatric Audiology, and contributes to pediatric-audiological projects to aid the work of the WHO. Her research topics are, among others, the implementation and evaluation of newborn hearing screening programs, the examination of language, voice, and hearing processes with neuroimaging methods, and audiological diagnostics and outcome in hearing impaired children. She works as associate editor for *Folia phoniatrica et logopaedica and Communication Disorders Quarterly*.

Rico Peterson is an associate professor in the ASL Interpreting Program at Northeastern University in Boston, Mass. An interpreter since 1973 and teacher of interpreting since 1985, he earned a doctorate in curriculum and instruction from the University of California, Riverside. Dr. Peterson works as a curriculum consultant for the National Consortium of Interpreter Education Centers, and has advised and consulted with developing interpreting programs in Thailand, the Philippines, Japan, and China. His publications include *The Unlearning Curve: Learning to Learn American Sign Language* and co-authorship of *ASL at Work*. His research interests include classroom interaction and interpreting in video settings.

Melissa Smith is an associate professor and director of the American Sign Language-English interpreting program at Palomar College in San Marcos, California. She holds doctoral and master's degrees in teaching and learning from the University of California, San Diego and a Bachelor's degree in Spanish from San Diego State University. Her dissertation, "More than Meets the Eye: Revealing the Complexities of K-12 Interpreting (2010)," explores the practices and decisions of interpreters working in public schools. Melissa served on the board of the San Diego chapter of ASLTA for seven years and has received the Interpreter Educator of the Year award from Region V of the Registry of Interpreters for the Deaf.

Index

Figures and tables are indicated by f and t following page numbers.